CLASSIC READERS THEATRE
FOR YOUNG ADULTS

2

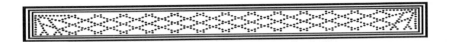

Classic Readers Theatre for Young Adults

Suzanne I. Barchers
Jennifer L. Kroll

2002
TEACHER IDEAS PRESS
Libraries Unlimited
A Division of Greenwood Publishing Group, Inc.
Greenwood Village, Colorado

TEACHER IDEAS PRESS
Libraries Unlimited
A Division of Greenwood Publishing Group, Inc.
7730 East Belleview Avenue, Suite A200
Greenwood Village, CO 80111
1-800-225-5800
www.lu.com/tips

Library of Congress Cataloging-in-Publication Data

Barchers, Suzanne I.
    Classic readers theatre for young adults / [adapted by] Suzanne I.
Barchers and Jennifer L. Kroll.
        p. cm.
      ISBN 1-56308-881-9
      1. Young adult drama, American. 2. Fiction--Adaptations. I. Kroll,
Jennifer L. II. Title.
      PS3552.A5988 C57 2002
      812'.54--dc21

                                                    2002006430

To Jeff and Charlotte Barchers,
a classic couple
—Suzanne I. Barchers

To my grandmother,
Josephine LeGrave Wautlet
—Jennifer L. Kroll

CONTENTS

INTRODUCTION

From short stories, such as "The Lady, or the Tiger?" to novels, such as *Hard Times,* classic literature has been an important part of the English curriculum. Combining the study of classic literature with readers theatre, a dramatic oral interpretation of a story, provides teachers and librarians with the ideal opportunity to enhance the English or language arts program in a lively fashion. *Classic Readers Theatre for Young Adults* includes a collection of scripts from a variety of authors who have been admired for their enduring role in English literature. Teachers and librarians undoubtedly will find that this collection includes several old favorites—along with a few surprises.

Using Readers Theatre

Readers theatre can be compared to radio plays. The emphasis is on an effective reading of the script rather than on a dramatic, memorized presentation. Students may paraphrase the scripts, and this should be encouraged. In some scripts, the narrators have long passages, and they should rehearse their lines carefully. Reading orally develops strong reading skills, and listening to scripts promotes active listening for students in the audience. The scripts also provide an opportunity for preparing a special program or for a diversion from the regular curriculum.

Preparing the Scripts

Teachers are always advised to preread a script to ensure that it is appropriate for the grade level and background knowledge of the students. Once scripts have been chosen, make enough copies for each character, plus an extra set or two for your use and a replacement copy. To help readers keep their place, have students use highlighter markers to designate their character's role within the copy. For example, someone reading the role of Narrator 1 could highlight the lines in blue, with another character highlighting the lines in yellow.

Photocopied scripts will last longer if you use a three-hole punch (or copy them on prepunched paper) and place them in inexpensive folders. The folders can be color-coordinated to the internal highlighting for each character's part. The title of the play can be printed on the outside of the folder, and scripts can be stored easily for the next reading. The preparation of the scripts is a good project for a student aide or volunteer parent. The preparation takes a minimum of initial attention and needs to be repeated only when a folder is lost.

Getting Started

For the first experience with a readers theatre script, consider choosing a short story or a script with many characters to involve more students. Gather the students informally. If the students have read the story or novel, explain that the script provides a dramatic interpretation. If the students are unfamiliar with the story or novel, consider sharing the summary or information about the author before reading the script together.

Next, introduce the script and explain that readers theatre does not mean memorizing a play and acting it out, but rather reading a script aloud with perhaps a few props and actions. Select volunteers to do the initial reading, allowing them an opportunity to review their parts silently before reading aloud. If the script is familiar, discuss how it is alike or different from what the students have previously read. Discuss definitions or pronunciations of challenging words as necessary. While these students are preparing to read their script, another group could brainstorm ideas for props or staging, if appropriate.

Before reading the first script, decide whether to choose parts after the reading or to introduce additional scripts to involve more students. If students are reading scripts based on short stories, a readers theatre workshop could be held, with each student belonging to a group that prepares a script for presentation. A readers theatre festival could be planned for a special day when several short scripts are presented consecutively, with brief intermissions between each reading. Consider grouping together related scripts. For example, *Frankenstein* could be grouped with *The Legend of Sleepy Hollow*, and both stories would be enjoyed near Halloween. *Captains Courageous* and *The Prince and the Pauper* share the theme of young men who discover how the "other half" live.

Once the students have read the scripts and become familiar with the new vocabulary, determine which students will read the various parts. Some parts are considerably more demanding than others, and students should be encouraged to volunteer for roles that will be comfortable for them. Once they are familiar with readers theatre, students should try a reading that is more challenging. Reading scripts is especially useful for remedial reading students and adult new readers of English. The adaptation is often written in simpler language with little description, giving readers an easier version of the story. Reading orally also serves to improve silent reading skills. Keep in mind that it is equally important for students to enjoy the literature.

Presentation Suggestions

For readers theatre, readers traditionally stand—or sit on stools, chairs, or the floor—in a formal presentation style. The narrators may stand with the scripts placed on music stands or lecterns slightly off to one or both sides. The readers may hold their scripts in black or colored folders.

The position of the reader indicates the importance of the role. For example, Harvey and Dan from *Captains Courageous* are key characters and should stand in the center with the other characters flanking them. On occasion, key characters might sit on high stools to elevate them above numerous other characters. For a long script with many main characters, such as *Little Women*, the characters could sit informally on a variety of chairs. The scripts include a few suggestions for positioning readers, but students should be encouraged to create interesting arrangements.

Props

Readers theatre has few props, if any. However, simple costuming effects, such as royal clothing or flowing gowns, plus a few props on stage will lend interest to the presentation. Suggestions for simple props or costuming are included; however, the students should be encouraged to decide how much to add to their reading. For some readers, the use of props or actions may be distracting, and the emphasis should remain on the reading rather than on an overly complicated presentation.

Delivery Suggestions

Few delivery suggestions are imbedded in the scripts. Therefore, it is important to discuss with the students what will make the scripts come alive as they read. During their first experiences with presenting a script, students are tempted to keep their heads buried in the script, making sure they don't miss a line. Students should learn the material well enough to look up from the script during the presentation. Students can learn to use onstage focus—to look at each other during the presentation. This is most logical for characters who are interacting with each other. The use of offstage focus—the presenters look directly into the eyes of the audience—is more logical for the narrator of characters who are uninvolved with onstage characters. Alternatively, have students who do not interact with each other focus on a prearranged offstage location, such as the classroom clock, during delivery. Simple actions, such as gestures or turning, can also be incorporated into readers theatre.

Generally the audience should be able to see the readers' facial expressions during the reading. On occasion, it might seem logical for a character to move across the stage, facing the other characters while reading. In this event, the characters should be turned so that the audience can see the reader's face.

About the Adaptations

When adapting a work of literature for readers theater, the authors strove to retain as much of the flavor of the author's original style as possible. For example, readers familiar with Louisa May Alcott's style will discover that much of the conversation among the family members is true to the original. Moderate adaptations were made for ease of understanding, appropriate length, and for reading aloud. With shorter works of literature, the plot is primarily intact. For long works, such as *Little Women*, *Captains Courageous*, or *The Prince and the Pauper*, chapters were omitted. Those who enjoy the play versions will find that there remains much to be discovered in the original novels. A good follow-up project for readers would be to compare the novel to the version in this book and prepare additional scenes from the omitted chapters.

The Next Step

Once students have enjoyed the reading process involved in preparing and presenting readers theatre, the logical next step is to involve them in the writing process by creating their own scripts. Students should also be encouraged to adapt other classic stories into scripts for sharing, perhaps beginning with other stories written by the authors in *Classic Readers Theatre for Young Adults*. Encourage students to choose stories that have ample conversation to make the process easier. Remember that the primary purpose of using readers theatre with classic literature is to enhance the English program. Curtain's up!

Little Women

Louisa May Alcott

Adapted by Suzanne I. Barchers

Summary

It's Christmas morning at the March home, and the four sisters are anticipating a modest celebration. Their father is helping with the war effort, but the girls face the new year willing to carry their "burdens." The year progresses and they develop a warm friendship with Laurie and his grandfather. The four sisters face their individual challenges, with Father's injury and Beth's illness the family's primary obstacles. This script, based on the first book about the March family, describes a variety of the family's adventures, leading to the following Christmas and Meg's engagement. This script is divided into two parts, which can be performed independently or together.

Background Information

Louisa May Alcott (1832–1888) was born in Germantown, Pennsylvania. Her parents started a school, which failed, prompting them to move to Boston and later Concord, Massachusetts, where her father tried to pursue other idealistic ventures. Alcott began writing dime novels to help support her parents and three sisters. She served as a nurse in the Civil War, where she contracted typhoid. In 1863, her father published revisions of her letters home during her recovery as *Hospital Sketches.* At the suggestion of her editor, she wrote *Little Women,* based largely on her life with her family in Concord, completing the manuscript in six weeks. After its successful publication in 1868, the public demanded a sequel, which came out in 1869.

Presentation Suggestions

The narrators can be sitting to the side. Jo, Meg, Beth, Amy, Mrs. March, and Laurie can be seated in chairs or on stools. Mr. Laurence, Mr. Davis, Hannah, Mr. Brooke, and Mr. March can enter for their lines.

Props

The characters can be dressed in clothes appropriate for the mid-1800s. The clothing should be simple, in keeping with the family's circumstances. Other props could include needlework, old-fashioned household items, and living room furniture.

Characters

- ❀ Narrators 1 and 2
- ❀ Jo, *fifteen years old*
- ❀ Meg, *sixteen years old*
- ❀ Beth, *thirteen years old*
- ❀ Amy, *twelve years old*
- ❀ Mrs. March, *mother*
- ❀ Laurie, *neighbor*
- ❀ Mr. Laurence, *Laurie's grandfather*
- ❀ Mr. Davis, *teacher*
- ❀ Hannah, *housekeeper*
- ❀ Mr. Brooke, *tutor*
- ❀ Mr. March, *father*

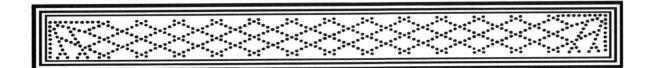

Little Women

PART I

Scene 1

Narrator 1: The firelight shines brightly on the four March children as they discuss Christmas. Their modest home is lonely without their father, who is a chaplain with the Union army.

Jo: Christmas won't be Christmas without any presents.

Meg: It's so dreadful to be poor!

Beth: We've got Father and Mother, and each other, anyhow.

Jo: *(Sadly.)* We haven't got Father—and shall not have him for a long time.

Meg: You know the reason Mother proposed not having any presents this Christmas was because it's going to be a hard winter for everyone. She thinks we ought not to spend money for pleasure when our men are suffering so in the army.

Jo: But I don't think the little we should spend would do any good. We've each got a dollar, and the army wouldn't be much helped by our giving that. I agree not to expect anything from Mother or you, but I do want to buy a book or two.

Beth: I planned to spend mine in new music.

Amy: I shall get a nice box of drawing pencils. I really need them.

Jo: Mother didn't say anything about our money, and she won't wish us to give up everything. Let's each buy what we want, and have a little fun. We grub hard enough to earn it.

Meg: I know *I* do—teaching those dreadful children nearly all day, when I'm longing to enjoy myself at home.

Jo: How would you like to be shut up for hours with a nervous, fussy old lady? Aunt March keeps me hopping—she's never satisfied until I'm ready to fly out the window or box her ears.

Beth: It's naughty to fret, but I think washing dishes and keeping things tidy is the worst work in the world. It makes me cross. My hands get so stiff I can hardly practice the piano.

Amy: I don't believe any of you suffer as I do. You don't have to go to school with impertinent girls, who plague you if you don't know your lessons, and laugh at your dresses, and label your father if he isn't rich, and insult you when your nose isn't nice.

3

Jo: If you mean *libel* I'd say so, and not talk about *labels,* as if Pa were a pickle bottle.

Meg: Don't peck at one another. Dear me, how happy and good we'd be if we had the money Papa lost when we were little.

Narrator 2: The sisters continue bickering until it's nearly time for their mother to return home. Beth puts a pair of slippers down to warm by the fire.

Jo: Marmee's slippers are quite worn out.

Beth: I thought I'd get her some with my dollar.

Amy: No, I shall!

Meg: I'm the oldest!

Jo: I'm the man of the family now Papa is away, and I shall provide the slippers.

Beth: Let's each get her something for Christmas and not get anything for us.

Jo: That's exactly like you, dear. What will we get?

Meg: I shall give her a nice pair of gloves.

Jo: Army shoes, best to be had.

Beth: Some handkerchiefs, all hemmed.

Amy: I'll get a little bottle of cologne. She likes it and it won't cost much. I'll have some money left to buy something for me.

Narrator 1: After making shopping plans, the girls rehearse their annual Christmas play until their mother arrives.

Mrs. March: Glad to find you so merry, my girls. How have you got on today? Has anyone called, Beth? How is your cold, Meg? Jo, you look tired to death. Come and kiss me, Amy. Girls, I have a treat for after dinner. It's a letter from your father.

Jo: Let's hurry up and get done with dinner!

Meg: I think it was so splendid of Father to go as a chaplain when he was too old to be drafted and not strong enough to be a soldier.

Beth: When will he come home, Marmee?

Mrs. March: Not for many months, dear, unless he becomes sick. He will stay and do his work faithfully as long as he can. Now come and hear the letter.

Narrator 2: The family draws together by the fire to hear the loving words from their father that end with his anticipation of returning even more proud and fond of his little women.

Jo: I'll try and be what he loves to call me, "a little woman," and not be rough and wild.

Mrs. March: Do you remember how you used to play Pilgrim's Progress when you were little? I'd tie bags on your backs for burdens and let you travel through the house. You'd have battles to fight and long journeys until you made it to the Celestial City.

Amy: I don't remember much about it, but if I wasn't too old for such things, I'd rather like to play it again.

Mrs. March: We are never too old for this my dear, because it's a play we are playing all the time. Our burdens are here, our road is before us, and we must see how far we can get before Father comes home.

Meg: It's only another name for trying to be good, and the story may help us. It's hard work to want to be good.

Mrs. March: Look under your pillows Christmas morning and you'll find something to help. And now it's time for bed, my dears.

Scene 2

Narrator 1: Jo is the first to wake in the gray dawn of Christmas morning. No stockings hang at the fireplace, and for a moment she feels disappointed. Then she remembers her mother's promise and finds a little crimson-covered book under her pillow. The others wake up and exclaim over their precious books, pledging to read them for guidance. They go downstairs, and Hannah, their beloved housekeeper, tells them that their mother has gone to help a beggar. They wait for her return, eager to give her their basket of gifts.

Mrs. March: Merry Christmas, little daughters!

Amy, Beth, Jo, Meg: Merry Christmas, Marmee!

Mrs. March: I want to say one word before we sit down to breakfast. Not far away from here lies a poor woman, Mrs. Hummel, with a newborn baby. Six children huddle in one bed to keep from freezing, for they have no fire. There is nothing to eat over there. My girls, will you give them your breakfast as a Christmas present?

Narrator 2: The girls are unusually hungry, having waited nearly an hour for Mrs. March to return before having breakfast. Then Jo speaks.

Jo: I'm so glad you came before we began!

Beth: May I help carry the things to the poor little children?

Amy: I shall take the cream and the muffins.

Mrs. March: I thought you'd do it. You shall all go and help me, and when we come back we will have bread and milk for breakfast and make it up at dinnertime.

Narrator 1: The family takes their breakfast to the desperate family, who receives it with great gratitude. Upon their return home, the children make a great ceremony of giving Mrs. March her gifts. After a good deal of laughing, kissing, and explaining, the family prepares for their Christmas play. An assortment of young friends enjoys the production. Afterward, Mrs. March invites the children to a lavish supper.

Amy: Have fairies come?

Beth: It's Santa Claus!

Meg: Mother did it!

Jo: Aunt March had a good fit and sent it, right?

Mrs. March: You're all wrong. Old Mr. Laurence sent it.

Meg: We don't know him. What in the world put such a thing into his head?

Mrs. March: Hannah told one of his servants about your breakfast party. He's an odd old gentleman, but that pleased him. He knew my father years ago, and he sent me a polite note this afternoon saying he hoped he could send a few trifles. I could not refuse, and so you have a little feast to make up for the bread and milk breakfast.

Jo: His grandson Laurie put it into his head. He's a capital fellow and I wish we could get acquainted. He looks like he'd like to know us, but he's bashful.

Amy: I hear he's proud and doesn't like to mix. He keeps his grandson shut up and makes him study dreadful hard.

Jo: He brought our cat back once and we talked over the fence. We need to know him better. I'm sure he needs fun.

Mrs. March: I like his manners, and he looks like a little gentleman. I've no objection to your knowing him if a proper opportunity comes. He brought these flowers himself, and he looked like he would have liked to stay and join in the fun.

Jo: I'm surprised you didn't invite him, Mother. But we'll have another play that he can see. Maybe he'll help act.

Meg: I've never had a bouquet before. How pretty it is.

Beth: I wish I could send a bunch to father. I'm afraid he isn't having such a merry Christmas as we are.

Scene 3

Narrator 2: The holidays pass with small entertainments, and the March sisters try to carry their individual burdens cheerfully. Determined to make the acquaintance of the Laurence boy, Jo takes advantage of Mr. Laurence's departure to toss a snowball at the window where the boy watches listlessly. He opens the window and begins to smile.

Jo: How do you do? Are you sick?

Laurie: I'm better, thank you. I've had a horrid cold.

Jo: I'm sorry. What do you amuse yourself with?

Laurie: Nothing. It's as dull as tombs up here.

Jo: Don't you read?

Laurie: Not much. Grandpa reads to me sometimes, but my books don't interest him. I hate to ask Brooke, my tutor, all the time.

Jo: Why don't you have someone come and see you then?

Laurie: I don't know anyone.

Jo: You know me.

Laurie: So I do! Will you come, please?

Jo: I'll ask my mother. Shut that window and wait till I come.

Narrator 1: Mrs. March agrees and soon Jo arrives with surprises.

Jo: Here I am, bag and baggage. Mother sent her love. Meg wanted me to bring some of her blancmange. And Beth thought her cats would be comforting.

Narrator 2: The kittens help Laurie get over his bashfulness, and they begin their acquaintance.

Laurie: Is Beth the rosy one, who stays at home a good deal, and sometimes goes out with a little basket?

Jo: Yes, that's Beth, a regular good one she is.

Laurie: The pretty one is Meg, and the curly-haired one is Amy, I believe?

Jo: How did you find that out?

Laurie: I often hear you calling to one another, and I can't help looking over at your house. You always seem to be having such good times. I beg your pardon for being so rude, but sometimes you forget to put down the curtain at the window where the flowers are. When the lamps are lighted, it's like looking at a picture to see the fire, and you all around the table with your mother. I can't help watching it. I haven't got a mother, you know.

Jo: We'll never draw that curtain any more, and I give you leave to look as much as you like. I just wish, though, that instead of peeping, you'd come over and see us. We'd have jolly times. Wouldn't your grandpa let you?

Laurie: I think he would, if your mother asked him. He's very kind, though he doesn't look it, and he lets me do what I like, pretty much.

Narrator 1: The youngsters continue to become friends when Mr. Laurence and the doctor interrupt them. Jo looks at a portrait of Mr. Laurence and talks to herself as she waits for Laurie to finish with the doctor.

Jo: I'm sure that I shouldn't be afraid of him, for he's got kind eyes, though his mouth is grim, and he looks as if he had a tremendous will of his own. He isn't as handsome as *my* grandfather, but I like him.

Narrator 2: Mr. Laurence, overhearing her, interrupts her monologue.

Mr. Laurence: Thank you, ma'am. So you're not afraid of me?

Jo: Not much, sir.

Mr. Laurence: And I've got a tremendous will, have I?

Jo: I only said I thought so.

Mr. Laurence: But you like me in spite of it?

Jo: Yes, I do, sir.

Mr. Laurence: You've got your grandfather's spirit. He was a brave and honest man, and I was proud to be his friend.

Jo: Thank you, sir.

Mr. Laurence: *(Gruffly.)* You think my boy needs cheering up?

Jo: Yes, he seems a little lonely, and young folks would do him good. We are only girls, but we should be glad to help if we could. We don't forget the splendid Christmas present you sent us.

Mr. Laurence: That was the boy's doing. . . . There's the bell for tea. Come and join us.

Narrator 1: Laurie, showing more energy, joins them. After tea, Jo and Laurie tour the conservatory, where Laurie cuts flowers for Mrs. March. When they return to the drawing room, Jo, drawn to the grand piano, convinces Laurie to play. Finally, after promises to visit again, Jo departs for home.

Narrator 2: The March sisters discover that Mr. Laurence, once thought gruff, is in truth a thoughtful, generous man. He takes a special interest in sweet Beth's love of music, giving her a little cabinet piano that had once belonged to a granddaughter he lost. Soon a warm friendship between the families has blossomed along with springtime.

Scene 4

Narrator 1: One afternoon Amy and Meg watch Laurie ride by on his horse.

Amy: I wish I had some of the money Laurie spends on that horse.

Meg: Why?

Amy: I'm dreadfully in debt, and it won't be my turn to have the rag money for a month.

Meg: What do you mean?

Amy: I owe the other girls at least a dozen pickled limes, and I can't pay them until I have the money. Marmee forbid my having anything charged at the shop.

Meg: Are limes the fashion now?

Amy: You see, the girls are always buying them, and unless you want to be thought mean, you must do it too. It's nothing but limes now, for everyone is sucking them in their desks during school. They trade them for pencils, bead-rings, or paper dolls at recess. If one girl likes another, she gives her a lime. If she's mad, she eats one in front of her. I've had ever so many, but haven't returned them. I ought to, for they are debts of honor, you know.

Meg: How much will pay them off and restore your credit?

Amy: A quarter would do it and leave a few cents over for a treat for you. Don't you like limes?

Meg: Not much. You may have my share. Here's the money—make it last as long as you can.

Amy: Oh, thank you! It must be so nice to have pocket money. I'll have a grand feast, for I haven't tasted a lime this week. I felt reluctant to take any, as I couldn't return them. I'm actually suffering for one.

Narrator 2: The next day Amy is rather late at school, but she cannot resist displaying a moist brown paper parcel before putting it in her desk. During the next few minutes, the rumor that Amy March has 24 delicious limes (she ate one on the way) and is going to treat, circulates through her set of friends, who lavish attention on her. Amy seizes the moment to let Jenny Snow understand that she, due to previous slights, will not be receiving a lime.

Narrator 1: Mr. Davis, the teacher, had declared limes a contraband article, and Jenny Snow wastes no time in informing him that Amy has a quantity of limes hidden in her desk.

Mr. Davis: Young ladies, attention, if you please. Miss March, come to the desk. Bring with you the limes you have in your desk.

Narrator 2: Amy takes all but half a dozen to Mr. Davis.

Mr. Davis: Is that all?

Amy: Not quite.

Mr. Davis: Bring the rest, immediately.

Narrator 1: With a despairing glance at her friends, Amy obeys.

Mr. Davis: You are sure there are no more?

Amy: I never lie, sir.

Mr. Davis: So I see. Now take these disgusting things, two by two, and throw them out of the window.

Narrator 2: There is a simultaneous sigh, as the last hope flees, and the treat disappears. Scarlet with shame and anger, Amy goes to and fro twelve times. As each pair of limes falls from her hands, a shout from the street completes the anguish of the girls, for it tells them that the street children below are enjoying their feast. Finally, the task is complete.

Mr. Davis: Young ladies, you remember what I said to you a week ago. I am sorry this has happened, but I never allow rules to be infringed, and I *never* break my word. Miss March, hold out your hand.

Narrator 1: Amy starts, and puts both hands behind her, turning on him an imploring look.

Mr. Davis: Your hand, Miss March.

Narrator 2: Amy sets her teeth, throws back her head defiantly, and bears without flinching several tingling blows on her little palm. For the first time in her life, she has been struck. The disgrace is as deep as if he had knocked her down.

Mr. Davis: You will now stand on the platform till recess.

Narrator 1: The fifteen minutes seem like an hour. Finally, he is done.

Mr. Davis: You can go, Miss March.

Narrator 2: Mr. Davis will not soon forget the reproachful look Amy gives him, as she silently gathers her things and leaves the place *forever,* as she passionately declares to herself.

Narrator 1: At home, Mrs. March does not say much, but comforts her afflicted little daughter in her most tender manner. Then Miss March writes a letter to Mr. Davis, which Jo delivers.

Mrs. March: Yes, you can have a vacation from school, but I want you to study a little with Beth every day. I don't approve of corporal punishment, especially for girls. I dislike Mr. Davis's manner of teaching, and I don't think the girls you associate with are doing you any good. I shall ask your father's advice before I send you anywhere else.

Amy: I wish all the girls would leave, and spoil his old school. It's perfectly maddening to think of those lovely limes.

Mrs. March: I am not sorry you lost them, for you broke the rules, and deserved some punishment for disobedience. I should not have chosen that way of mending a fault. But I'm not sure it won't do you more good than a milder manner. You are getting to be altogether too conceited and important, my dear. You have a good many little gifts and virtues, but there is no need of parading them.

Amy: So it's nice to have accomplishments and be elegant, but not to show off.

Mrs. March: These things are always seen and felt in a person's manner and conversation, if modestly used. But it is not necessary to display them.

Jo: Any more than it's proper to wear all your bonnets, gowns, and ribbons at once that folks may know you've got them!

Narrator 2: And the lecture ends with laughter all around.

Scene 5

Narrator 1: Meg and Jo are getting ready to go out, and Amy is curious about their plans.

Amy: Girls, where are you going?

Jo: Never mind. Little girls shouldn't ask questions.

Amy: Do tell me where you are going. Beth is fussing over her dolls and I haven't anything to do. I'm so lonely.

Meg: I can't dear, because you aren't invited.

Jo: Be quiet, Meg, or you'll spoil it all. You can't go, Amy, so don't be a baby and whine about it.

Amy: You're going somewhere with Laurie! Right?

Jo: Yes, we are. Now do be still, and stop bothering us.

Amy: Are you going to the theater to see the "Seven Castles?" Yes, that's it! Please let me go. I have some money, and I've been sick with this cold so long. I'm dying for some fun. I'll be ever so good.

Meg: *(To Jo.)* What if we take her? I don't believe mother would mind.

Jo: If she goes, I won't, and Laurie won't like it. He invited us, not Amy.

Amy: But I *shall* go! Meg will let me and if I pay for myself, Laurie hasn't anything to do with it.

Jo: You can't sit with us, for our seats are reserved, and you mustn't sit alone. So Laurie will give you his place, and that will spoil our pleasure. Or he'll get another seat for you, and that isn't proper when you weren't asked. Just stay where you are.

Narrator 2: Amy sits on the floor and begins to cry. Laurie calls from below, and the two girls hurry down, leaving their sister wailing.

Amy: *(Loudly.)* You'll be sorry for this, Jo March!

Jo: Fiddlesticks!

Narrator 1: Meg, Jo, and Laurie have a charming time, though Jo is reminded of Amy by the fairy queen's golden curls. When they get home, they find Amy reading in the parlor. Although Amy has an injured air, all seems well. The next day, however, Jo makes a discovery that produces a tempest.

Jo: Has any one taken my story?

Meg, Beth: No!

Jo: Amy, you have it!

Amy: No, I haven't.

Jo: You know where it is, then!

Amy: No, I don't.

Jo: That's a fib!

Amy: It isn't. I haven't got it, don't know where it is now, and don't care.

Jo: You know something about it, and you'd better tell at once.

Amy: Scold as much as you like, you'll never get your silly old story again.

Jo: Why not?

Amy: I burnt it.

Jo: What! My little book I worked over and meant to finish before Father got home? Have you really burnt it?

Amy: Yes, I did! I told you I'd make you pay for being so cross yesterday, and I have.

Jo: *(Angrily.)* You wicked, wicked girl! I never can write it again, and I'll never forgive you as long as I live!

Narrator 2: Meg flies to rescue Amy, and Beth tries to pacify Jo, but Jo is beside herself. With a parting box on Amy's ear, she rushes out of the room. When Mrs. March comes home, she makes Amy realize the wrong she's done her sister. Jo is considered the literary talent of the family, and Jo had worked over her stories, hoping to make something good enough to sell. Amy's deed has consumed the loving work of several years. Amy tries to make amends at teatime.

Amy: Please forgive me, Jo. I'm very, very sorry.

Jo: I never shall forgive you.

Narrator 1: No one speaks of the trouble until Mrs. March gives Jo her goodnight kiss.

Mrs. March: *(Quietly.)* My dear, don't let the sun go down on your anger. Forgive each other. Help each other and begin again tomorrow.

Jo: It was an abominable thing, and she doesn't deserve to be forgiven.

Narrator 2: The next morning Jo is getting her skates, planning to ask Laurie to skate with her. Amy hears the clash of skates and remembers that Jo has promised to take her the next time she goes skating.

Amy: That Jo! She promised I should go skating next time, for this is the last ice we shall have.

Meg: You *were* very naughty, and it's hard to forgive the loss of her book. But I think she might forgive you by now. Go after them, and once Jo is skating and feeling better, do some kind thing, and I'm sure she'll be your friend again.

Amy: I'll try.

Narrator 1: Amy hurries after Jo and Laurie. It is not far to the river, but both are ready before Amy reaches them. Jo sees her coming and turns her back. Laurie does not see her because he is carefully skating along the shore, checking the ice, for a warm spell had preceded the cold snap.

Laurie: I'll go on to the first bend and see if it's all right before we begin to race.

Narrator 2: Jo hears Amy panting, trying to put her skates on, but Jo never turns. She goes slowly, zigzagging down the river, enjoying her anger. Laurie turns back and shouts.

Laurie: Keep near the shore! It isn't safe in the middle.

Narrator 1: Jo hears, but Amy does not catch a word. Jo is just at the turn and Laurie has vanished round the bend. Amy heads out toward the smoother ice in the middle. Jo stops, resolving to go on, but something makes her turn around just in time to see Amy throw up her hands and go through the ice. She tries to call Laurie, but her voice is gone. Laurie rushes by her.

Laurie: Bring a fence rail! Quick!

Narrator 2: Jo never knows how she did it, but she obeys Laurie, who is lying flat on the ice, holding up Amy with his arm and hockey stick. Using the rail for support, they get Amy out, more frightened than hurt.

Laurie: We must get her home as fast as we can. Pile our things on her while I get off my skates.

Narrator 1: They wrap their coats on Amy and get her home, shivering, dripping, and crying. Jo hardly speaks, but flies about, with her dress torn and her hands cut and bruised from the ice and fence rail. When Amy is asleep, Mrs. March tends to Jo's hurt hands.

Jo: *(Whispering.)* Are you sure she is safe?

Mrs. March: Quite safe, dear; she is not hurt, and won't even take cold. You were so sensible in covering her and getting her home quickly.

Jo: Laurie did it all. I only let her go. Mother, if she *should* die, it would be my fault. It's my dreadful temper. I try to curb it. I think I have, and then it breaks out worse than ever. What shall I do?

Mrs. March: Never tire of trying and never think it's impossible to conquer your fault. Remember this day and resolve that you will never know another like it. We all have our temptations. My temper used to be just like yours.

Jo: Yours, Mother? Why, you are never angry!

Mrs. March: I've been trying to cure it for forty years, and have only succeeded in controlling it. I am angry nearly every day, but I've learned not to show it.

Narrator 2: Mrs. March continues to counsel and comfort Jo. When Jo expresses her regrets again, Amy opens her eyes and holds out her arms to Jo with a smile. Neither says a word, but they hug each other close, and all is forgiven and forgotten.

PART II

Scene 1

Narrator 1: It's the first day of June, and the children are expressing their excitement about the summer ahead. Meg has been teaching the King children, and Jo has been serving as a companion to Aunt March.

Meg: The Kings are off to the seashore tomorrow and I'm free! Three months vacation! How I shall enjoy it!

Jo: Aunt March left today. I was afraid she'd ask me to go with her, but I left before she had a chance and raced home.

Beth: Jo came in looking as if bears were after her!

Amy: What shall you do with all your vacation?

Meg: I shall lie in bed and do nothing. I've gotten up early all winter and had to spend my days working for other people. Now I'm going to rest and revel to my heart's content.

Jo: I'm going to spend my time reading on my perch in the old apple tree when I'm not having larks with Laurie.

Amy: Don't have us do any chores and lessons for a while, Marmee. Let us play and rest as girls are meant to do.

Beth: I want to learn some new songs, and my children need fixing up for the summer. They are really suffering for clothes.

Meg: May we have some time off, Mother? Perhaps as an experiment?

Mrs. March: I'll let you try your experiment for a week. I think by Saturday night you will find that all play, and no work, is as bad as all work, and no play.

Meg: Oh, no! It will be delicious, I'm sure.

Narrator 2: They all toast their plans with lemonade and begin their experiment by lounging for the rest of the day. Next morning, Meg doesn't appear until ten o'clock. Her solitary breakfast doesn't taste good, and the room seems lonely and untidy, for the girls have not done their usual chores. Marmee's corner looks neat as usual.

Narrator 1: Jo spends the morning on the river with Laurie and spends the afternoon reading in the apple tree. Beth rummages in her closet for things for her family of dolls, but leaves it before finishing to go to her music. Amy puts on her best white frock and sits down to draw under the honeysuckles, hoping someone will admire the young artist. Finally teatime arrives.

Meg: How has your day been?

Jo: It's been delightful! But I spent too long on the river and my nose hurts from sunburn.

Beth: I still need to clean my closet, but I started learning three new songs.

Meg: Did you finish one?

Beth: No.

Amy: I enjoyed my drawing, but I forgot about Katy's party tomorrow and now I have nothing to wear. But it was still charming to be free of the usual chores.

Narrator 2: And so the week progresses. The days keep getting longer and longer. The tempers are as variable as the weather. Jo quarrels with Laurie. Meg gets so tired of having nothing to do that she tries to refurbish some clothes, spoiling them in the process. Beth forgets that it is *all play* and falls back into her old ways. Amy fares worst of all for she doesn't like dolls and can't draw all the time.

Narrator 1: No one will admit that they are tired of the experiment. But by Friday night each one is secretly glad the week is almost over. When they get up Saturday morning, there is no fire in the kitchen, no breakfast in the dining room, and no mother anywhere to be seen.

Jo: Mercy on us! What has happened?

Narrator 2: Meg runs upstairs to Mrs. March's room and comes back with a report.

Meg: Mother isn't sick, only very tired, and she says she is going to stay quietly in her room all day and let us do the best we can. She doesn't act a bit like herself. But she says it *has* been a hard week for her, so we mustn't grumble, but take care of ourselves.

Jo: That's easy enough. I'm aching for something to do—that is, some new amusement, you know.

Narrator 1: In fact, it is an immense relief to them to have a little work. But they soon realize that housekeeping is not so easy. Meg and Jo get breakfast started.

Meg: I shall take some up to Mother, though she said we were not to think of her, for she'd take care of herself.

Narrator 2: Mrs. March receives the bitter tea, scorched omelet, and lumpy biscuits with thanks, laughing after they depart. Jo decides to invite Laurie to dinner while Meg tries to hastily tidy up the parlor.

Meg: You'd better see what we have before you think of having company.

Jo: Oh, there's corned beef, and plenty of potatoes. I shall get some asparagus and a lobster. I'll have lettuce for a salad. I don't know how, but the book tells. I'll fix blancmange and strawberries for dessert.

Meg: Don't try too many messes, Jo. You can't make anything but gingerbread and molasses candy. I wash my hands of this. You may just take care of this.

Jo: Won't you give me advice if I get stuck?

Meg: Yes, but I don't know much, except about bread. You'd better ask Mother's permission before you order anything.

Narrator 1: Jo puts the request to her mother.

Mrs. March: Get what you like and don't disturb me. I'm going out to dinner. You can worry about things at home. I'm glad to take a vacation today. I'm going read, write, go visiting, and amuse myself.

Narrator 2: The sight of her mother reading and rocking early in the morning disturbs Jo. She hurries into the parlor, feeling out of sorts, only to find Beth crying over her canary, Pip.

Beth: It's all my fault! I forgot him. There isn't a seed or drop left. Oh, Pip! How could I be so cruel to you?

Jo: Oh dear, he is dead. Here, let me get a little box and we'll bury him.

Amy: Put him in the oven and maybe he'll get warm and revive.

Beth: He's been starved, and he shan't be baked, now he's dead. I'll never have another bird. I'm too bad to own one.

Jo: We'll have a funeral this afternoon, and we will all go. Don't cry, Bethy. It's a pity, but nothing goes right this week, and Pip has had the worst of the experiment. Make a shroud and lay him in the box. We'll have the funeral after the dinner party.

Narrator 1: Jo goes to the kitchen, where the preparations begin with one calamity after another. The rising bread has been forgotten and run over the pans. Jo boils the asparagus until the heads fall off. The bread burns while she struggles with the salad dressing. She hammers the lobster until the shell reveals its meager portions. The potatoes don't get done, and the strawberries are not fully ripened. The blancmange is lumpy.

Narrator 2: Jo rings the bell a half an hour later than usual and surveys the "feast" dispiritedly. At least the fruit and cream look pretty, but upon the first taste, they discover that instead of sugar, salt has been stirred into the cream. The meal is such a disaster that Jo can't help but laugh until tears run down her cheeks. They finish the meal with bread, butter, and olives.

Jo: I haven't the strength to clear up now, so we will have our funeral.

Narrator 1: After the funeral, the afternoon flies by with guests calling, requiring the making of tea. As twilight falls, the girls gather on the porch.

Jo: What a dreadful day this has been.

Meg: It's been shorter than usual, but so uncomfortable.

Amy: Not a bit like home.

Beth: It can't seem so without Marmee and little Pip.

Narrator 2: Just then Mrs. March comes home and joins them.

Mrs. March: Are you satisfied with your experiment, girls, or do you want another week of it?

Jo: I don't!

Meg, Beth, Amy: Nor I!

Mrs. March: Do you think that it's better to have a few duties?

Jo: I'm tired of lounging. I mean to go to work at something right off.

Mrs. March: Suppose you learn plain cooking. That's a useful accomplishment.

Meg: Mother, did you go away and let everything be, just to see how we'd get on?

Mrs. March: Yes, I wanted you to see how the comfort of all depends on each doing their share faithfully. While Hannah and I did your work, you got on pretty well, though I don't think you were very happy or amiable. So I thought I would show you what happens when every one thinks only of herself. Don't you feel that it's better to help one another? Doesn't leisure time seem sweet when it comes after some work?

Meg, Jo, Beth, Amy: Yes, Mother!

Mrs. March: Then let me advise you to take up your little burdens again. Though they seem heavy sometimes, they are good for us and lighten as we learn to carry them.

Jo: We'll work like bees, and love it too. I'll learn plain cooking.

Meg: I'll learn to sew, even though I'm not fond of it.

Beth: I'll do my lessons every day and not spend so much time with my music and dolls.

Amy: I shall learn to make buttonholes and attend to my parts of speech.

Mrs. March: Very good! Then I am quite satisfied with the experiment. I don't think we'll have to repeat it. Work and play makes each day useful and pleasant. Don't forget.

Narrator 1: And the girls always remember the lessons of the experiment.

Scene 2

Narrator 1: The summer and fall pass pleasantly, and in no time the March family faces November.

Meg: November is the most disagreeable month in the whole year.

Beth: If something pleasant happened now, we'd think it a delightful month.

Jo: I wish I could fix things for you as I do my storybook heroines. I'd have some rich relation leave you a fortune.

Meg: People don't have fortunes left them in that style nowadays. Men have to work and women to marry for money. It's a dreadfully unjust world.

Amy: Jo and I are going to make fortunes for you all. Just wait ten years and see if we don't!

Meg: Two pleasant things are going to happen now. Marmee is coming down the street, and Laurie is tramping through the garden as if he had something nice to tell.

Laurie: Won't you come for a drive? I've been working away at mathematics until my head is in a muddle. I'm going to freshen my wits by a brisk turn. Come, Jo and Beth.

Jo: Of course, we'll come.

Meg: I'm busy.

Narrator 2: A sharp ring interrupts them and Hannah comes in with a letter.

Hannah: It's one of those horrid telegram things, mum.

Narrator 1: Mrs. March snatches the telegram, reads it, and drops into her chair as white as if the little paper had sent a bullet to her heart. Jo reads it aloud.

Jo, Mrs. March: Your husband is very ill. Come at once. S. Hale, Blank Hospital, Washington.

Narrator 2: The room is still. The whole world seems to change as the girls gather around their mother.

Mrs. March: I shall go at once, but it may be too late. Oh, children, I'll need your help to bear this.

Narrator 1: The family gathers around, trying to comfort each other.

Hannah: The Lord keep the dear man! I won't waste my time crying, but will get your things ready right away, mum.

Mrs. March: She's right. There's no time for tears. Let's be calm and I'll try to think. Laurie, send a telegram saying I will come at once. The next train goes early in the morning. I'll take that.

Laurie: Of course, Mrs. March. What else?

Mrs. March: I'll write a note for you to take to Aunt March. I'll need her help with the fare.

Narrator 2: Soon Laurie is on his way, riding as if for his life. Mrs. March continues writing.

Mrs. March: Jo, run to the store and get the things on this list. I must be prepared for nursing your father, and hospital stores are not always good. Amy, tell Hannah to get down the black trunk. Beth, go tell Mr. Laurence what has happened, in case Laurie didn't stop on his way to Aunt March's. Girls, you will have to help out with the Hummel family in my absence. Meg, help me find my things, for I'm half bewildered.

Meg: You sit and let us do the work. We'll get it all organized.

Narrator 1: Mr. Laurence hurries back with Beth, bringing every comfort he can think of for Mr. March.

Mr. Laurence: Now, Mrs. March, don't worry about the girls. I'll do everything I can to ensure that the girls are safe in your absence. Can I escort you on your journey?

Mrs. March: No, no, I wouldn't think of troubling you so for that.

Mr. Laurence: Then I have another idea. I'll be back directly.

Narrator 2: Soon Laurie's tutor, Mr. Brooke, appears.

Mr. Brooke: I'm very sorry to hear of this, Mrs. March. May I escort you to Washington? Mr. Laurence has commissions for me there, and I would be happy to be of service for you, too.

Mrs. March: How kind of you! That will be a comfort, to be sure.

Narrator 1: By this time Laurie has returned with an envelope from Aunt March. Soon the errands are done, but Jo has not returned from her trip to the store. Finally, she comes in with a strange look on her face, placing a roll of bills in her mother's hands before removing her coat and bonnet.

Mrs. March: Twenty-five dollars! Where did you get it? I hope you haven't done anything rash!

Jo: No, it's mine. I earned it, and I don't think you'll blame me, for I only sold what was my own.

Narrator 2: As she speaks, Jo takes off her bonnet. Everyone cries out as they realize her abundant hair has been cut short.

Meg: Your hair! Your beautiful hair!

Mrs. March: Oh, Jo, how could you? There was no need of this!

Beth: She doesn't look like my Jo any more!

Narrator 1: As Beth hugs her, Jo assumes an indifferent air, which doesn't deceive any one of them.

Jo: I was getting too proud of my hair anyway. It will do my brains good to have that mop taken off. My head feels deliciously light and cool, and the barber said I will soon have a curly crop. I'm satisfied, so please take the money and let's have supper.

Narrator 2: The family discusses Jo's sacrifice, marveling at her courage and generosity throughout the evening. Finally, everyone settles down in bed, with varying degrees of anxiety and regret.

Scene 3

Narrator 1: For a week, the family works hard at keeping busy. Jo catches a cold from neglecting to cover her shorn head. Then Beth remembers that the Hummel family has been neglected since Mrs. March left.

Beth: Meg, I wish you'd go and see the Hummel family. You know mother told us not to forget them.

Meg: I'm too tired to go this afternoon.

Jo: I can't go with this cold.

Meg: Can't you go, Beth?

Beth: I have been going, but the baby is sick, and I don't know what to do with it. Mrs. Hummel goes away to work, but it gets sicker. I think you or Hannah should go. Besides, my head aches.

Jo: Ask Hannah for some treats for them and take it around. The air will do you good.

Meg: Amy will be back soon and perhaps she will go for us.

Beth: Well, I'll rest a little and wait for her.

Narrator 2: Beth lies down on the sofa and the girls get absorbed in their tasks. After an hour, Amy hasn't arrived, so Beth quietly prepares a basket for the Hummels and leaves. She returns late, and no one notices her creep upstairs and shut herself in her mother's room. Soon Jo finds her there, looking very grave, with a camphor bottle in her hand.

Jo: Beth! What's the matter?

Beth: You've had scarlet fever, haven't you?

Jo: Years ago. Why?

Beth: Oh, Jo! The Hummel baby's dead! It died in my lap before she got home!

Jo: Oh, my poor Beth. How dreadful for you.

Beth: It wasn't dreadful, only sad. Her sister Lotty said her mother had gone for a doctor, so I took the baby so Lotty could rest. All of a sudden the baby gave a little cry, trembled, and then lay still. I knew it was dead.

Jo: What did you do?

Beth: I just sat and held it until Mrs. Hummel came with the doctor. He said it was dead and looked at Heinrich and Minna, who have sore throats. He said it was scarlet fever and that she should have gotten him early. He told me to go home and take belladonna right away, or I'd get the fever.

Jo: No you won't! If you should get sick, I could never forgive myself. What shall we do?

Beth: Don't be frightened. I guess I shan't have it badly. I looked in mother's book, and it said it begins with headache, sore throat, and feelings like mine, so I did take some belladonna and I feel better.

Jo: If mother were only home!

Narrator 1: Jo grabs the book and reads for a few minutes.

Jo: You've been seeing the baby for days, so I'm afraid you're going to have it. I'll get Hannah. She'll know what to do.

Beth: Can you and Meg get it again?

Jo: I don't think so, but it would serve me right for being so selfish.

Narrator 2: Jo consults Hannah, who reassures her that people treated properly do not die of scarlet fever.

Hannah: I'll tell you what we'll do. We will have Dr. Bangs come to take a look at Beth and see that we start right. Then we'll send Amy off to Aunt March's to keep her out of harm's way. Then one of you girls can stay and amuse Beth for a day or two.

Jo: I'll do it, of course.

Meg: I shall stay. I'm the oldest.

Hannah: There's only need of one. Which will you have, Beth?

Beth: Jo, please.

Narrator 1: Meg, who dislikes nursing, is a bit relieved, and leaves to tell Amy that she must go to Aunt March's. Amy complains to Hannah and Laurie.

Amy: I'd rather get the fever than go there!

Hannah: Bless your heart, child. It's to keep you well. You don't want to be sick.

Amy: But it's dull at Aunt March's, and she is so cross.

Laurie: I'll pop in every day to tell you how Beth is and take you out gallivanting.

Amy: Will you come every day and take me out for rides?

Laurie: Of course. And I'll bring you home as soon as Beth is well.

Narrator 2: The doctor comes and predicts that Beth's case will be light, prompting the sisters to resist sending a telegram to their mother. Amy reluctantly settles in with the gruff Aunt March.

Narrator 1: As November slips into December, Meg and Jo wait anxiously for Beth to improve. The doctor comes twice a day. Hannah stays up with her at night, and Jo rarely leaves her side. Finally the doctor says that they should send for Mrs. March. Jo confides her fears to Laurie.

Jo: The doctor told us to send for Mother.

Laurie: It has gotten that bad?

Jo: She doesn't recognize us. She doesn't even look like our Beth, and there's nobody to help us bear it.

Narrator 2: Laurie holds Jo's hands, comforting her.

Laurie: Keep hoping for the best. That will help you lots, Jo. Soon your mother will be here, and then everything will be right.

Jo: I'm so glad father is getting better, but it seems all the troubles come in a heap.

Laurie: I don't think she'll die. She's so good, and we all love her so much.

Jo: The good and dear people always do die.

Laurie: Jo, I'm going to tell you something that will lift your spirits. I telegraphed your mother yesterday, and Brooke answered that she'd come at once. She'll be here tonight. Everything will be all right. Aren't you glad I did it?

Narrator 1: Jo jumps up and throws her arms around his neck.

Jo: Oh, Laurie! I'm so glad! What made you send the telegram?

Laurie: Grandpa and I got worried and thought your mother would want to know.

Narrator 2: No sleep comes to the girls and Hannah as they keep their watch. At midnight, a shadow seems to fall upon Beth's wan face. Laurie leaves for the station, worried that the train will be delayed due to falling snow. At two in the morning, Beth lays so still that Jo prepares to kiss her dear sister goodbye. Then Hannah stirs from her sleep, and feels Beth's hands and face.

Hannah: The fever's turned! She's sleeping natural, her skin's damp, and she's breathing easily. Praise be given!

Narrator 1: The sun rises soon, and never has the world seemed so lovely to Meg and Jo. They look outside at the snow.

Meg: It looks like a fairy world.

Jo: Listen!

Laurie: *(Whispering.)* Girls! She's come! She's come!

Scene 4

Narrator 2: As Christmas approaches, there is an unseasonably warm spell of weather. Beth improves steadily, and Mr. March begins to talk of returning early in the new year. The morning of Christmas, the sisters enjoy their thoughtful gifts. Just when they think they can't be any happier, Laurie opens the parlor door.

Laurie: Here's another Christmas present for the March family.

Narrator 1: Laurie steps aside, and in his place appears a tall man, muffled up to his eyes, leaning on the arm of another tall man. Everyone is shocked into silence as they throw their arms around Mr. March. Mr. Brooke, who has also arrived, kisses Meg—entirely by mistake, he later claims.

Narrator 2: Mr. March tells how he had longed to surprise them and how the warm weather prompted his doctor to release him. He praises Mr. Brooke for his help, while watching Meg to see if she betrays any signs of affection for Mr. Brooke. Finally, the family settles down to dinner.

Jo: Just a year ago we were groaning over the dismal Christmas we expected to have. Do you remember?

Meg: Rather a pleasant year on the whole!

Amy: I think it's been a pretty hard one.

Beth: I'm glad it's over, because we've got Father back.

Mr. March: Rather a rough road for you to travel, my little pilgrims, especially the latter part of it. But you have got on bravely. I think the burdens are about to tumble off very soon. I've noticed several things about you all today.

Jo: What have you discovered?

Mr. March: First, look at Meg's hand. I remember a time when this hand was white and smooth and your first care was to keep it so. It is much prettier now. I'm sure the sewing done by these pricked fingers will last a long time. These hands will keep a happy home. I'm proud to shake this good, industrious little hand.

Beth: What about Jo?

Mr. March: I don't see the Jo I left a year ago. I see a young lady whose face has grown gentler. Her voice is lower; she doesn't bounce, but moves quietly. She takes care of a certain little person in a motherly way. I rather miss my wild girl, but if I get a strong, helpful, tenderhearted woman in her place, I shall feel quite satisfied.

Amy: Now, Beth.

Mr. March: There's so little of her, I'm afraid to say much, afraid she will slip away altogether. However, she is not so shy as she used to be. I've got you safe, my Beth, and I'll keep you so, please God.

Narrator 1: With those words, he draws Beth close.

Mr. March: I noticed that Amy ran errands for her mother all afternoon, gave Meg her place tonight, and that she does not fret much or call attention to herself. I conclude she has learned to think of other people more and of herself less. I am glad of this, for I shall be proud of a lovable daughter with a talent for making life beautiful to herself and others.

Narrator 2: The family ends their Christmas, grateful to hear their dear Beth singing sweetly while playing on her little piano.

Narrator 1: The next day the family enjoys having Mr. March nearby. Jo notices that Mr. Brooke has left his umbrella, and Meg blushes when his name is mentioned. When the youngsters tease Meg about the growing affection between Brooke and her, Meg protests that she is still young and that they are just friends. At this point the subject of their discussion, John Brooke, enters to retrieve his umbrella. Jo leaves to tell Father he's there, leaving him alone with Meg.

Meg: Mother would like to see you. Please sit down and I'll call her.

Mr. Brooke: Don't go. Are you afraid of me, Margaret?

Meg: How can I be afraid when you have been so kind to Father? I only wish I could thank you for it.

Mr. Brooke: Shall I tell you how?

Narrator 2: Mr. Brooke holds Meg's hand and looks at her lovingly.

Meg: Oh no, please don't—I'd rather not.

Mr. Brooke: I won't trouble you. I only want to know if you care for me a little. I love you so much.

Meg: *(Softly.)* I don't know.

Mr. Brooke: Will you try and find out?

Meg: I'm too young . . .

Mr. Brooke: I'll wait. In the meantime, you could be learning to like me. Would that be a hard lesson? Please choose to learn it.

Narrator 1: Meg feels excited, but doesn't know how to handle all the feelings growing in her.

Meg: I *don't* choose. I'm too young to be worried about such things.

Mr. Brooke: May I hope you'll change your mind? I'll wait and say nothing until you've had more time.

Meg: Don't think of me at all. I'd rather you wouldn't.

Narrator 2: Mr. Brooke is grave and pale now, looking at her wistfully. Just then Aunt March hobbles in to see Mr. March. Mr. Brooke vanishes into the study.

Aunt March: Bless me! What's all this?

Meg: It's Father's friend. I'm *so* surprised to see you!

Aunt March: That's evident. But what is Father's friend saying to make you look like a peony. There's mischief going on. I insist on knowing what it is!

Meg: Mr. Brooke came to get his umbrella.

Aunt March: Ah. I understand now. I heard that he was after you. You haven't gone and accepted him, child? Do you mean to marry him? If you do, not one penny of my money goes to you. Remember that and be a sensible girl.

Meg: I shall marry whom I please, Aunt March, and you can leave your money to any one you like.

Aunt March: Is that what you think of my advice? You'll be sorry for it when you've tried love in a cottage.

Meg: It can't be worse than what some people find in big houses.

Aunt March: You should marry well and help your family.

Meg: Father and Mother like John, even though he is poor. He is rich in friends. And Mr. Laurence is going to help him get started in his business.

Aunt March: So you intend to marry a man without money, position, or business, and go on working harder than you do now, when you might be comfortable all your days by minding me and doing better? I thought you had more sense, Meg.

Meg: I couldn't do better if I waited half my life! John is good and wise, talented and brave. I'm proud to think he cares for me.

Aunt March: He knows you have rich relations, child. That's the secret of his liking, I suspect.

Meg: How dare you say such a thing? John is above such meanness, and I won't listen to you a minute if you talk so. I'm not afraid of being poor, and I know I shall be happy with him because he loves me, and I . . .

Aunt March: Well, I wash my hands of the whole affair! You've lost more than you know by this folly. Don't expect anything from me when you're married.

Narrator 1: Slamming the door, Aunt March drives off. Meg stands for a moment, undecided whether to laugh or cry. Suddenly she is interrupted in her thoughts.

Mr. Brooke: I couldn't help hearing, Meg. Thank you for defending me and for caring for me.

Meg: I didn't know how much, till she abused you.

Mr. Brooke: May I stay and be happy?

Meg: *(Whispering.)* Yes, John.

Narrator 2: Mr. and Mrs. March meet with Meg and Mr. Brooke, and the first romance of the family becomes official. Later the family discusses the latest turn of events.

Mrs. March: In most families there comes, now and then, a year full of events. This has been such a one, but it ends well, after all.

Laurie: Don't you wish you could take a look forward and see where we shall all be in three years? I do.

Jo: I think not, for I might see something sad. Everyone looks so happy now. I don't believe they could be much improved.

Narrator 1: And so the curtain falls on Meg, Jo, Beth, and Amy, the "Little Women."

The End

Episodes from *Don Quixote*

Miguel de Cervantes

Adapted by Jennifer L. Kroll

Summary

A middle-aged Spanish gentleman named Don Quixote loses his mind and begins to think that he is a knight. A number of his humorous "adventures" follow. He sets out to be knighted, challenges travelers he meets on the road, recruits a local farmer as his "squire," and mistakes windmills for giants. Meanwhile, his niece, housekeeper, and friends try to figure out a way to keep him at home.

Background Information

Spanish poet, playwright, and novelist Miguel de Cervantes Saavedra lived from 1547 to 1616. He is probably the most celebrated and famous figure in Spanish literature. Cervantes's first poem was published in 1569, when he was 21. His most famous work is the novel *Don Quixote*, first published in 1605. *Don Quixote* is a long, humorous work, which pokes fun at the tradition of heroic knight-at-arms tales. It is an episodic novel. This play only details a very few of Don Quixote's many adventures as described by Cervantes in the longer work.

Presentation Suggestions

Seat Don Quixote front and center. You may wish to seat him on a stool or higher chair, so that he is a bit higher than other readers. Seat Sancho Panza beside Don Quixote. Place the Narrators to the side. Seat Don Quixote's Niece and Housekeeper, the Priest, and Nicholas the Barber in one group. Seat the Maids and Innkeeper in another group. Seat the Merchants and the Young Man in a third group. As the play progresses, you might wish to have Don Quixote move to take a seat or stand near the various groups of readers.

Props

Don Quixote and Sancho Panza can use mops or brooms as their "steeds." Don Quixote can wear some sort of armor and sport a yardstick or other object as his "lance." He might wear a pot, bucket or bowl on his head as a helmet. The Maids and Housekeeper can wear aprons. The Priest can wear a robe of some sort. The Housekeeper, Niece, Nicholas, and the Priest should have some books to examine during Scene 6.

Characters

- ❀ Narrators 1, 2, and 3
- ❀ Don Quixote, *a middle-aged gentleman who thinks he's a knight*
- ❀ Niece of Don Quixote
- ❀ Maids 1 and 2
- ❀ Innkeeper
- ❀ Merchants 1 and 2
- ❀ Young Man
- ❀ Housekeeper of Don Quixote
- ❀ Priest, *a friend of Don Quixote*
- ❀ Nicholas the Barber, *a friend of the Priest*
- ❀ Sancho Panza, *a local peasant farmer*

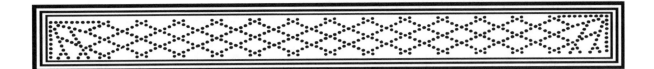

Episodes from *Don Quixote*

Scene 1

Narrator 1: In the village of La Mancha in Spain there once lived a gentleman of about fifty who loved to read books about knights and heroes and their great adventures. Because he was a reasonably wealthy man, he had plenty of time for reading.

Don Quixote: This is such a beautiful passage, Niece. Listen. *(Reading.)* The high heavens that with their stars divinely fortify you in your divinity and make you deserving of the desert that your greatness deserves.

Niece: But Uncle, that doesn't mean anything. It's pure nonsense. And this story you've been reading me—it could never have really happened.

Don Quixote: What do you mean? Of course it happened! Everyone knows that Amadis of Gaul was the greatest knight that ever lived!

Niece: But even the greatest knight couldn't have killed three giants with a single sword stroke. To begin with, there's no such thing as a giant. And even if giants existed, how could anyone kill three in one blow? It's impossible. Why don't you put that book down, uncle, and come have some dinner?

Don Quixote: Not now! Not now! First I must see whether our hero is able to rescue the fair Princess Paulina from the dreadful ogre holding her captive.

Narrator 2: Don Quixote buried himself in books. He spent the nights reading from twilight till daybreak and the days from dawn till dark. Eventually, from little sleep and much reading, his brain dried up, and he lost his wits.

Narrator 3: Then Don Quixote fell into the strangest fancy that ever a madman had. He decided that he should become a knight errant, a knight traveling through the world on a horse and wearing armor, in search of adventures.

Niece: What are you doing, Uncle?

Don Quixote: I'm cleaning my armor, Niece.

Niece: *Your* armor? But that suit of armor has been standing in a back corner of the house for years, rusting and collecting dust.

Don Quixote: It is very important for a knight errant to keep his armor well cleaned.

Niece: A knight errant? What are you talking about?

Don Quixote: *(Ignoring her.)* Hmmm. This is very bad. This helmet has no visor. What am I going to do about a visor?

Niece: Uncle, I'm getting worried about you.

Don Quixote: *(Still ignoring her.)* I'll have to get some pasteboard and make one.

Niece: You're making a visor out of pasteboard? Uncle, the heat must be getting to you. Come and have a cold drink with me.

Don Quixote: *(Turning to her.)* I've decided to name my steed Rocinante. I think the name has a truly grand sound to it, very noble and distinguished. What do you think?

Niece: What steed are you talking about, Uncle? You can't mean your old hunting horse out in the barn. That horse is nothing but skin and bones.

Don Quixote: *(In a reverie.)* Rocinante! Rocinante! I shall ride forth on Rocinante and do great deeds in the name of the Lady Dulcinea del Toboso!

Niece: Who is this Lady Dulcinea? We don't know any Lady Dulcinea.

Don Quixote: She is a princess, the fairest and most virtuous lady in all the world. She inspires me in everything I do.

Niece: Uncle, I'm fairly certain that there are no princesses in Toboso. There are only merchants' wives and farm girls. Uncle, are you sure you're feeling OK? Should I call for the doctor?

Scene 2

Narrator 1: The next morning, Don Quixote begins his career as a knight errant. He puts on his armor and his helmet with its pasteboard visor, slings on his shield, grabs his lance, and mounts Rocinante.

Narrator 2: He is only barely out into the open country, however, when he discovers a problem with his plan.

Don Quixote: Oh no! I just remembered! The laws of chivalry forbid my taking arms against any other knight until I have been knighted, and I have not been properly knighted!

Narrator 3: After mulling over this problem for a while, Don Quixote comes up with a solution.

Don Quixote: I'll just have to have myself knighted by the first man I meet on the road. I've read a number of books in which it was done this way.

Narrator 1: Satisfied with this solution, Don Quixote rides on, talking to himself.

Don Quixote: Who can doubt that in ages to come the story of my famous deeds shall be widely told. How fortunate those ages will be, for my deeds shall be worthy to be engraved in bronze, carved in marble, and painted on wood.

Narrator 2: Sometimes he calls out the name of Dulcinea . . .

Don Quixote: O Princess Dulcinea, mistress of this captive heart! You commanded me not to appear in your beauteous presence, and that has wounded me deeply. Be merciful toward the one who suffers so much for you!

Narrator 3: By nightfall, both Don Quixote and his horse are weary and very hungry. Don Quixote looks in all directions for a shepherd's hut or a castle where he might take shelter. Finally, he spots an inn, which seems to him to be a fortress with four towers, a drawbridge, and a deep moat.

Narrator 1: A short distance from the inn, Don Quixote stops. He waits for a dwarf to sound a trumpet from the castle wall, announcing his approach, for this is what always happens to knights in the books he reads. Two maids standing at the door to the inn watch his strange behavior with fascination.

Maid 1: What's he doing, sitting there like that?

Maid 2: And why is he wearing that ridiculous getup?

Narrator 2: Somewhere nearby, a swineherd blows a horn to call his hogs together. Don Quixote thinks a dwarf is giving notice of his arrival at the castle. He rides up to the inn door.

Don Quixote: *(To the peasant women.)* Good evening, fair ladies.

Narrator 3: Both women back away from the crazy-looking man who is approaching with a spear in one hand.

Maid 1: Did he just call us fair ladies?

Don Quixote: I beg you, ladies, not to run away in fear, for I follow the code of chivalry and would harm no innocent being, especially not fair maidens of your high rank.

Narrator 1: Both women start laughing.

Maid 2: Listen to him! He thinks we're fair maidens of high rank!

Narrator 2: The innkeeper comes to the door, where he sees the ridiculous looking Don Quixote and the laughing women. He decides to get in on the fun.

Innkeeper: If your worship is looking for a place to rest, Sir Knight, we have plenty of everything at this inn, except for beds. It's not a fancy place, and there are no beds left, but we will give you whatever other hospitality we can.

Don Quixote: For me, sir, whatever you have is enough. My only ornaments are my arms. My rest is the bloody fray.

Narrator 3: The women erupt into more hysterical laughter and continue laughing while Don Quixote awkwardly dismounts from Rocinante and hands the reins to the Innkeeper.

Don Quixote: Please take good care of my steed, for no better piece of horseflesh ever munched oats in all the world.

Narrator 1: The Innkeeper stares at the bony body of Rocinante, then winks at the maids. When he returns from stabling the horse, the Innkeeper finds the two women helping Don Quixote get out of his armor.

Maid 1: Well, I've got the rest of it, but I can't get this helmet off. We'll have to cut these ribbons that are holding the pasteboard visor on.

Don Quixote: No! No! Don't cut off my visor! I spent so much time attaching it.

Maid 2: I just don't think there's any other way we can get your helmet off.

Don Quixote: Then I shall leave it on.

Maid 1: _(Laughing.)_ As you wish, Sir Knight.

Maid 2: Would you like anything to eat, Sir Knight?

Don Quixote: I would gladly take some food, for I think there is nothing that would come more opportunely.

Narrator 2: The maids set Don Quixote a table and bring him some baked fish and blackened bread. He soon finds that he can't get anything into his own mouth while wearing his helmet and visor. The maids have to help him eat.

Narrator 3: Drinking proves to be even more difficult for Don Quixote in his helmet. The laughing maids have to pour wine into Don Quixote's mouth through a straw.

Scene 3

Narrator 1: Once he is finished eating, Don Quixote finds the innkeeper, who is in the stables. Don Quixote falls on his knees before the innkeeper.

Don Quixote: Never will I arise from where I am till you grant me the favor I beg of you. I ask you to do a thing that will bring you much honor and will benefit the whole human race, as well.

Innkeeper: Sir, please get up. You're kneeling in mud.

Don Quixote: I will not rise until you promise me that you will grant the favor I ask.

Innkeeper: OK, OK. I'll grant the favor.

Don Quixote: I had expected no less from your great magnificence, dear sir.

Innkeeper: Now please get up.

Narrator 2: Don Quixote gets up.

Don Quixote: The favor I ask is this: will you knight me tomorrow morning? This night I will keep watch over my armor in the chapel of your castle, as is customary. And tomorrow, if you will honor me by knighting me, my dearest wish will be fulfilled and I will have the right to ride through all corners of the world in search of adventures.

Innkeeper: _(To himself.)_ Wow! This man is really nuts! I can have some real fun with him! _(To Don Quixote.)_ I am more than happy to grant you the favor you ask, sir. For in my youth, I, too, devoted myself to the honorable profession of knighthood. In my search for adventures, I even made it as far as the Fish Market of Malagra, the Tavern of Toledo, and the Little Market Place at Segovia. Those were the days!

Don Quixote: And then you retired to this castle.

Innkeeper: I did. And a fine "castle" it is, too! But sir, I'm sorry to have to report to you that this castle does not have a chapel.

Don Quixote: No chapel? Impossible! Everyone knows that all castles have chapels.

Innkeeper: Well our chapel had to be pulled down in order to be rebuilt, you see. You can watch your armor in the hallway tonight, if that will do, or out in the yard.

Narrator 3: Don Quixote decides to watch his armor in the yard that lies on one end of the inn. He gathers all the parts of his armor together and lays it all down on a stone watering trough next to a well. Then he buckles on his shield and begins to pace up and down in front of the trough.

Narrator 1: Shortly after nightfall, a package carrier who has been staying at the inn realizes that he has forgotten to give his mules any water. The carrier comes down to fill the watering trough. He decides to move the armor from the trough. But before he can touch it, Don Quixote calls out.

Don Quixote: You, whoever you are, rash knight, who comes to touch the armor of the famed Don Quixote de la Mancha, take heed what you do! Do not touch this armor unless you wish to lose your life!

Narrator 2: The carrier pays no attention to Don Quixote's speech. He throws the armor off of the trough and onto the ground.

Don Quixote: Lady Dulcinea, let not your favor and protection fail me as I face this first trial of my knightly career!

Narrator 3: Don Quixote raises his lance in both hands and bonks the carrier on the head. The man falls down, unconscious. Don Quixote gathers his armor and places it back on the trough. He begins pacing again.

Narrator 1: A little later, another man comes to water his mules at the trough. Once again, Don Quixote attacks when the man dares to touch his armor.

Don Quixote: O beauteous Lady Dulcinea! Now is the time to turn your magnificent eyes on this, your captive knight, and assist him.

Narrator 2: When the innkeeper realizes that his guests are being attacked, he decides that he had better "knight" Don Quixote as soon as possible and end the "watching of arms" in the yard. He goes down to have a word with Don Quixote.

Innkeeper: Seeing as there is no chapel in the castle, it seems to me that there is no need for us to go through a whole night of arms watching. You have watched your arms for four hours, and I know for a fact that the minimum required of a knight-to-be is actually two hours.

Don Quixote: Two hours? Are you sure? I thought the watching of arms had to go on all night.

Innkeeper: I'm quite certain that two hours is sufficient. Let me see if the fair maidens you met earlier will assist with the ceremony.

Narrator 3: The innkeeper and the maids perform a fake knighting ceremony. The innkeeper reads out of his bookkeeping ledger in a ceremonial tone of voice, mumbling so that Don Quixote cannot hear what he is reading. The two maids try their hardest to keep from giggling. At the end of the reading, the innkeeper taps Don Quixote's shoulders with his sword.

Innkeeper: I dub thee Sir Don Quixote de la Mancha.

Maid 1: May your worship become world famous and have great luck in all battles.

Don Quixote: Thank you, fair lady. Thank you all. And now, I must be going. The open road calls and there are many who need my assistance.

Scene 4

Narrator 1: Don Quixote rides off in search of adventures. Sometime the next morning, he comes to a crossroads. He stops to consider which road to take.

Don Quixote: I believe I will let my horse make the decision. This is what knights errant do in the books I've read.

Narrator 2: Don Quixote drops the reins. Immediately, Rocinante begins heading toward his home stable, which is not too far away.

Narrator 3: Don Quixote rides along for a couple more miles. Suddenly, in the distance, he sees a group of merchants approaching. Believing a knightly adventure is heading his way, he positions himself in the middle of the road with his lance in his hands. As the merchants come within earshot, he calls out.

Don Quixote: You who wish to pass this way—confess that there is not in the whole world a more beauteous maiden than the Empress of la Mancha, the peerless Dulcinea del Toboso.

Merchant 1: This man must be insane. Look at his armor! He's dressed up like a knight!

Merchant 2: He wants us to say something about some lady named Dulcinea before he'll let us pass.

Merchant 1: *(To Don Quixote, jokingly.)* Sir Knight, we do not know who this good lady is that you speak of. Show her to us and, if she is as beauteous as you say, we will most willingly acknowledge her beauty.

Don Quixote: If I were to show her to you, then her beauty would be obvious. There wouldn't be any point in your acknowledging it. You must confess her to be the most beautiful woman in the world without seeing her. If you will not, you must do battle with me!

Merchant 2: Sir Knight, we are not about to swear to something that we don't know is true. Show us at least a small portrait of this Lady Dulcinea.

Merchant 1: Yes, yes! We want to see a portrait of your lady. Even if the picture shows us that she squints or is humpbacked or that her eyes drip, we will still do what you ask.

Don Quixote: Her eyes do not drip, vile scoundrels! She is not squinting or humpbacked! You shall pay for this blasphemy!

Narrator 1: With these words he begins to charge at the merchants with his lance aimed at them. Fortunately for the merchants, Rocinante trips on a stone and sends Don Quixote flying head over heels into a field.

Narrator 2: Don Quixote finds that he cannot get up because his armor is too heavy. He struggles, attempting to rise.

Don Quixote: Flee not, you band of cowards! It is not my fault, but my horse's that I lie here.

Narrator 3: One of the merchants, in a bad mood, dismounts from his own horse and kicks Don Quixote several times in the ribs. Then the merchant grabs Don Quixote's lance and breaks it into little pieces.

Don Quixote: Vile scoundrel! Villain!

Narrator 1: The merchants all ride off, laughing. They leave Don Quixote lying by the side of the road, unable to rise. He spends the next several hours in this position. To pass the time, he begins reciting poems about famous battles.

Narrator 2: Finally, a young man from his own village passes by.

Young Man: What's this?

Narrator 3: As the young man gets nearer, he hears Don Quixote's voice.

Young Man: Sir? Sir? Why are you lying there? Are you OK?

Narrator 1: Don Quixote continues reciting poetry. The young man lifts up Don Quixote's visor, dusts off his face, and recognizes him.

Young Man: Master Quixote! Why are you wearing this armor? And who has done this to you?

Narrator 2: With great effort, the young man hoists Don Quixote up off the ground and onto Rocinante. Then he leads the battered Don Quixote back to his own home.

Scene 5

Narrator 3: Hearing a noise in the yard, Don Quixote's niece and housekeeper rush out of the house. The local priest accompanies them. Both of the women throw their arms around Don Quixote.

Niece: Oh thank heavens you're home! We've all been worried sick about you!

Don Quixote: Cease to embrace me, dear ladies, for I am sorely wounded through the fault of my steed. Carry me to my bed and, if possible, call the great Dr. Urganda to examine and cure my wounds.

Young Man: I found him lying in a field, reciting poems about chivalry. He was delirious.

Housekeeper: Confound those books of chivalry! They have caused all of this! Well, we'll know how to cure him here, and we won't need the great Dr. Urganda. *(To Don Quixote.)* Come along to your room, sir.

Narrator 1: They take Don Quixote straight to his bed.

Priest: I don't really see any wounds on him, just a lot of bruises.

Don Quixote: Indeed, I am bruised all over due to a grievous fall during a fight with ten of the most monstrous and horrible giants to be found anywhere on earth.

Priest: So now there are giants in the deal! Well, don't worry, sir. We'll take care of those giants. You just rest now.

Scene 6

Narrator 2: The next day, as Don Quixote sleeps, his niece, housekeeper, and priest all meet in the family library. The priest's friend, Nicholas the Barber, has also joined them.

Housekeeper: Here, I'll open this window. Then we can throw all of his books straight out into the yard and make a giant bonfire out of them.

Priest: We might find some books that don't deserve to be burned. We had better go through them carefully.

Niece: No. Let's not bother. None of these books should be pardoned. They are all guilty of causing my uncle's trouble. Throw them all out into the courtyard. Or else we can cart them off into the back-yard. The bonfire will be less of a nuisance there.

Priest: Well, I think we should at least read the titles first . . . Nicholas, you hand me the books one at a time, and we'll all decide whether each book should be saved or burned.

Nicholas: Here's the first one.

Narrator 3: The priest reads the title.

Priest: *Amadis of Gaul.* I have heard that this was the first book about chivalry printed in this country. It inspired the others that followed. Therefore, it seems to me, we should condemn it to the flames without mercy.

Nicholas: No, sir. We shouldn't burn that one! I've heard it's the best book of its kind ever written. Therefore, it should be pardoned.

Priest: Alright. We'll grant this one mercy then.

Narrator 1: He sets the book aside.

Priest: Let's take a look at that other one you've got there.

Nicholas: This one's called *The Exploits of Esplandian, the son of Amadis of Gaul.*

Priest: We've spared the father, but let's burn the son. He'll be the foundation of our bonfire. Mistress Housekeeper, throw him into the yard!

Narrator 2: The housekeeper takes pleasure in throwing the thick book out of the window.

Narrator 3: The book sorting process continues for about an hour, until suddenly the group in the library hears Don Quixote shouting upstairs.

Don Quixote: Rally around me, valorous knights! We must not lose this tournament!

Narrator 1: They all rush upstairs, where they find Don Quixote running around his bedroom, waving his sword in all directions.

Priest: Well, sir, it seems to me that you weren't wounded after all. You're up and about already.

Don Quixote: I am not wounded, but I have been bruised and battered in this tournament.

Niece: Please, uncle, get back into bed. You shouldn't be running around like this. Your health is at risk.

Narrator 2: They coax Don Quixote back into bed. That night, the housekeeper rounds up all the remaining books in the library and other rooms of the house. She builds a huge bonfire.

Priest: Let's board up the library door and plaster over it, too, just for good measure.

Niece: Yes. That's a good idea. When my uncle asks about his books and library, I'll just make up some kind of a story.

Narrator 3: They act quickly. Two days later, when Don Quixote gets up again, the first thing he does is stroll down toward his library . . .

Don Quixote: That's funny. I used to have a library here. I'm sure of it. But now there is only this wall.

Narrator 1: He stops his housekeeper and niece as they come down the hall.

Don Quixote: Where is my library? I'm sure it was here a few days ago.

Housekeeper: What library? You never had a library.

Don Quixote: But I'm sure I did. I had hundreds of books.

Housekeeper: There are no books here.

Narrator 2: Don Quixote looks confused.

Niece: You see, Uncle, an enchanter came one night after you went away. He got down from the dragon he was riding on and went into your library.

Narrator 3: Don Quixote's eyes light up with interest.

Niece: I don't know what he did inside, but there was a terrible amount of smoke and fire. When we dared to look again, the library and all the books were gone. The enchanter said that his name was the Sage Munaton and that he was acting out of an old grudge that he bore against the owner of the books.

Don Quixote: He must have said that his name was Freston.

Housekeeper: Yes, come to think of it, his name might have been Freston. In any case, his name ended with a "ton."

Don Quixote: Yes, Freston it must have been. He is a great enchanter and an old enemy of mine. I knew that he bore me a grudge. Well, well. I shall have to avenge myself for this great wrong. I must saddle up Rocinante at once and find the evil Freston!

Niece: But wouldn't it be better to stay peacefully at home, Uncle? Aren't you enjoying getting some rest?

Don Quixote: For a knight errant, my dear niece, there is never rest.

Scene 7

Narrator 1: Despite these words to his niece, Don Quixote stays at home quietly for fifteen days. He shows no signs of any desire to return to his strange behavior.

Niece: I believe my uncle's mental health may be better at last.

Housekeeper: Burning those books was the best thing we ever did.

Narrator 2: What Don Quixote's niece and housekeeper do not know is that all this while, Don Quixote has been looking after some new knightly business. He has been trying to convince a local peasant farmer, Sancho Panza, to become his squire and come along on his knightly expeditions.

Don Quixote: If you come with me, Sancho, sooner or later an adventure is going to occur in which we win an island. And when we do, I promise that I shall leave you there as governor.

Sancho Panza: As governor? Really? Me?

Don Quixote: Absolutely. But you must be ready to set out with me the day after tomorrow.

Sancho Panza: Well, all right. I would like to become governor of an island someday.

Don Quixote: Just remember to bring some saddlebags. I'll take care of the rest.

Sancho Panza: I'm planning to ride on this good donkey of mine.

Don Quixote: A donkey? I'm not sure I can allow that.

Sancho Panza: What's wrong with riding a donkey?

Don Quixote: Well, I've never read about a knight's squire riding on a donkey. I don't think it's the done thing.

Sancho Panza: But this is a very fine donkey.

Don Quixote: Well, alright. Bring the donkey, then.

Scene 8

Narrator 3: Two days later, Don Quixote and Sancho Panza ride out together. Sancho is mounted on his donkey.

Sancho Panza: Remember what you promised me, Sir Knight. Don't forget about the island. I'm looking forward to governing it.

Don Quixote: I haven't forgotten my promise, and I intend to keep it. The knights of old used to give their squires many fine gifts, and I plan to follow that custom. You may wind up not only as a governor, but also as a count or duke. There is a chance you may even be made king of some distant land or other.

Sancho Panza: Wow! A king! That would be even better than governor!

Narrator 1: At that moment, the two riders catch sight of thirty or forty windmills standing in the distance on the plane.

Don Quixote: Fortune has smiled upon us, Sancho. Look over there, where more than thirty monstrous giants appear! We shall do battle with them. Once we have wiped this wicked brood off the face of the earth, we can take the spoils and begin to get rich.

Sancho Panza: Giants? I don't see any giants.

Don Quixote: Over there—with the long arms. Did you know that some giants have arms up to 60 miles long?

Sancho Panza: Those aren't giants! They're windmills! You're mistaking their sails for arms!

Don Quixote: It's quite clear, Sancho, that you are totally inexperienced in the matter of adventures. They are indeed giants. If you're afraid, then just step aside and stay out of the action.

Narrator 2: Saying this, Don Quixote digs his spurs into Rocinante and heads off toward the windmills.

Don Quixote: Do not run away, cowards!

Sancho Panza: Come back! I'm certain that those aren't giants! They're windmills!

Narrator 3: At that moment, a wind arises and the sails of the windmills begin to turn.

Don Quixote: _(Addressing the windmills.)_ No matter how many arms you have, I do not fear you!

Narrator 1: Don Quixote lifts his eyes to the skies.

Don Quixote: Dearest Lady Dulcinea, my soul is yours forever!

Narrator 2: Covering himself with his shield and readying his lance, Don Quixote charges the nearest windmill, thrusting his lance into the sail.

Narrator 3: With his lance caught up in the quickly turning sail, Don Quixote is thrown into the air and sent rolling across the plain. The lance snaps into a number of pieces. Seeing that Don Quixote is hurt, Sancho rushes to his side.

Sancho Panza: I told you those giants were only windmills!

Don Quixote: Silence, friend Sancho. Battle situations are always unpredictable. These monstrous forms may now appear to be windmills, but that is only because the enchanter Freston has transformed them.

Sancho Panza: But why would an enchanter do such a thing?

Don Quixote: Have I not told you of the great grudge that Freston bears against me? He is the same enchanter who robbed me of my books and library. And now he intends to rob me of the glory I would have gained in conquering a hoard of giants.

Sancho Panza: Here, sir, let me give you a hand.

Narrator 1: Don Quixote collects the pieces of his lance, and Sancho helps him onto his horse.

Don Quixote: I remember reading about a certain Spanish knight named Diego Perez de Vargas. When his weapon was broken in battle, he tore a huge limb from an oak tree and performed great, heroic deeds using that limb as a weapon.

Sancho Panza: Careful with that arm, sir. I think you've hurt it badly.

Don Quixote: I intend to tear off an even greater oak limb than the one used by Sir Diego Perez. I will do such deeds with that huge branch that you shall consider yourself lucky to have witnessed it all.

Sancho Panza: I believe you will, sir. I believe everything you say. But for now, Sir Knight, if you could just sit a little bit more upright. You seem to be riding lopsided.

This is just the beginning of the many adventures of Don Quixote de la Mancha and his squire, Sancho Panza. To read more, pick up a copy of Don Quixote *by Miguel de Cervantes.*

The End

The Necklace

Guy de Maupassant

Adapted by Suzanne I. Barchers

Summary

The young Mathilde resents her simple life-style, yearning to have wealth and a lifestyle more consistent with her beauty. When her husband is invited to an elegant reception, they agree that she will buy an elegant dress. Mathilde borrows a diamond necklace from a wealthy friend. After the reception, the necklace disappears on their way home. They borrow heavily to replace it, taking ten years to repay the debt. Mathilde ages dramatically, and her friend hardly recognizes her when they meet by chance. Mathilde decides to tell her about the loss and replacement of the necklace, whereupon her friend informs her that it was simply costume jewelry.

Background Information

Guy de Maupassant (1850–1893) was born in Normandy, a province of France. He served in the French army during the Franco-Prussian War and worked in Paris as a clerk while trying to find a publisher for his work. Gustave Flaubert proved to be a valuable mentor, helping him to polish his writing. His first story, "Ball of Fat," was met with critical acclaim. During his career, de Maupassant wrote sixteen volumes of short stories, six novels, and several volumes of travel sketches. This story reflects his understanding of life in Paris in the late 1800s.

Presentation Suggestions

Arrange the characters in the following order: Narrator 1, Narrator 2, Mathilde, Monsieur Loisel, and Madame Forestier.

Props

Mathilde and Monsieur Loisel should be dressed in simple yet serviceable clothing. Madame Forestier should be dressed in a more elegant style. The narrators can wear black shirts and pants, with neckerchiefs around their necks.

Characters

- ❀ Narrators 1 and 2
- ❀ Mathilde, *wife of M. Loisel*
- ❀ M. Loisel, *clerk*
- ❀ Mme. Forestier, *wealthy friend*

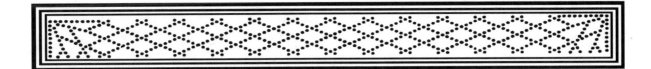

The Necklace

Scene 1

Narrator 1: Mathilde is a pretty and charming girl, born, as if by an accident of fate, into a family of clerks. With no dowry, no prospects, no way of being met, understood, loved, and married by a man both prosperous and famous, she finally marries a minor clerk from the Ministry of Education.

Narrator 2: Mathilde dresses plainly because she cannot afford fine clothes, and she is as unhappy as a woman who has come down in the world. She grieves incessantly, feeling that she has been born for all the luxuries of a rich woman's life. She grieves over the shabbiness of her apartment. Things that another woman of her class would not notice gnaw at her and make her furious. She even resents the sight of the maid she employs to keep her humble home clean.

Narrator 1: Mathilde dreams of having a grand home and holding fashionable dinner parties. She has no evening clothes, no jewels, nothing. But she feels that was the kind of life she should have had. She has a well-to-do friend, a classmate from her school days, whom she no longer goes to see, simply because she feels so distressed upon returning home. Then one evening, Mathilde's husband comes home proudly holding out a large envelope.

M. Loisel: Look, I've got something for you.

Mathilde: What is it?

M. Loisel: I'll read it. "The Minister of Education and Madame George Ramponneau beg Monsieur and Madame Loisel to do them the honor of attending an evening reception at the Ministerial Mansion on Friday, January 18."

Mathilde: What good is that to me?

M. Loisel: My dear, I thought you'd be thrilled to death. You never get a chance to go out, and this is a real affair, a wonderful one! I had an awful time getting an invitation. Everybody wants one; it's much sought after, and not many clerks have a chance at one. You'll see all the most important people there.

Mathilde: What do you think I have to go in?

M. Loisel: Why, the dress you wear when we go to the theater. That looks quite nice, I think.

Narrator 2: He stops talking, dazed and distracted to see two large tears slowly roll down from the corners of her eyes to the corners of her mouth.

M. Loisel: Why, what's the matter? What's the trouble?

41

Mathilde: Oh, nothing. Only I don't have an evening dress and therefore I can't go to that affair. Give the invitation to some friend at the office whose wife can dress better than I can.

M. Loisel: Let's see, Mathilde. How much would a suitable outfit cost—one you could wear for other affairs too—something very simple?

Narrator 1: She thinks it over for several seconds, going over her allowance and thinking also of the amount she could ask for without bringing an immediate refusal and an exclamation of dismay from the thrifty clerk.

Mathilde: I'm not sure exactly, but I think with four hundred francs I could manage it.

Narrator 2: He turns a bit pale, for he has set aside just that amount to buy a rifle so that, the following summer, he can join some friends who are getting up a group to shoot larks on the plain near Nanterre.

M. Loisel: All right. I'll give you four hundred francs. But try to get a nice dress.

Narrator 1: As the day of the party approaches, Mathilde seems sad, moody, and ill at ease. Her outfit is ready, however.

M. Loisel: What's the matter? You've been out of sorts for three days.

Mathilde: It's embarrassing not to have a jewel or a gem—nothing to wear on my dress. I'll look like a pauper. I'd almost rather not go to that party.

M. Loisel: Why not wear some flowers? They're very fashionable this season. For ten francs you can get two or three gorgeous roses.

Mathilde: No! There's nothing more humiliating than to look poor among rich women.

M. Loisel: My, but you're silly. Go see your friend Madame Forestier and ask her to lend you some jewelry. You and she know each other well enough for you to do that.

Mathilde: Why, that's so! I hadn't thought of it.

Narrator 2: The next day Mathilde pays her friend a visit and tells her of her predicament. Madame Forestier takes out a large jewel box from a closet and opens it.

Mme. Forestier: Pick something out, my dear.

Narrator 1: Mathilde tries on a pearl necklace, a Venetian cross, and other adornments.

Mathilde: Haven't you something else?

Mme. Forestier: Oh, yes, keep on looking. I don't know just what you'd like.

Narrator 2: All at once she finds, in a black satin box, a superb diamond necklace. Her hands tremble as she clasps it around her neck. She stands in ecstasy, looking at her reflection.

Mathilde: Could I borrow that, just that and nothing else?

Mme. Forestier: Why, of course.

Narrator 1: Mathilde throws her arms around her friend, kisses her warmly and flees with her treasure.

Scene 2

Narrator 2: The day of the party arrives. Mathilde is a sensation. She's the prettiest one there, fashionable, gracious, smiling, and wild with joy. All the men turn to look at her and beg to meet her. All the cabinet officials ask to waltz with her. Even the minister notices her.

Narrator 1: She dances madly, delirious with pleasure, giving no thought to anything in the triumph of her beauty and success. Finally, they leave around four o'clock in the morning. Monsieur Loisel throws her modest wrap over her shoulders. Not wanting to be seen by the women in their furs, Mathilde hurries away.

M. Loisel: Hold on! You'll catch cold outside. I'll call a cab.

Mathilde: Let's start on our way. We'll find a carriage soon enough.

Narrator 2: They walk toward the Seine but can't find a cab. Finally, on the docks they find one of those carriages that one sees in Paris only after nightfall, as if they were ashamed to show their drabness during daylight hours. It drops them at their door, and they climb wearily up to their apartment. Mathilde looks in the mirror to admire herself once again as she removes her wrap.

Mathilde: Oh no!

M. Loisel: What's the trouble?

Mathilde: I . . . I . . . I don't have Madame Forestier's necklace.

M. Loisel: What! You can't mean it! It's impossible!

Narrator 1: They hunt everywhere, through the folds of the dress, through the folds of the coat, in the pockets. They find nothing.

M. Loisel: Are you sure you had it when leaving the dance?

Mathilde: Yes, I felt it when I was in the hall of the ministry.

M. Loisel: But if you had lost it on the street, we'd have heard it drop. It must be in the cab.

Mathilde: Yes. Quite likely. Did you get its number?

M. Loisel: No. Didn't you notice it either?

Mathilde: No.

M. Loisel: I'll retrace our steps on foot to see if I can find it.

Narrator 2: He goes out while she slumps in a chair. He returns at about seven o'clock.

M. Loisel: No luck. I'll go to the police, the cab companies, and put a notice in the newspaper. If we offer a reward, perhaps it will turn up.

Narrator 1: That evening Loisel returns from work. He is pale, his face lined.

M. Loisel: We'll have to write your friend to tell her you have broken the catch and are having it repaired. That will give us a little time to turn around.

Narrator 2: At the end of the week they have given up all hope.

M. Loisel: We must think how to replace that piece of jewelry. We'll take the case to jewelers to see if we can find a replacement.

Mathilde: I've looked around some and found a similar string of diamonds in a shop in Palais Royal.

M. Loisel: How much is it?

Mathilde: It's 40,000 francs, but he will sell it for 36,000 francs.

M. Loisel: Let's go see him. We'll need to negotiate a price in case we can return it. We can use the 18,000 francs I inherited from my father. Somehow I'll borrow the rest.

Narrator 1: The jeweler agrees to take back the necklace for 34,000 if the lost one is found before the end of February. Loisel goes about raising the money, asking a thousand francs from one, four hundred from another, a hundred here, sixty there. He signs notes, makes ruinous deals, does business with loan sharks, runs the whole gamut of moneylenders.

Narrator 2: He compromises the rest of his life, risks his signature without knowing if he'll be able to honor it, and then, terrified by the outlook for the future, by the blackness of despair about to close around him, he goes to claim the new necklace. They return it to Madame Forestier, hoping she won't notice the substitution.

Scene 3

Narrator 1: Thereafter, Mathilde experiences the horrible life of the needy. She dismisses her maid, and she and her husband are forced to rent a garret under the eaves. She learns to clean, cook, and do the laundry. Clad like a peasant, she bargains with the fruit dealers, the grocer, the butcher—and is insulted by all of them.

Narrator 2: Monsieur Loisel labors at work and at an evening job, paying off some notes, renewing others. This goes on for ten years. Finally all is paid back, including the exorbitant rates of the loan sharks and accumulated compound interest. Mathilde appears to be an old woman, but sometimes she sits near the window and thinks of that long-ago evening when, at the dance, she had been so beautiful and admired. What would have happened if she had not lost that necklace?

Narrator 1: One Sunday Mathilde goes for a walk on the Champs Élyseés to relax a bit from the week's labors. She notices a woman strolling with a child. It's Madame Forestier, still young looking, still beautiful, still charming. Should Mathilde speak? Should she tell her the whole story now that everything is paid off? Why not?

Mathilde: Hello, Jeanne.

Mme. Forestier: But . . . Madame . . . I don't recognize . . . you must be mistaken.

Mathilde: No, I'm Mathilde Loisel.

Mme. Forestier: Oh, my poor Mathilde. How you've changed!

Mathilde: Yes, I've had a hard time since last seeing you. And plenty of misfortunes—and all on account of you!

Mme. Forestier: Of me? How do you mean?

Mathilde: Do you remember that diamond necklace you loaned me to wear to the dance at the ministry?

Mme. Forestier: Yes, but what about it?

Mathilde: Well, I lost it.

Mme. Forestier: You lost it! But you returned it.

Mathilde: I brought you another just like it. And we've been paying for it for ten years now. You can imagine that wasn't easy for us who had nothing. Well, it's over now, and I am glad of it.

Mme. Forestier: You mean to say you bought a diamond necklace to replace mine?

Mathilde: Yes. You never noticed, then? They were quite alike.

Mme. Forestier: Oh, my poor Mathilde. But mine was only paste. Why, at most it was worth five hundred francs.

The End

A Christmas Carol

Charles Dickens

Adapted by Jennifer L. Kroll

Summary

Ebenezer Scrooge, an old miser, lives alone and runs a loan office. He is humorless, unpleasant, and has no compassion for others. On Christmas Eve, the ghost of his dead business partner, Jacob Marley, visits Scrooge. The ghost warns Scrooge that he is headed down a disastrous path. Later, three other spirits appear to Scrooge: the Ghost of Christmas Past, the Ghost of Christmas Present, and the Ghost of Christmas Yet to Come. Showing Scrooge scenes from the past, present, and the probable future, the ghosts teach Scrooge to be a better person.

Background Information

Charles Dickens was an English writer who lived from 1812 to 1870. Difficulties he faced in childhood became the subject of and inspiration for many of his novels. When Dickens was twelve years old, his father was sent to prison for failure to pay debts. While the rest of his family joined Mr. Dickens in prison, young Charles was sent to work in a blacking factory, where shoe polish was made. The experience seems to have been a horrific one that haunted him for the rest of his life. Many of Dickens's writings deal with the subject of poverty and the class division between rich and poor. As a young adult, Dickens became a freelance reporter. His first novel, *The Pickwick Papers*, was published in installments in a literary magazine during 1836 and 1837. *A Christmas Carol* was first published in December of 1844 and became the first in a series of popular shorter works written for the Christmas season.

Presentation Suggestions

Use a table or a series of chairs as Scrooge's bed. Place the "bed" on one side of the room. Seat the four ghosts near the "bed." Place other readers in a central location. Have the Scrooge and ghost readers move back and forth between the "bed" location and the other cluster of readers at appropriate moments in the script.

Props

Scrooge and the Gentlemen can wear top hats. The Cratchits might wear ragged clothing. The ghosts can be dressed in robes or draped with sheets or dark blankets. Jacob Marley's ghost might rattle a chain during his part. A gong or chime of some kind can be used when the clock chimes in the script.

Characters

- Narrators 1, 2, and 3
- Ebenezer Scrooge, *an old miser*
- Fred, *Scrooge's nephew*
- Gentlemen Collecting for Charity 1 and 2
- Bob Cratchit, *Scrooge's employee*
- The Ghost of Jacob Marley
- Church Chime
- The Ghost of Christmas Past
- Frances "Fan" Scrooge, *Scrooge's sister*
- Young Ebenezer Scrooge
- Fellow Apprentice, *a friend of young Scrooge*
- Belle, *young Scrooge's fiancée*
- Belle's Husband
- Ghost of Christmas Present
- Mrs. Cratchit, *Bob Cratchit's wife*
- Young Cratchit Boy
- Martha Cratchit
- Young Cratchit Girl
- Tiny Tim Cratchit
- Fred's Wife, *wife of Scrooge's nephew*
- Ghost of Christmas Yet to Come (*possible nonspeaking part*)
- Merchants 1, 2, and 3, *businessmen of London*
- Maid
- Laundry Woman
- Shopkeeper, *owner of a seedy trading and pawn shop*
- Wife
- Husband
- Boy

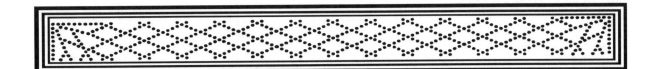

A Christmas Carol

Scene 1

Narrator 1: It is Christmas Eve. Ebenezer Scrooge sits counting money in the front office of his loan company. A sign on the front door of the building reads "Scrooge and Marley."

Narrator 2: Bob Cratchit, Scrooge's clerk, sits in a small office to the side of Scrooge's. The fire heating Cratchit's office has died down to a mere coal. He sits shivering in the cold, knowing that his employer is too miserly to allow any more fuel to be used for the fire.

Narrator 3: The front door to the office bursts open, and a pleasant-looking, middle-aged man enters.

Fred: A merry Christmas, Uncle!

Narrator 1: Scrooge looks up from his counting.

Scrooge: Bah! Humbug!

Fred: Christmas a humbug, Uncle? You don't mean that, I am sure.

Scrooge: I do. What reason do you have to be merry? You're poor enough.

Fred: *(Cheerfully.)* What right do you have to be so morose? You're rich enough.

Scrooge: Bah! Humbug!

Fred: Don't be cross, Uncle.

Scrooge: What else can I be, when I live in such a world of fools? What's Christmas time to you but a time for paying bills without money; a time for finding yourself a year older, but not an hour richer.

Fred: I have always thought of Christmas time as a kind, forgiving, charitable, pleasant time. It's the only time of year when men and women seem to fully open their hearts to their fellow human beings. And therefore, Uncle, though it has never put a scrap of gold or silver in my pocket, I believe that Christmas has done me good, and can do us all good. Come, sir! Dine with us tomorrow.

Scrooge: I've no interest in your Christmas dinner. Now, good afternoon!

Fred: I'm sorry that you won't be coming to dinner. Oh, well. I did my best. I came down here to invite you, just as I do every year. Merry Christmas, Uncle!

Scrooge: Good afternoon!

Fred: And a Happy New Year!

Scrooge: Good afternoon!

Narrator 2: As Scrooge's nephew leaves the office, two other men enter.

Gentleman 1: Scrooge and Marley's, I believe. Have I the pleasure of addressing Mr. Scrooge or Mr. Marley?

Scrooge: Mr. Marley has been dead these seven years. He died seven years ago, this very night.

Gentleman 2: We have no doubt that his generosity is well represented in his surviving partner.

Narrator 3: Scrooge realizes that the men are about to ask him to make a donation, and he frowns.

Gentleman 1: At this festive season of the year, Mr. Scrooge, it is usual to give some small amount to the poor and destitute. Many thousands go in need of basic necessities and common comforts, sir.

Scrooge: What about the prisons and poorhouses? Aren't they in business anymore?

Gentlemen 2: Yes, sir. I wish I could say they were not.

Scrooge: Oh! I was afraid, from what you said at first, that something had occurred to stop the prisons and poorhouses from conducting their useful business.

Gentlemen 1: Since these institutions don't provide much Christmas cheer, a few of us are trying to raise a fund to buy the poor some meat and drink, and means of warmth. What shall I put you down for?

Scrooge: Nothing! I choose to see to my own business and not to interfere with other people's. Good afternoon, gentlemen!

Narrator 1: Scrooge holds the door open as the two disappointed gentlemen depart.

Narrator 2: Not long afterward, it is time to close up the office for the evening.

Scrooge: *(To Cratchit.)* You'll want all day tomorrow, I suppose?

Cratchit: If quite convenient, sir.

Scrooge: It's not convenient, and it's not fair. I have to pay you, but you don't have to work. Christmas is just an excuse for picking a man's pocket! But I suppose you must have the whole day. Be here all the earlier the next morning!

Cratchit: I will, sir.

Scene 2

Narrator 3: After the office is closed, Scrooge eats dinner at his usual restaurant, reads the newspaper as usual, and heads home to his gloomy apartment. He is about to open his front door when a strange thing happens.

Narrator 1: As Scrooge looks at the doorknocker, he suddenly finds himself staring at the face of his deceased partner, Jacob Marley.

Scrooge: Marley!

Narrator 2: The vision of Jacob Marley fades.

Scrooge: No, no. I'm imagining things. Must have been something I ate.

Narrator 3: Scrooge goes into his apartment, feeling strange and a little nervous. Inside, everything seems to be in its ordinary place. Scrooge feels a little better. He puts on his pajamas and slippers.

Narrator 1: Suddenly, Scrooge spots Marley's face again, this time staring back from out of a decorative tile.

Scrooge: Wha—?

Narrator 2: Then, Scrooge begins to hear a clanking noise, as if some person were dragging a heavy chain through the cellar. Scrooge hears the cellar door fly open with a boom. He hears the clanking, dragging sound coming straight toward his door.

Scrooge: There are no ghosts! This is humbug! I won't believe it.

Narrator 3: Scrooge pales as the apparition of Marley enters his bedroom, straight through the heavy, closed door. He recognizes the face, the clothing, the hair.

Narrator 1: The ghost carries a heavy chain which is fastened about its waist. Scrooge can see that the chain is made of cash boxes, keys, padlocks, ledgers, legal documents, and heavy purses made from steel.

Scrooge: *(Shakily.)* Wh . . . wh . . . who are you?

Ghost of Jacob Marley: In life I was your partner, Jacob Marley.

Scrooge: Jacob! Jacob! You're all in chains!

Marley: I wear the chain I forged in life. I made it link by link, and yard by yard. Is its pattern strange to you?

Narrator 2: Scrooge looks at the ledgers and cash boxes that weigh down Marley. He trembles.

Marley: Would you like to know the weight and length of the chain you bear yourself? It was as heavy and as long as this, seven Christmas Eves ago. You have worked on it, since. It is a heavy chain!

Scrooge: Old Jacob Marley, you were my friend. Don't tell me this! Speak some words of comfort.

Marley: I have none to give. And I am allowed only a very little time here. I cannot rest or linger anywhere. Because my spirit never walked beyond the counting-house in life, it is doomed to wander after death. Oh for the chance to live my life over—to take advantage of the opportunities that I misused!

Scrooge: *(As if to comfort the ghost.)* You were always a good man of business, Jacob.

Marley: Business! Mankind was my business. The common welfare of all people was my business. The dealings of my trade were but a drop of water in the ocean of my business!

Narrator 3: Scrooge begins to tremble violently.

Marley: Hear me! My time is nearly gone.

Scrooge: I'm listening.

Marley: I am here tonight to warn you, that you have yet a chance and hope of escaping my fate. It's a chance and hope that I have won for you.

Scrooge: You were always a good friend to me. Thank you!

Marley: Three spirits shall haunt you. Without their visits, you cannot hope to avoid the path I tread. Expect the first tomorrow, when the bell tolls one o'clock.

Scrooge: Couldn't I take them all at once and have it over, Jacob?

Marley: Expect the second on the next night at the same hour. The third upon the next night when the last stroke of twelve has ceased to vibrate. Look to see me no more; and look that, for your own sake, you remember what has passed between us.

Narrator 1: The ghost steps slowly toward the closed window. As it does, the window opens, little by little. The ghost of Jacob Marley disappears through the open window.

Narrator 2: Scrooge sits dazed, for a minute, staring after the ghost. Then he gets up and fastens the window. Finally, exhausted, he collapses into his bed and falls fast asleep.

Scene 3

Narrator 3: Scrooge wakes. It is dark in his room. He hears the chimes of a neighboring church clock strike twelve.

Scrooge: Twelve! It was past two when I went to bed. The clock must be wrong. It isn't possible that I can have slept through a whole day and far into another night.

Narrator 1: Scrooge goes to his window and looks outside. The world is silent and pitch dark. He gets back into bed and tries to fall back asleep, but he cannot. The words of Marley's Ghost echo in his head. He lies there for an hour, until finally he hears the church chimes sound once again.

Church Chime: Ding, dong!

Scrooge: A quarter past.

Church Chime: Ding, dong!

Scrooge: Half past.

Church Chime: Ding, dong!

Scrooge: A quarter to the hour.

Church chime: Ding, dong!

Scrooge: *(Triumphantly.)* The hour has come, and no ghost! I must have imagined it all before!

Narrator 2: Scrooge speaks too soon. As he finishes speaking, a ghostly hand draws back the curtain around his bed.

Scrooge: Wh . . . what? Who's there?

Narrator 3: Scrooge finds himself face to face with a strange-looking being. Although the creature has the size and figure of a small child, it has the face of a very old person.

Ghost of Christmas Past: I am the Ghost of Christmas Past.

Scrooge: Long past?

Ghost of Christmas Past: No. Your past.

Scrooge: Wh . . . what's your business here?

Ghost of Christmas Past: Your welfare! Rise and walk with me!

Narrator 1: The ghost points toward the window, which begins to open by itself.

Scrooge: I can't go out through the window! I'll fall!

Ghost of Christmas Past: Touch my hand, and I'll hold you up.

Narrator 2: Scrooge reluctantly touches the spirit's hand and immediately finds that his bedroom has vanished. Instead, he is standing on a familiar-looking country road, with fields on either side.

Scrooge: Good Heaven! I know this place! I was a boy here!

Ghost of Christmas Past: Strange that you forgot it for so many years! Let us go on.

Narrator 3: As they pass into a small town, Scrooge can see that the place is decorated for Christmas. Small boys, newly released from school for the holidays, run through the streets. Scrooge smiles and waves to each boy, calling each by his remembered name. The boys don't appear to see him.

Ghost of Christmas Past: The school is not quite deserted. A solitary child, neglected by his friends and family, remains there for the holidays.

Scrooge: I know! I know! That child was me!

Narrator 1: Scrooge begins to weep. He and the spirit pass into the dreary hall of a boarding school and glance through the doors of many cold, poorly furnished rooms.

Narrator 2: At the back of the building, they enter a long, bare room, filled with empty desks. There, a single boy sits reading in front of a small fire. Scrooge sits down next to the image of his past self and continues sobbing.

Narrator 3: The scene before his eyes suddenly shifts. Now he sees himself as an older boy, a young teen, alone in the same room. This time, he is pacing the floor. Suddenly, the school room door flies open and a young girl enters. She runs up and hugs young Scrooge.

Frances "Fan" Scrooge: Dear brother! I have come to bring you home!

Narrator 1: She claps her hands with joy.

Fan: Father is so much kinder than he used to be! He spoke gently to me one night and I was not afraid to ask once more if you might come home. And he said yes and sent me in a coach to bring you. We'll be together all the Christmas long and have the merriest time in the world.

Young Scrooge: Oh, Fan! Thank you so much!

Narrator 2: The little girl hugs her big brother once more, then takes him by the hand and drags him to the schoolroom door.

Old Scrooge: Dear little Fan! How I miss her!

Ghost of Christmas Past: She was always a delicate, sickly little thing. But she had a large heart.

Old Scrooge: So she had.

Ghost of Christmas Past: She didn't die until she was a grown woman. She had, I think, children.

Scrooge: One child.

Ghost of Christmas Past: Yes. Your nephew.

Narrator 3: The scene begins to shift again. Scrooge finds himself looking into the warehouse where he was apprenticed to a merchant named Fezziwig.

Narrator 1: Unlike his own dreary loan office, the warehouse is decorated for Christmas. Inside, Scrooge and another apprentice are enjoying a small Christmas party being thrown for them by their employer. Scrooge, young again, dances across the warehouse floor to fiddle music, accompanied by one of Master Fezziwig's three daughters.

Scrooge: Old Fezziwig! Bless his heart. Dear old Fezziwig.

Narrator 2: Scrooge thoroughly enjoys reliving the Christmas dance. He listens to his former self praising Fezziwig.

Young Scrooge: Dear Fezziwig is a really splendid fellow!

Fellow Apprentice: There isn't a better man in all the world, bless him.

Ghost of Christmas Past: You were silly back then, to be so full of gratitude over something so small. The man only spent a few dollars on that party.

Old Scrooge: Small! It wasn't small! He was our employer. He had the power to make us happy or unhappy, to make our service a pleasure or a burden. The happiness he gave us was so great that it might as well have cost a fortune!

Narrator 3: Scrooge feels the spirit's eyes on him, and stops.

Ghost of Christmas Past: What is the matter?

Scrooge: Nothing in particular.

Ghost of Christmas Past: Something, I think?

Scrooge: No—well, yes. I would like to be able to say a word or two to my clerk just now! That's all.

Narrator 1: The scene is already shifting as Scrooge speaks. Scrooge sees himself again, only now he is older, a young man in the prime of life. His face doesn't yet have the harsh and rigid lines of later years, but it has begun to show the signs of worry and greed.

Narrator 2: By his side sits a young woman with tears in her eyes.

Belle: You feel nothing for me anymore. You have another passion in life, which has replaced your passion for me. I hope it can cheer and comfort you in the times to come, as I would have done.

Young Scrooge: What passion are you talking about?

Belle: All your other hopes have merged into the hope for money.

Scrooge: I'm wiser than I used to be and more frugal. But what of it? I haven't changed in my attitude toward you.

Narrator 3: She shakes her head.

Belle: We became engaged long ago. Back then, we were both poor. It didn't matter to you that I have no family connections, no dowry. You were another man.

Young Scrooge: I was a boy.

Belle: In any case, you have changed. And what would once have brought us happiness could now only bring us misery. Though it pains me to do so, I must break our engagement.

Scrooge: Spirit, show me no more! Take me home. Why do you delight to torture me?

Ghost of Christmas Past: My time is short, but I must show you one more shadow.

Narrator 1: The same woman appears before Scrooge's eyes again, only now she is much older. She is baking in a house full of Christmas decorations, surrounded by laughing children and grandchildren. The door of the house opens and her husband enters.

Belle's Husband: Belle, I saw an old friend of yours this afternoon.

Belle: Who was it?

Belle's Husband: Mr. Scrooge. I passed his office window. Because it was not shut up, and he had a candle inside, I could scarcely help seeing him. His partner lies upon the point of death, I hear; and there he sat alone. Quite alone in the world, I do believe.

Scrooge: Spirit! Remove me from this place!

Ghost of Christmas Past: I only show you things that have been. That they are what they are is not my fault.

Scrooge: Remove me! I cannot bear it!

Ghost: Very well. I have done my part.

Narrator 2: Scrooge suddenly finds himself back in his bed and quite alone. He sighs with relief, then sinks into a deep sleep.

Scene 4

Narrator 3: Scrooge awakens in the middle of a loud snore, and sits up in bed to get his thoughts together.

Scrooge: It must be nearly one in the morning—Oh dear!

Narrator 1: The church bell chimes one o'clock. Scrooge braces himself, but no spirit appears. He sits in his bed, heart thumping, for five minutes, then ten minutes.

Narrator 2: Finally, he notices a strange light that seems to be coming from the next room. He gets out of bed and walks to the door. As soon as his hand is on the doorknob, he hears a voice.

Ghost of Christmas Present: Enter, Ebenezer Scrooge!

Narrator 3: Scrooge turns the knob and is surprised to find himself looking into his own bedroom. The room, however, is transformed. Green light fills it, and the walls and ceilings are hung with holly, mistletoe, ivy, and pine boughs.

Narrator 1: The room is heaped with holiday foods, and decorated as if for a holiday party. Sitting on Scrooge's own bed is a jolly-looking giant, who holds a flaming torch.

Ghost of Christmas Present: Come in!

Narrator 2: Scrooge enters timidly, hanging his head before this spirit. He feels ashamed to look the spirit in the eye.

Ghost of Christmas Present: I am the Ghost of Christmas Present. Look upon me!

Scrooge: (*Submissively.*) Spirit, take me wherever you please. I went forth with one of your fellows last night, and I learnt a lesson that is working now. Teach me whatever I need to know.

Ghost of Christmas Present: Touch my robe!

Narrator 3: Scrooge does as he is told, and the bedroom vanishes. Scrooge finds himself out on the streets of the city now, accompanied by the giant ghost.

Narrator 1: The streets are full of sooty snow and ice, but the people racing around in them seem to be in a happy mood. Men and women and boys and girls shovel off walkways and roofs, laughing as they throw an occasional snowball at one another.

Narrator 2: People hurry into and out of the local bakery, butcher shop, and grocery store, greeting each other in cheerful voices and rushing to make last-minute purchases before the stores close. It is Christmas Day.

Narrator 3: Scrooge and the spirit move through the streets until they reach a dingy northern suburb of London. There, they enter the four-room house occupied by Scrooge's clerk, Bob Cratchit, and his large family.

Mrs. Cratchit: What's keeping your precious father and Tiny Tim? And Martha didn't get off work this late last year!

Narrator 1: Mrs. Cratchit is dressed in poor, worn-out clothing. She has tried to make the clothing appear festive by attaching colorful ribbons to it. Mrs. Cratchit's second oldest daughter, who is not yet employed, wears similar clothes. The two of them are busy over pots and pans on the stove.

Young Cratchit Boy: Here's Martha, mother!

Mrs. Cratchit: Why, bless your heart alive, my dear, how late you are!

Martha Cratchit: We'd a lot of work to finish up last night, and we had to clear away this morning.

Mrs. Cratchit: Well! Never mind so long as you are come. Sit down before the fire, my dear.

Young Cratchit Girl: There's Father coming!

Narrator 2: Bob Cratchit enters, dressed in shabby, patched up clothes. He carries his youngest son, Tiny Tim, on his shoulder. He sets down Tiny Tim, then hands the small, crippled boy his crutch.

Mrs. Cratchit: And how did little Tim behave?

Bob Cratchit: As good as gold.

Narrator 3: He pats the boy on the head.

Bob: Our Tim is growing strong and hearty.

Narrator 1: Scrooge can see from Bob Cratchit's expression, and the glance he exchanges with Mrs. Cratchit, that this isn't true.

Narrator 2: Scrooge watches as the Cratchits sit down to their Christmas dinner of goose, applesauce, stuffing, potatoes, and pudding. As the meal reaches its conclusion and all platters have been cleared, Bob proposes a toast to his family.

Bob: A Merry Christmas to us all, my dears. God bless us!

Narrator 3: The Cratchits all echo Bob's toast.

Tiny Tim: God bless us every one!

Narrator 1: Tiny Tim sits on a stool near his father, who gently holds his withered little hand. Scrooge looks into Bob's face. In it, he sees how much this man loves his son and fears to lose him. Scrooge's heart suddenly is moved with pity.

Scrooge: Spirit, tell me if Tiny Tim will live.

Ghost of Christmas Present: I see a vacant seat, in the poor chimney-corner, and a crutch without an owner, carefully preserved. If things continue on as they are going now, the child will die.

Scrooge: No, no! Oh, no, kind Spirit! Say he will be spared.

Ghost of Christmas Present: I cannot tell you that. I cannot alter the future.

Narrator 2: Once again, Bob Cratchit raises his glass in a toast.

Bob: To Mr. Scrooge, the founder of the feast.

Mrs. Cratchit: *(Angrily.)* The Founder of the Feast, indeed! I wish I had him here. I'd give him a piece of my mind to feast upon, and I hope he'd have a good appetite for it.

Bob: My dear! The children are listening! And it's Christmas Day.

Mrs. Cratchit: It would have to be Christmas Day, before I would consider drinking to the health of such a stingy, hard, unfeeling man as Mr. Scrooge. You know he is, Robert! Nobody knows it better than you do!

Bob: My dear! It's Christmas Day!

Mrs. Cratchit: I'll drink his health for your sake and the day's, not for his. Long life to him. A merry Christmas and a happy new year!

Narrator 3: The children all toast glumly. Only Tiny Tim seems perfectly cheerful.

Tiny Tim: *(Toasting.)* God bless us everyone!

Narrator 1: The scene of the Cratchit household fades, and the Ghost of Christmas Present whisks Scrooge on to other sights. The two pass into the home of a miner, who lives in abject poverty. Inside his stone and mud hut, his family happily sings Christmas songs.

Narrator 2: Scrooge is taken next to a desolate lighthouse, far from civilization. Inside it, two weathered looking lighthouse keepers make toasts and wish one another happy holidays.

Narrator 3: Finally, Scrooge and the Ghost venture unseen into the home of Scrooge's nephew, Fred. Fred and his wife are laughing together, as they sit before the fire with friends and relatives.

Fred: *(Laughing.)* He said that Christmas was a humbug! He believed it too!

Fred's Wife: More shame on him, Fred!

Fred: He's a comical old fellow. That's the truth. And he's not very pleasant. However, his sins carry their own punishment, and I have nothing to say against him.

Fred's Wife: I have no patience with him.

Narrator 1: Fred's sisters-in-law chime in, expressing their agreement with Fred's wife.

Fred: I couldn't be angry with him if I tried. Who suffers by his ill whims? Himself, always. Here, he takes it into his head to dislike us, and he won't come and dine with us. What's the consequence? He loses out on a wonderful dinner and some pleasant moments, which could do him no harm. I am sure we are all much pleasanter companions than he can find in his own thoughts, either in his moldy old office or his dusty apartment. I mean to give him the same chance to come to dinner every year, whether he likes it or not.

Narrator 2: Scrooge and the Ghost of Christmas Present leave the home of Scrooge's nephew and enter other homes. During this night of travels, Scrooge begins to notice that the ghost is aging rapidly. At first, he says nothing about this. Finally, when the spirit looks ancient and gray, Scrooge asks.

Scrooge: Are spirits' lives so short?

Ghost of Christmas Present: My life upon this globe lasts only for one night. It is nearly midnight, and I am nearly through.

Narrator 3: The church clock begins to strike twelve and Scrooge finds himself back in his bed once again. He looks around for the Ghost of Christmas Present, but this ghost has vanished. He falls asleep, once again, but sleeps fitfully, waiting for the third ghost to come.

Scene 5

Narrator 1: As the final chime rings out midnight, Scrooge awakens to see another phantom crossing the floor toward him. This one is cloaked and hooded, with its face hidden. The sight of it strikes gloom and terror into Scrooge's heart. The spirit comes and stands beside Scrooge, but remains silent.

Scrooge: Am I in the presence of the Ghost of Christmas Yet to Come?

Narrator 2: The spirit doesn't answer but points toward the window with its hand. All Scrooge can see of the ghost is its bony, ghostly hand and its black shroud. He quakes with fear.

Scrooge: Ghost of the Future! I fear you more than the other two ghosts. But as I know your purpose is to do me good, and as I hope to live to be another man from what I was, I am prepared to bear you company and do it with a thankful heart. Will you not speak to me?

Narrator 3: The ghost gives no reply.

Scrooge: Well, lead on then, Spirit!

Narrator 1: The phantom moves away from Scrooge, who follows in its footsteps. In an instant, he finds himself back in the city. It is daylight, and some familiar merchants stand on the street corner in a group, having a conversation.

Merchant 1: No, I don't know much about it, either way. I only know he's dead.

Merchant 2: When did he die?

Merchant 1: Last night, I believe.

Merchant 3: Why, what was the matter with him? I thought he'd never die.

Merchant 1: *(Yawning.)* Who knows?

Merchant 2: What has he done with his money?

Merchant 1: I haven't heard. Left it to his company, perhaps. He hasn't left it to me. That's all I know.

Narrator 2: They all laugh.

Merchant 1: It's likely to be a very cheap funeral. I don't know of anybody who'll go to it. Maybe we should be good sports and volunteer.

Merchant 3: I don't mind going if a lunch is provided. But I wouldn't go otherwise.

Narrator 3: They all laugh again.

Narrator 1: Scrooge and the ghost leave behind the merchants and the busy downtown street and go into a gloomy, smelly run-down part of the city. Scrooge has never been in this particular slum before.

Narrator 2: He and the ghost enter a junk shop in the slum. On the shop floor lie heaps of rusty keys, nails, chains, hinges, files, scales, all kinds of scrap metal, as well as old clothes and other household items.

Narrator 3: The dirty old shopkeeper sits smoking his pipe, as three clients enter the shop with merchandise to sell to him. The three seem startled to suddenly recognize each other. Then they all laugh.

Maid: Every person has a right to take care of him or herself, I guess. He always did!

Laundry Woman: That's true, indeed! No man more so.

Maid: *(To the Laundry Woman.)* Who's the worse off? A dead man doesn't need these things.

Laundry Woman: No, indeed!

Maid: Anyhow, if he had been a natural, normal person, he would have had somebody to look after him while he was dying. He wouldn't have been lying there, gasping out his last breath, alone by himself.

Laundry Woman: That's the truest word that ever was spoken.

Shopkeeper: Well, let's see what you three have got.

Narrator 1: The man, an undertaker's assistant, unwraps his little bundle first. In it lies a pencil case, a pair of sleeve buttons, and a brooch of no great value. The shopkeeper adds up the value of the items and shows the number to the man.

Shopkeeper: That's my offer, and I won't give a penny more. Who's next?

Narrator 2: The laundry woman unwraps her bundle. In it lie sheets and towels, as well as some clothes, two old-fashioned silver teaspoons, a pair of sugar-tongs, and a few boots. The shopkeeper shows her a total.

Shopkeeper: I'm being generous, so don't you dare ask for more. Now what's next?

Narrator 3: The maid gives the shopkeeper her bundle. After undoing many knots, he drags out a large and heavy roll of some dark stuff.

Shopkeeper: What are these? Bed curtains?

Narrator 1: The maid crosses her arms and laughs.

Maid: That's what they are. Bed curtains.

Shopkeeper: You don't mean to say you took them down, rings and all, with him lying there?

Maid: Yes I do. Why not?

Shopkeeper: Are these his blankets?

Maid: Who else's would they be? He isn't likely to take cold without 'em, I dare say.

Narrator 2: Scrooge shudders and tries to turn away from the scene in the shop.

Scrooge: Spirit! I see, I see. The case of this unhappy man might be my own. My life is going that way, now. Merciful Heaven, what is this!

Narrator 3: Scrooge jumps back, noticing that the scene has changed. Now he is almost touching a bed—a bare, uncurtained bed. On the bed, the body of a person lies covered completely by single ragged sheet. The room is very dark. All Scrooge can see is the covered body on the bed. He glances toward the phantom.

Narrator 1: The phantom makes a silent gesture, indicating that he wants Scrooge to pull back the sheet. Scrooge is gripped with horror.

Scrooge: Spirit, this is a fearful place. I have already learned its lesson. Now, let's go!

Narrator 2: The ghost continues pointing to the dead man's covered head.

Scrooge: I understand you, and I would pull back the sheet, if I could. Please, let's go. Show me somebody in this town who feels some emotion over this man's death. Spirit, I beg you!

Narrator 3: The phantom seems to agree to Scrooge's request. He sweeps up Scrooge and carries him away from the bed and off to a small room elsewhere, occupied by a mother and children. The mother paces, anxiously awaiting someone. She seems terribly worried.

Narrator 1: After some time, a man comes in who is clearly her husband. His face is careworn and depressed, although he is young. There is an odd expression on his face. He appears to be delighted, but is struggling to repress his look of delight, as if embarrassed by it.

Wife: What's the news? Are we ruined?

Husband: No. There is hope yet.

Wife: If he is willing to wait for our payment, there's hope.

Husband: He is dead.

Wife: Dead? To whom will our debt be transferred?

Husband: I don't know. But at least we'll be dealing with somebody else. It seems unlikely that our new creditor could possibly be as heartless as that old man was.

Narrator 2: The scene begins to fade, and Scrooge suddenly becomes aware of the fact that his time with the ghost is growing small.

Scrooge: Phantom, something informs me that our parting moment is at hand. I know it, but don't know how. Tell me what man these people are talking about. Who was it that we saw lying dead?

Narrator 3: The Ghost of Christmas Yet To Come once again seems willing to honor Scrooge's request. He pulls Scrooge quickly through familiar streets, until finally the two near Scrooge's own home.

Scrooge: I know we are in a hurry now, Spirit, but I can see my own house. Let me behold what I shall be, in days to come.

Narrator 1: The spirit points away from the house.

Scrooge: The house is over there. Why do you point away?

Narrator 2: The spirit continues pointing. Scrooge accompanies the spirit until they reach the iron gate of a churchyard. The place is dismal. It is overrun by grass and weeds, and overfull of graves.

Narrator 3: The spirit stands among the graves and points down to one. Scrooge takes a step toward the grave, then stops.

Scrooge: Before I draw nearer to that stone, answer one question. Are these the shadows of the things that *will* be, or are they shadows of things that *may* be?

Narrator 1: The silent ghost continues to point downward to the grave by which it stands.

Scrooge: The course of lives can be changed. Say it is true!

Narrator 2: The spirit stands pointing and makes no other gesture. Scrooge creeps toward the grave, trembling.

Narrator 3: Following the spirit's finger, he reads upon the stone of the neglected grave his own name, Ebenezer Scrooge.

Scrooge: Am I that man who lay upon the bed?

Narrator 1: Scrooge sinks to his knees. The ghost points his finger at the grave, then back at Scrooge, indicating that the two are one and the same.

Scrooge: No, Spirit! Oh no, no, no! Tell me that I yet may change these images you've shown me, by changing the way I live my life! I promise that I will honor Christmas in my heart all year long. Oh, tell me I may erase the writing on this stone!

Narrator 2: In desperation, Scrooge reaches out to grab the ghost's hand. The ghost shakes Scrooge off. Then, suddenly, his hood and cloak collapse and shrink, and the phantom disappears.

Scene 6

Narrator 3: Scrooge suddenly wakes up and finds himself in his own bed.

Scrooge: I'm back in my room! This bed is my own! This house is my own! Best of all, the time before me is my own! I can use it to make up for all I have and have not done!

Narrator 1: Scrooge reaches up and touches the bed-curtains around his bed.

Scrooge: The curtains are not torn down! They are here! I am here! The future the phantom showed me can still be prevented! It will be!

Narrator 2: Scrooge struggles to put his clothes on. In his haste, he turns his pants inside out and buttons his shirt wrong. He laughs as he rebuttons his shirt.

Scrooge: I don't know what to do with myself! I am as light as a feather, I am as happy as an angel, I am as merry as a schoolboy.

Narrator 3: Scrooge dances across his apartment.

Scrooge: I don't know what day it is, but I feel like a baby. I've just been reborn!

Narrator 1: A church bell starts to ring out. Scrooge runs to the window and throws it open. He spots a boy passing beneath his window in Sunday clothes.

Scrooge: What's today?

Boy: Pardon me, Mister?

Scrooge: What's today, my fine fellow?

Boy: Today? Why, it's Christmas Day.

Scrooge: *(To himself.)* It's Christmas Day! I haven't missed it. The spirits have done all their work in one night. *(Shouting to the boy.)* Hallo, my fine fellow!

Boy: Yes, sir?

Scrooge: Do you know the grocery store at the corner of the next street?

Boy: Why yes, sir. Of course, sir.

Scrooge: *(To himself.)* An intelligent boy! A remarkable boy! *(To the boy.)* Do you know whether they've sold the prize turkey that was hanging up there? Not the little prize turkey, but the big one?

Boy: What, the one as big as me? It's hanging there now.

Scrooge: Is it? Go and buy it! Tell the grocer to bring it here, and I'll give him directions for where to take it. Come back with the man, and I'll give you a shilling. Come back with him in less than five minutes, and I'll give you half a crown!

Narrator 2: The boy immediately scampers off.

Scrooge: *(Laughing to himself.)* I'll send it to Bob Cratchit's! I won't tell him I sent it. It's twice the size of Tiny Tim. What a wonderful joke!

Narrator 3: Scrooge writes down Bob Cratchit's address and waits in his doorway for the delivery man to arrive. Soon, the grocery man comes hurrying up the walk, accompanied by the boy.

Scrooge: Why, here it is now. *(To the delivery man.)* How are you? Merry Christmas!

Narrator 1: Scrooge stares at the huge turkey, then looks back at the delivery man.

Scrooge: Why, it's impossible for you to carry that to Camden Town! I'll call you a cab.

Narrator 2: After the delivery man is packed into his cab and the boy is paid for his help, Scrooge shaves and puts on his finest clothes. Then, he ventures out into the street. He smiles at everyone he sees.

Scrooge: Good morning, sir! A Merry Christmas to you! Good morning, Madam!

Narrator 3: By chance, he quickly comes upon one of the men who entered his shop on Christmas Eve, looking for a charitable donation.

Scrooge: My dear sir, how do you do?

Narrator 1: Scrooge grabs the hands of the surprised gentleman.

Scrooge: I hope you had success yesterday and collected a great sum for your wonderful cause. It was very kind of you.

Gentleman 1: Mr. Scrooge? Is that you?

Scrooge: Yes. That is my name, and I fear it may not be pleasant to you. Allow me to ask your pardon. And will you have the goodness to accept for your cause a donation of—

Narrator 2: Scrooge leans over and whispers a sum in the man's ear.

Gentleman 1: Lord bless me! My dear Mr. Scrooge, are you serious?

Scrooge: I'm completely serious. I wouldn't think of giving you a penny less!

Gentleman 1: Thank you!

Scrooge: No! Thank you! I thank you fifty times. Bless you!

Narrator 3: Scrooge goes to Christmas church service, then walks around the streets, greeting more people. Wherever he goes, he pats children on the head, gives money to beggars, and talks to everyone. In the afternoon, he walks to his nephew's house. It takes him some time to get up the courage to knock.

Fred: Why bless my soul! Who's that?

Scrooge: It's I. Your Uncle Scrooge. I have come to dinner. Will you let me in, Fred?

Narrator 1: Fred's face lights up with joy as he leads Scrooge into the house. Scrooge spends the evening with his nephew's family. By the end of an hour, Fred's wife and her sisters have all changed their minds about not liking Uncle Scrooge.

Narrator 2: The next morning, Scrooge arrives at his office early. It's quarter after nine when Bob Cratchit comes puffing into the office, whipping off his hat and coat.

Cratchit: I am very sorry I'm late, sir.

Scrooge: *(In a stern voice.)* Yes. I think you are.

Narrator 3: Scrooge tries to hide his smile.

Cratchit: Christmas is only once a year, sir. I was making rather merry yesterday, sir.

Scrooge: *(Still stern.)* Now, I'll tell you what, my friend, I am not going to stand this sort of thing any longer! And therefore—therefore, I am about to raise your salary!

Narrator 1: Bob stares at Scrooge, not understanding.

Scrooge: A merry Christmas, Bob! I want to help your struggling family. Let's discuss your affairs this afternoon, over a cup of hot chocolate!

Narrator 2: A slow smile spreads across Bob Cratchit's face.

Scrooge: And Bob, put some more coal on the fire and order another shipment of it. It's too cold in this place!

Epilogue

Narrator 3: In the days to come, Scrooge keeps his promise to Bob. In fact, he does more than just give Bob a raise. He begins to take a personal interest in Bob's family and eventually becomes like a second father to Tiny Tim, who does not die after all.

Narrator 1: The people around town don't know quite what to make of the new Scrooge, and some even laugh at him, but he never cares. He simply laughs right back.

Narrator 2: Scrooge has no more dealings with ghosts, but he always remembers the lessons he learned from them. He never again speaks ill of Christmas, and he always celebrates it.

Narrator 3: And so that is the story of the transformation of Ebenezer Scrooge. In the words of Tiny Tim, God bless us everyone!

The End

Hard Times

Charles Dickens

Adapted by Jennifer L. Kroll

Summary

The story is set in a bleak industrial city in the north of England during the 1800s. Mr. Gradgrind, a school superintendent, believes that children should be exposed only to facts, nothing fanciful, artistic, or sentimental. He raises his teenaged son and daughter according to his own educational theories. Gradgrind is eventually made to see the error of his ways when his children become unhappy adults. Young Tom develops a gambling habit. Tom's sister Louisa enters into a loveless marriage with a rich man. Their lives intersect with those of poor local mill workers when Tom robs a bank to pay off his debts and frames one of the mill workers. This script is divided into two parts, which can be performed in two sittings.

Background Information

Charles Dickens was an English writer who lived from 1812 to 1870. Difficulties he faced in childhood became the subject of and inspiration for many of his novels. When Dickens was twelve years old, his father was sent to prison for failure to pay debts. While the rest of his family joined Mr. Dickens in prison, young Charles was sent to work in a blacking factory, where shoe polish was made. The experience seems to have been a horrific one that haunted him for the rest of his life. Many of Dickens' writings deal with the subject of poverty and the division between rich and poor people. As a young adult, Dickens became a freelance reporter. His first novel, *The Pickwick Papers*, was published in installments in a literary magazine during 1836 and 1837. *Hard Times* was also first printed in installments. Sections of the novel appeared weekly in a periodical called *Household Words* in 1854.

Presentation Suggestions

Place the following well-off characters on one side of the room: Mr. Gradgrind, Mrs. Gradgrind, Louisa, Tom, Jane, Mr. Bounderby, Mr. Harthouse, and Mrs. Sparsit. Place the poor mill workers and townspeople on the other side: Bitzer, Sissy, Mr. Childers, Stephen Blackpool, Rachel, Joanna, Mrs. Pegler, and the Doctor. Narrators may be placed in any suitable location. Place four or five chairs or stools front and center. Have readers move from the sides to the front chairs or stools when they interact.

Props

When using the presentation strategy described above, decorate the "well-off" side of the classroom in bright colors. You might place flowers, plants, or a nice piece of furniture on that side of the room. Decorate the "poor" side of the room in dark colors. Readers can dress in clothing that denotes their character's social status. Poor characters can wear shabby clothes. Rich characters can wear dressy clothes, such as suit jackets and ties.

Characters

- Narrators 1, 2, and 3
- Mr. Thomas Gradgrind, *superintendent of schools*
- Cecilia "Sissy" Jupe, *a young student*
- Bitzer, *a young student*
- Louisa Gradgrind, *Mr. Gradgrind's sixteen-year-old daughter*
- Mr. Bounderby, *a rich banker and merchant in his late forties*
- Mrs. Gradgrind, *mother of Louisa, Thomas, and Jane*
- Mr. E. W. B. Childers, *a circus performer*
- Stephen Blackpool, *a poor factory worker in his late thirties*
- Rachel, *a poor factory worker in her mid thirties*
- Joanna, *wife of Stephen*
- Mrs. Sparsit, *housekeeper to Mr. Bounderby*
- Servant
- Mrs. Pegler, *visitor to Coketown*
- Mr. James Harthouse, *a gentleman in his mid thirties*
- Thomas "Tom" Gradgrind Jr., *younger brother of Louisa*
- Jane Gradgrind, *younger sister of Louisa*
- Doctor

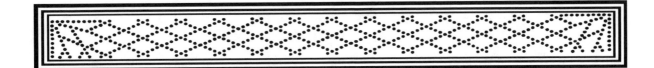

Hard Times

PART I

Scene 1

Narrator 1: The setting is England in the mid-1900s. Mr. Thomas Gradgrind, the superintendent of schools in the city of Coketown, is visiting the classroom of Mr. Choakumchild.

Gradgrind: Now, what I want is facts. Teach these boys and girls nothing but facts. Facts alone are wanted in life. Plant nothing else, and root out everything else. This is the principle on which I bring up my own children, and this is the principle on which I bring up these children. Stick to facts, sir.

Narrator 2: Mr. Choakumchild nods in approval at the words of his supervisor. The children in the classroom look terrified.

Gradgrind: Girl number twenty—I don't know who you are. Speak up and tell me your name, child.

Narrator 3: Cecilia Jupe, a young girl in ragged clothing, stands and curtseys.

Cecilia "Sissy" Jupe: My name is Sissy Jupe, sir.

Gradgrind: Sissy is not a real name. Don't call yourself that. Call yourself Cecilia.

Sissy: It's my father who calls me Sissy, sir.

Gradgrind: Then he has no business to do it. Tell him he mustn't. Cecilia Jupe. Let me see. What is your father?

Sissy: He belongs to the traveling circus, sir. He rides horses.

Gradgrind: We don't want to know anything about the circus here, girl. Never speak of it again. And when you speak of your father, don't say that he rides horses in a circus! Call him a horse trainer, a horse breaker, a veterinarian, something respectable.

Sissy: Yes, sir.

Gradgrind: Very well, then. He is a horse breaker. Give us your definition of a horse.

Narrator 1: Sissy stands there with her mouth open. She has no idea what to say.

Gradgrind: Girl number twenty is unable to define a horse! Girl number twenty knows no facts in reference to one of the commonest of animals! Someone else give a definition of a horse then. You, Bitzer.

67

Narrator 2: A cold-eyed, pale little boy stands up.

Gradgrind: Bitzer—your definition of a horse.

Bitzer: Quadruped. Plant eater. Forty teeth, namely, twenty-four grinders, four eyeteeth, and twelve incisors. Sheds coat in the spring. In marshy countries, sheds hoofs, too.

Narrator 3: Bitzer continues on like this for several minutes. When he is finished, Gradgrind nods in satisfaction and Bitzer returns to his seat.

Gradgrind: Now, girl number twenty, you know what a horse is.

Scene 2

Narrator 1: That afternoon, after leaving the school, Mr. Gradgrind walks home past the place where the circus is performing. As he passes around the back of the main tent, he spots a number of children and teens that are trying to catch a glimpse of the act.

Gradgrind: For shame! These vagabond circus people are attracting the children from my school! The children's minds will be corrupted with all this nonsense! Children don't need circuses! They need facts!

Narrator 2: Suddenly, Mr. Gradgrind catches sight of two of his own children. His sixteen-year-old daughter, Louisa, is kneeling and peering through a crack in the tent. His fourteen-year-old son, Thomas Jr., is lying in the dirt, trying to see under the edge of the tent.

Gradgrind: Louisa! Thomas!

Narrator 3: Both rise, looking sheepish.

Gradgrind: In the name of wonder, idleness, and folly! What are you doing here?

Louisa Gradgrind: We wanted to see what it was like.

Gradgrind: What it was like?

Louisa: Yes, father.

Narrator 1: Mr. Gradgrind looks angry.

Gradgrind: You two have been trained to value facts. You have had excellent educations. What could possibly have brought you to occupy yourselves in this way?

Louisa: We were tired.

Gradgrind: Tired? Of what?

Louisa: I don't know of what—of everything, I think.

Gradgrind: I don't know what you are talking about, Louisa, but you will both be coming home with me this instant.

Narrator 2: The two sullen teenagers follow their father away from the tent.

Gradgrind: For shame! For shame! What would your friends say? What would Mr. Bounderby say?

Scene 3

Narrator 3: At the Gradgrind residence, Mrs. Gradgrind sits in the formal drawing room, listening to a story told by Mr. Gradgrind's best friend, Mr. Bounderby.

Narrator 1: Bounderby is a banker, merchant, manufacturer, and a very rich man who controls the lives of thousands of workers in Coketown. He is in his late forties, but looks a good bit older. He has a loud, booming voice and a puffed-up looking face.

Mr. Bounderby: When I was a boy, I hadn't a shoe for my foot. As for a sock, I didn't know such a thing existed. I passed the day in a ditch and the night in a pigsty. That's the way I spent my tenth birthday. Not that a ditch was new to me, for I was born in a ditch.

Mrs. Gradgrind: Oh dear. I hope at least it was a dry ditch.

Mr. Bounderby: No! It was sopping wet! A foot of water was in it.

Mrs. Gradgrind: That's enough to give a baby a cold.

Mr. Bounderby: Cold? I was born with inflammation of the lungs—and of everything else. For years, ma'am, I was one of the most miserable little wretches ever seen. I was so sick and ragged and dirty that you wouldn't have touched me with a pair of tongs.

Mrs. Gradgrind: You poor child!

Mr. Bounderby: How I fought through it, I don't know. I was determined, I suppose. I have been a determined character all my life. Here I am, Mrs. Gradgrind, with nobody to thank for my being here but myself.

Mrs. Gradgrind: I hope that your mother—

Narrator 2: Bounderby cuts her off.

Mr. Bounderby: *My* mother? She bolted, ma'am!

Narrator 3: Mrs. Gradgrind gasps.

Mr. Bounderby: My mother left me to my grandmother, and she was the wickedest and the worst old woman who ever lived. If I got a little pair of shoes by any chance, she would take them off and sell them for drink. Of course I ran away as soon as I could, only to become a starving vagabond.

Mrs. Gradgrind: How terrible!

Mr. Bounderby: How I pulled through it all, I'm not sure. I went from vagabond to errand boy, then laborer, porter, clerk, chief manager, small partner, until finally I became who I am today, Josiah Bounderby of Coketown.

Narrator 1: Mr. Bounderby's story is interrupted by the arrival of Mr. Gradgrind, Louisa, and Tom.

Gradgrind: Louisa, look, it's Mr. Bounderby. Give him a kiss. Thomas, say hello.

Narrator 2: The two teens sullenly obey their father.

Mr. Bounderby: *(To Louisa.)* What are you two so in the dumps about?

Louisa: We were watching the circus and Father caught us.

Mrs. Gradgrind: Dear me! Watching the circus! How could you do such a thing? Why couldn't you just go and look at all the shells and minerals and things provided for you? You have so many facts that you need to learn! Go and be somethingological immediately!

Narrator 3: As Louisa and Tom slump off, Mr. Gradgrind pulls up a chair.

Gradgrind: Bounderby, you are always so interested in my young people. Perhaps you can help me to understand what happened today. Tell me, where does their alarming curiosity come from?

Mr. Bounderby: I'll tell you where it comes from—idle imagination.

Gradgrind: I feared that might be the case. Do you think that, in spite of all my precautions, some storybook might have got into the house? How else would Louisa and Thomas even know about circuses?

Mr. Bounderby: Didn't you say that one of the circus performers has a child in the school?

Gradgrind: Yes, that's true. The girl's name is Cecilia Jupe.

Mr. Bounderby: Well, it's all clear, then. The Jupe girl must have been spreading nonsense about the circus around. Perhaps you had better go and speak to her father.

Gradgrind: I will do so immediately. Will you come with me?

Scene 4

Narrator 1: Mr. Bounderby and Mr. Gradgrind walk through Coketown toward the circus. Coketown is a depressing place. Tall chimneys spew out smoke and grime that covers everything. The canal that runs through the center of town is black and smells terrible, having been polluted by the local factories.

Narrator 2: As the two men near the row of shacks where the circus people are living, Sissy Jupe comes tearing out into the road with a terrified look on her face.

Gradgrind: Stop! Why are you tearing about the streets in this improper manner?

Sissy: *(Panting.)* I was being run after, sir, and I wanted to get away.

Narrator 3: Suddenly, Bitzer, the pale boy who defined "horse" earlier in the day, comes racing around the corner.

Gradgrind: What are you doing, boy? *(To Sissy.)* Was this boy chasing you?

Sissy: *(Reluctantly.)* Yes, sir.

Bitzer: No, I wasn't! She's lying. Everybody knows that the circus people are all liars. Can't believe a thing they say. They are stupid, too. They don't even know their multiplication tables!

Sissy: He was making terrible faces at me!

Bitzer: I never did! I just asked her if she would know how to define a horse tomorrow and offered to tell her again, and she ran away, and I ran after her.

Gradgrind: Bitzer, you turn around and take yourself home. *(To Sissy.)* This gentleman and I wish to see your father.

Narrator 1: Mr. Gradgrind notices that Sissy is holding a bottle.

Gradgrind: What have you got in that bottle you are carrying?

Mr. Bounderby: It's alcohol, no doubt. These lazy circus people are all big boozers.

Sissy: It's the nine oils, sir.

Mr. Bounderby: The what?

Sissy: The nine oils, sir. To rub father with. When any of our people get hurt in the ring, we rub them with the nine oils. Sometimes they get bruised pretty badly.

Mr. Bounderby: Serves them right for being idle. You know, girl, when I was four or five years younger than you, I had worse bruises upon me than ten oils, twenty oils, or forty oils would have rubbed off.

Narrator 2: Sissy takes the two men to the shack where she and her father live.

Sissy: Father must have gone down to the ticket booth, sir. I don't know why he would go there, but he must have. I'll bring him in a minute.

Narrator 3: Sissy runs off, her long, dark hair streaming behind her.

Gradgrind: What does she mean? Back in a minute? That booth is more than a mile off!

Narrator 1: Before Bounderby can reply, a young man appears in the door and introduces himself as Mr. E. W. B. Childers. He is another performer from the circus show.

Mr. E. W. B. Childers: I believe that you were wishing to see Mr. Jupe?

Gradgrind: We were. His daughter has gone to fetch him, but we don't have time to wait for him to return. We would prefer to leave a message, if that's possible.

Mr. Bounderby: You see, my friend, we are the kind of people who know the value of time, and you are the kind of people who don't know the value of time.

Narrator 2: Childers looks irritated but ignores Bounderby's rudeness.

Childers: *(To Gradgrind.)* If you leave a message, it's doubtful that Mr. Jupe will ever receive it.

Gradgrind: Why is that?

Childers: Jupe has missed his tip very often lately.

Gradgrind: Has—what has he missed?

Childers: He's missed his tip. He was short in his leaps and bad in his tumbling. He has been jeered off the stage very often.

Gradgrind: What has this got to do with my leaving a message?

Childers: I think Jupe has come to the end of his rope. His joints are turning stiff, and he's getting all used up. He's been very close to losing his job, and I think he may have sneaked away before that could happen.

Mr. Bounderby: Are you saying that the man has run off and left his daughter behind? You know, I myself was born in a ditch and my mother ran away from me. And look at me now! I'm a great success!

Childers: Jupe sent his daughter out on an errand not an hour ago, and then was seen to slip out himself, with his hat over his eyes and a bundle tied up in a handkerchief under his arm. The girl will never believe it of him, but he has cut away and left her.

Gradgrind: Why won't she believe it of him?

Childers: Because those two were always together. Up until this time, he seemed to dote upon her. He even had her enrolled in that fancy local school. He was so pleased that she was learning to read and write. But now she'll have to quit and get some kind of a job.

Gradgrind: Actually, I came to tell Mr. Jupe that his daughter would have to quit the school. Her connections in the circus world have been causing problems.

Childers: Poor Sissy. It was her father's greatest dream for her that she would get a proper education.

Narrator 3: Mr. Gradgrind suddenly has a wild idea.

Gradgrind: Bounderby, let me have a word with you.

Narrator 1: The two men step aside and whisper to each other. Childers can only hear bits of their conversation.

Mr. Bounderby: No. I say no. I advise you not to. By no means should you do this.

Gradgrind: But think of it this way. The girl's plight would serve as an example to Thomas and Louisa. They could see firsthand what comes of curiosity and idleness. Think of that, Bounderby.

Narrator 2: After a period of arguing, the two men approach Childers again.

Gradgrind: Then it's settled. Mrs. Gradgrind and I shall take Cecilia Jupe into our household, and she shall continue at the school.

Scene 5

Narrator 3: Sissy Jupe moves in with the Gradgrinds. She has difficulty adjusting to her new life and is constantly tempted to run away. School is a constant source of anguish.

Sissy: How I wish I were you, Miss Louisa!

Louisa: You do? Why?

Sissy: I would know so much then. All that is so hard for me would be so easy then.

Louisa: You might not be the better for it, Sissy.

Sissy: I certainly couldn't be the worse.

Louisa: I don't know that. You are more useful to my mother, and more pleasant with her than I can ever be. You are pleasanter than anyone else in this family.

Sissy: But I am so stupid! All through the school day I make mistakes. Mr. Choakumchild calls on me, and I mess up every time.

Louisa: Tell me some of your mistakes.

Sissy: Today, for instance, our teacher was explaining to us about natural prosperity.

Louisa: National, I think it must have been.

Sissy: Yes, it was. But isn't it the same?

Louisa: You had better say national as he said to do.

Sissy: National prosperity. And he said, "Now, this schoolroom is a nation. And in this nation, there are fifty million pounds. Isn't this a prosperous nation? Girl number twenty, isn't this a thriving state?"

Louisa: What did you say?

Sissy: I said I didn't know. I thought I couldn't know whether it was prosperous and thriving unless I knew who had the money and whether any of it was mine. But Mr. Choakumchild said that had nothing to do with anything.

Louisa: Hmm. That was a big mistake you made.

Sissy: Yes, Miss Louisa. I know that now. Then Mr. Choakumchild said he would let me try again. And he said, "This schoolroom is an immense town, and in it there are a million inhabitants, and only 25 starve to death in the streets in the course of a year. Isn't the town prosperous?" And I said that I thought it must be just as hard on those who starved, whether the others were a million or a million million. And that was wrong, too.

Louisa: Of course it was.

Scene 6

Narrator 1: Meanwhile, in a far corner of Coketown, a power loom weaver named Stephen Blackpool is walking home from work.

Stephen Blackpool: *(To himself.)* Where is Rachel? I don't see her yet.

Narrator 2: Stephen stops and stands on a corner. He waits some minutes, as groups of young female mill workers pass him by with their shawls drawn over their heads.

Stephen: *(Sounding disappointed.)* I must have missed her.

Narrator 3: Suddenly Stephen spots another shawled figure.

Stephen: Rachel!

Narrator 1: The woman in the shawl turns and smiles at Stephen. She is about 35 years old, with dark hair and a kind but tired face.

Rachel: Stephen, is that you?

Stephen: You're late tonight.

Rachel: Yes. I never know what time I'll get out.

Narrator 2: They walk together a short way in silence.

Rachel: I've been thinking, Stephen, that we had better not walk together every night.

Stephen: I know you're right. People might start to talk. Even of someone as good and sweet as you, people might say bad things.

Narrator 3: He sighs.

Stephen: Yes, Rachel lass. It's always such a muddle. Such a muddle.

Narrator 1: They stop on the corner of the street where she lives, and she puts her hand in his.

Rachel: Good night, dear Stephen. Keep your chin up.

Stephen: Good night, dear lass. Good night.

Narrator 2: She turns down the dark, narrow street, and he continues on to his own little one room apartment, located over the top of a shop.

Narrator 3: Stephen enters the room and moves to set his candle down on a little table. As he does, he stumbles against something. The something turns out to be a very dirty, drunken woman with matted, tangled hair who lies crumpled up on the floor. The woman sits up.

Stephen: Mercy, woman! You've come back again.

Narrator 1: Cursing and clawing her hair out of her eyes, the woman looks at Stephen.

Joanna: Yes, I'm back again. And why not? This is my home, too. I'll come and go as I please and take what I want.

Narrator 2: Stephen sits down on his narrow bed with his head in his hands.

Joanna: Come away from that bed! It's mine! I'm your wife! I've a right to it!

Narrator 3: He moves away, and the woman throws herself onto the bed. In a moment, she is snoring loudly. Stephen sinks into a chair, where he spends the rest of the night.

Scene 7

Narrator 1: Mr. Bounderby sits sipping sherry in a leather chair near a roaring fire. His housekeeper, Mrs. Sparsit, sits across from him. A servant enters the room.

Servant: There is a Stephen Blackpool here to see you, sir. Should I let him in?

Mr. Bounderby: *(Thinking.)* Blackpool . . . Blackpool . . . He is one of my mill workers. Yes, I think it's alright to let him in. He has never been one of the more troublesome ones.

Narrator 2: Moments later, Stephen enters the parlor.

Mr. Bounderby: Now, Stephen, what's the matter with you?

Narrator 3: Stephen bows slightly and looks uneasy.

Mr. Bounderby: We have never had any difficulty with you. You have never been one of the unreasonable workers. You don't expect to be fed on turtle soup and venison with a pure gold knife and spoon, like the others do.

Stephen: No, sir. I haven't come to ask for anything like that.

Mr. Bounderby: Very well, then. Let's hear what you've got to say, lad.

Stephen: I have come to ask you for your advice. I need it badly. I got married on Easter, nineteen long, dreary years ago. The girl I married was well thought of and pretty. But she went bad almost as soon as we were married. Goodness knows it didn't happen because I was unkind to her.

Mr. Bounderby: I've heard all of this before and it rather bores me. She took to drinking, right? She left off working, sold the furniture, pawned the clothes, and so forth.

Stephen: I was patient with her.

Mr. Bounderby: *(Mumbling to his sherry glass.)* The bigger fool you are, then, I'd say.

Stephen: I was very patient with her. I tried to wean her off of the booze, over and over again. I tried this, I tried that, I tried the other. I have gone home many a time and found all my earthly possessions vanished and her lying in a stupor on the bare ground. I haven't done it just once—but twenty times.

Mr. Bounderby: Sounds like you should have thought twice before getting married in the first place. But I guess it's too late for that now, eh?

Stephen: I have come to ask you, sir, how I can be rid of this woman.

Mr. Bounderby: What are you talking about? You married her for better or worse!

Stephen: But I can't bear this anymore. If it wasn't for the help and support of the dearest lass in the world . . .

Mrs. Sparsit: I see what he's getting at! He wants to be rid of his wife so that he can marry another woman!

Narrator 1: Mrs. Sparsit raises her eyebrow disapprovingly.

Stephen: I want to be with Rachel. We have been friends since we were in school. We are both getting older . . . I read in the papers how rich folks are able to get out of their unfortunate marriages and marry again. They divide up the belongings and go their separate ways. I've read about rich people who break up their marriages over much smaller problems than the ones I've got . . . I want to know how to do it—how to get out.

Mr. Bounderby: There's no way out.

Stephen: If I flee from my marriage, is there a law to punish me?

Mr. Bounderby: Of course there is.

Stephen: If I marry the other dear lass, is there a law to punish me?

Mr. Bounderby: Of course there is.

Stephen: Please, sir! Show me the law that can help me!

Mr. Bounderby: Marriage is sacred, dear Stephen. You must simply stick it out.

Stephen: But I can't stick it out any longer. My case is such a terrible one. You know there's a law that can help me. Tell me what it is.

Mr. Bounderby: Okay, okay. Yes, there is such a law. But it costs money to get a divorce. It costs a *mint* of money.

Stephen: How much money?

Mr. Bounderby: You'd have to take your suit to three different courts and then get an act of Parliament to enable you to marry again. You couldn't do all that for less that one thousand to fifteen hundred pounds.

Stephen: There's no other law?

Mr. Bounderby: Certainly not.

Narrator 2: Stephen's face goes white, and his eyes go wide.

Stephen: It's all such a muddle, such a muddle. The sooner I'm dead, the better.

Mr. Bounderby: Pooh pooh! Don't talk nonsense, my good fellow.

Scene 8

Narrator 3: Stephen dejectedly descends the steps leading away from Bounderby's house. He crosses the street with his eyes on the ground. Suddenly, he feels a touch on his arm.

Mrs. Pegler: Pray tell me, sir, didn't I see you come out of that gentleman's house?

Stephen: Yes, missus.

Mrs. Pegler: And how did he look, sir? Was he portly, bold, and outspoken?

Stephen: Oh yes. He was all of that.

Mrs. Pegler: And healthy?

Stephen: He was eating and drinking and looked big and round as a bumblebee.

Mrs. Pegler: Thank you! Thank you!

Narrator 1: She continues walking along beside Stephen.

Mrs. Pegler: Coketown sure is a busy place, isn't it?

Stephen: Sure is. Very busy. You must be from the country, then?

Mrs. Pegler: Yes, yes. I came forty miles on the train this morning. I walked nine miles to the station. I'll walk the nine miles back again tonight. That's pretty good for someone my age, sir!

Stephen: Yes, it sure is. I hope you don't have to do it too often, missus.

Mrs. Pegler: No, no. Once a year. I spend my savings doing this once a year. I come to wander about the streets and see the gentleman, Mr. Bounderby.

Stephen: Only to see him?

Mrs. Pegler: That's enough for me. I ask no more.

Narrator 2: Later, when Stephen returns home, he finds Rachel sitting beside the bed where the dirty, disheveled woman still lies asleep.

Rachel: I'm glad you've come at last, Stephen. The doctor has already been here and left.

Stephen: Thank you so much for looking after her. I don't know how I would even go on if it wasn't for your friendship and help.

Rachel: You don't need to thank me, Stephen. You are like family to me.

Narrator 3: Stephen takes a seat beside Rachel and the two of them sit together in silence, gazing down at the prematurely aged face of the sleeping woman.

PART II

Scene 1

Narrator 1: Several years pass, and Stephen Blackpool's life becomes even bleaker. When he refuses to participate in a strike that his fellow workers are organizing, he becomes an outcast among the mill workers. Only Rachel stands by him.

Narrator 2: Young Tom Gradgrind goes to work in Mr. Bounderby's bank. At the same time, he develops a bad gambling habit and begins sinking deeper and deeper into debt.

Narrator 3: Louisa Gradgrind, motivated in part by a desire to help Tom financially, agrees to marry Mr. Bounderby. Her parents encourage her to do so, even though she is thirty years younger than Bounderby and does not love him.

Narrator 1: Sissy Jupe remains living in the Gradgrind household. When Mrs. Gradgrind dies, she becomes the caretaker and companion of the youngest Gradgrind child, Jane. Louisa and Sissy do not maintain a friendship. Louisa cannot stand being around Sissy because she feels that Sissy pities her for her marriage to Bounderby.

Narrator 2: It is evening. Mrs. Sparsit, Mr. Bounderby's old housekeeper who now lives at the bank, sits talking to the bank's porter. The porter is a young man named Bitzer who once defined "horse" for Sissy and chased her down the street.

Sparsit: Has it been a busy day, Bitzer?

Bitzer: Not a very busy day, my lady. About an average day.

Sparsit: The clerks, I presume, are all trustworthy, punctual, and hardworking?

Bitzer: Yes, ma'am. With the usual exception. I don't trust Mr. Thomas at all. He's an idler and not worth his salt. He'd have been out of here long ago, I think, if his sister weren't married to our dear employer.

Narrator 3: Mrs. Sparsit gives a sad shake of her head.

Bitzer: I only hope that she is not supplying her brother with the money that keeps him going. Otherwise . . . we both know where that money comes from!

Sparsit: Indeed we do!

Bitzer: Tom Gradgrind is as irresponsible as the worst of the workers in this town.

Sparsit: They would all do well to follow your example, Bitzer.

Bitzer: Thank you, ma'am. I have saved some money, even though my pay is small. The bonus I receive at Christmas—I never touch it. Why can't the others do as I have done?

Sparsit: I'm sure I don't know, Bitzer.

Bitzer: As for the workers needing recreations, ma'am, that's a lot of nonsense. I never take any recreation, myself. And I don't understand why they waste their money marrying and having children. I always say, "While my hat covers my family, I have only one to feed, and that's the person I like most to feed."

Narrator 1: There is a knock at the door. Bitzer goes to answer it, then returns.

Bitzer: If you please, ma'am, a gentleman wishes to see you.

Sparsit: Thank you, Bitzer.

Narrator 2: Mrs. Sparsit walks out into the entryway.

Sparsit: I believe, sir that you wished to see me?

Narrator 3: The gentleman in the hallway is tall, handsome, extremely well dressed, and about thirty-five. He wears a slightly bemused expression on his face and lounges carelessly against a banister.

Mr. James Harthouse: Ma'am, is this town always as black and sooty as it is tonight?

Sparsit: Indeed, sir, generally more so.

Harthouse: Astonishingly black! Even the river! But where are my manners? I am Mr. James Harthouse. I've come with a letter of introduction for Mr. Bounderby.

Narrator 1: Harthouse holds out the introductory letter, which is signed by Mr. Gradgrind.

Sparsit: I'm afraid Mr. Bounderby does not live here, but I will gladly point out the direction of the home that he shares with his wife.

Harthouse: His wife! Yes, Gradgrind's daughter! I've heard so much about her that I can hardly wait to meet her.

Sparsit: Indeed?

Harthouse: Tell me, is she absolutely unapproachable? Repellingly and stunningly clever? I see by your smile that you think not. As to her age, is she 35, 40?

Sparsit: She was no more than twenty when she married last year.

Harthouse: Remarkable! Remarkable! Well, thank you very much. I will be on my way.

Narrator 2: Harthouse leaves, heading in the direction that Mrs. Sparsit has indicated.

Sparsit: What do you think of that gentleman, Bitzer?

Bitzer: Spends a lot of money on his dress, ma'am.

Sparsit: It must be admitted that his clothes are tasteful.

Bitzer: If that's worth the money . . . He looks to me like the sort who drinks and gambles.

Scene 2

Narrator 3: Harthouse introduces himself at the Bounderby residence and in no time becomes a regular visitor there. He takes work in the bank and strikes up a friendship with young Tom. His fascination with Louisa grows. He makes a project out of trying to understand her and find out what's beneath her cool, aloof exterior.

Narrator 1: Harthouse, Tom, and Louisa are all sitting together in the Bounderby parlor one afternoon, when Bounderby sends for Stephen Blackpool. Bounderby assumes that because his fellow workers shun Stephen, he will be happy to play the role of spy, reporting on the activities of his coworkers.

Mr. Bounderby: Well, Stephen, what's this I hear? What have the pests that you work with been doing to you? Come in and speak up?

Narrator 2: Stephen stands by the door with his hat in his hand.

Mr. Bounderby: This is the man I was telling you about, Harthouse.

Narrator 3: Harthouse, who has been sitting near Louisa on the sofa, gets up and dawdles over to the hearth where Mr. Bounderby stands.

Harthouse: *(In a bored voice.)* Oh, really?

Mr. Bounderby: Now, Stephen Blackpool, speak up!

Stephen: What is it that you want with me?

Mr. Bounderby: Speak up and tell us all about what your fellows have been up to with their union and their strike plans.

Stephen: I'm sorry, sir, but I have nothing to say about it.

Mr. Bounderby: Will you believe this, Harthouse? Even though the others have ostracized him, he is such a slave to them still that he's afraid to open his lips about them.

Stephen: I said I had nothing to say, sir, not that I was fearful of opening my lips.

Mr. Bounderby: I know what you said. More than that, I know what you mean, you see. Not always the same thing. You had better tell us all at once: Is that fellow Slackridge in town, stirring up the people to mutiny? He's a scoundrel. Go on and tell us, Stephen.

Stephen: I'm as sorry as you are, sir, when the people's leaders are bad. They take whatever leaders they can get.

Narrator 1: Mr. Bounderby's big, puffy face is getting redder and redder, as he gets angry.

Mr. Bounderby: Pray, Mr. Blackpool, may I take the liberty of asking you how it happens that you refused to be in this union?

Stephen: How it happens? Well, I'd rather not get into that, but if I must, I must. I made a promise. My friend Rachel was afraid that the union organizing might lead to trouble. I promised her I wouldn't get involved.

Mr. Bounderby: Mr. Harthouse, have you ever met with anything like this man before? He defends the rascals and rebels who despise him.

Narrator 2: Stephen turns to Louisa and appeals to her.

Stephen: They're not rascals and rebels, ma'am. They're nothing of the kind. They've done me no kindness, but they've done what they've done believing it to be their duty to each other and to themselves.

Mr. Bounderby: So what have you come here to complain of? *(To Harthouse.)* They've always got something to complain of, these workers.

Stephen: I didn't come here to complain. Someone sent for me.

Mr. Bounderby: Then, what do your people, in general, complain of?

Stephen: Sir, look around the town, as rich as it is, and see the number of people who've been brought here to work on machines, day and night. They work their whole lives and never get any closer to any goal—except death.

Mr. Bounderby: It's clear to me that you are one of those chaps who always have a complaint. You are such an annoying chap that even your own people will have nothing to do with you. I never thought those fellows could be right in anything. But I'll tell you what! I'll go along with them and have nothing to do with you either.

Narrator 3: Stephen's face turns white.

Mr. Bounderby: Just finish off whatever you're working on and look for work elsewhere.

Stephen: Sir, you know that if I can't get work at your factories, I can't get work anywhere else around here either.

Mr. Bounderby: I have no more to say about this matter.

Stephen: *(Sighing.)* Heaven help us all in this world.

Scene 3

Narrator 1: It is near dark when Stephen comes out of Mr. Bounderby's house. Nothing is further from his thoughts than the strange old woman he encountered after his last meeting with Bounderby. Yet there she is, walking with Rachel.

Stephen: Rachel, my dear! Madam, how have you been?

Mrs. Pegler: I have been rather troubled with shortness of breath and so put off my visit this year till the weather was fine and warm. Instead of going straight back on the evening train, I'm staying tonight in a room at the traveler's lodge.

Narrator 2: The old woman chatters away happily, completely oblivious to Stephen's misery.

Mrs. Pegler: I have heard of Mr. Bounderby being married. I read it in the paper, where it looked like a grand wedding! Have you seen Mr. Bounderby's wife? Tell me, is she young and handsome?

Stephen: Yes, misses. I have seen the lady, and she is young and handsome.

Mrs. Pegler: Yes! Yes! And what a happy wife.

Stephen: Well . . . yes, I suppose she's happy . . .

Narrator 3: Stephen casts a doubtful look at Rachel.

Mrs. Pegler: You suppose she is? She *must* be! She's your master's wife!

Stephen: He's not my master anymore. That's all ended now.

Rachel: *(Anxiously.)* Have you left Mr. Bounderby's work, Stephen?

Stephen: It left me.

Rachel: Oh no! What will you do now? Where will you go?

Stephen: I don't know tonight. I have no idea where to turn. *(To Mrs. Pegler.)* Come up to my poor little place, misses, and take a cup of tea. Rachel will come, too, and then I'll make sure that you make it safely to the traveler's lodge.

Mrs. Pegler: Why, thank you. I believe I will.

Narrator 1: Back at Stephen's apartment, Rachel and Stephen begin fixing tea for Mrs. Pegler. A few minutes later, Louisa and Tom knock at the door. Stephen lets them in.

Louisa: I've come to speak with you, Mr. Blackpool, about what just happened. I'd like to be helpful, if you'll let me.

Narrator 2: She addresses herself to Rachel, who stands near Stephen. Mrs. Pegler stands back, watching the conversation.

Louisa: Has he told you what has passed between himself and my husband?

Rachel: I've heard the end of it, young lady.

Louisa: Did I understand that, being rejected by one employer, he would probably be rejected by all?

Rachel: The chances are very small—next to nothing—that he'll be able to work in this town again.

Narrator 3: Louisa turns to Stephen.

Louisa: What will you do?

Stephen: Well, ma'am, when I've finished what I'm working on, I must leave this part of the country and try another. There's nothing else to do.

Louisa: How will you travel?

Stephen: On foot, my kind lady, on foot.

Narrator 1: Louisa pulls a bunch of bills out of her purse. She lays the money on the table and turns again to Rachel.

Louisa: Will you convince him to take this?

Rachel: Bless you for thinking of the lad with such tenderness.

Stephen: I'll take only a few dollars, and I'll take that as a loan. It will be sweet work, paying it back, because I'll be reminded of this act of kindness.

Narrator 2: Louisa gets up to leave.

Tom: Just wait a moment, Lou! Before we go, I'd like to speak with him a moment. Something has come into my head. If you'll just step out on the stairs, Blackpool, I'll mention it.

Narrator 3: Stephen follows Tom out, and Tom closes the door.

Tom: *(In a whisper.)* I think I can do you a good turn. Don't ask me what it is, because it may not come to anything. When do you think you're leaving town?

Stephen: Today's Monday . . . I'll probably go about Friday or Saturday night.

Tom: Very well. When you leave work each night this week, just hang around the bank for an hour or so, will you? If I get things arranged as I wish, I'll send the bank porter with a note or message for you. Otherwise, there won't be any word. Do you understand?

Stephen: I understand, sir.

Tom: Look here, be sure you don't make any mistake then, and don't forget.

Stephen: I won't.

Tom: Very well, then.

Narrator 1: Tom and Stephen step back inside.

Tom: Time to go. Come along, Lou!

Narrator 2: Tom and Louisa depart. After a short time, Stephen and Rachel walk the old woman down to the traveler's lodge. On the way back, they console each other about their upcoming separation and promise to write to one another.

Scene 4

Narrator 2: The next day, Louisa and James Harthouse stroll together around the Bounderby garden, coming suddenly upon Tom. He seems to be in a particularly bad mood and is ripping moss off the trees with a stick.

Harthouse: What are you doing there, Tom, carving some girl's name?

Tom: I wouldn't be interested unless the girl had a fabulous fortune at her disposal. Then I wouldn't care if she was horribly ugly.

Harthouse: Tom, you are a money-grubber. You'll do anything for money.

Tom: A money-grubber, eh? Who isn't? Just ask my sister.

Louisa: Are you so sure that's a failing of mine?

Tom: You know whether the title suits you, Lou.

Harthouse: Tom is just in a bad and cruel mood today, as all bored people are now and then. Don't listen to him, Mrs. Bounderby. He knows better.

Narrator 3: They walk a small distance farther, then Louisa heads inside.

Harthouse: Tom, what's the matter?

Tom: Oh! Mr. Harthouse! I am hard up for money! You have no idea what a state I've gotten myself into. My sister could get me out of it, only she won't.

Harthouse: Tom, you're inconsiderate. You expect too much of your sister. You have gotten plenty of money from her, and you know it. And what if she doesn't have any money to give you just now?

Tom: She could get some if she really tried. Or else why bother being married to that horrible old, rich Bounderby?

Scene 5

Narrator 1: On Saturday morning, Harthouse lies lounging in the Bounderby garden. Suddenly, Mr. Bounderby comes bursting through the shrubbery.

Mr. Bounderby: Harthouse! Have you heard?

Harthouse: Heard what?

Mr. Bounderby: The bank's been robbed!

Harthouse: You don't mean it!

Mr. Bounderby: It was robbed last night, robbed with a false key.

Harthouse: Of much?

Mr. Bounderby: Well, no. Not of much. But it might have been!

Harthouse: How much was taken?

Mr. Bounderby: About a hundred and fifty pounds. But the sum isn't important!

Harthouse: Do you have any idea who might have done it?

Mr. Bounderby: Well, we've got two suspects. The first one is that Stephen Blackpool fellow. He was seen hanging around the bank looking suspicious every night this week.

Harthouse: And the other?

Mr. Bounderby: Some old woman who people say they've seen lurking around. I'm off to the police station now and then back to the bank. If you see Louisa, tell her I'll probably be back quite late tonight.

Harthouse: I will.

Narrator 2: At the news that Bounderby won't be around for the day, Harthouse smiles.

Scene 6

Narrator 3: Later that afternoon, as Louisa sits in the garden at the Bounderby residence, Harthouse finds her and surprises her with a declaration of love.

Louisa: Why did you come here? I'm married. We shouldn't be together like this.

Harthouse: My dearest love! What could I do? Knowing you were alone, was it possible that I could stay away from you?

Narrator 1: Louisa hangs her head, refusing to make eye contact with Harthouse.

Harthouse: You cannot deny that you have feelings for me. Often, I have noticed the special way you look at me. And anyone can see that you don't love Bounderby.

Narrator 2: He puts his arm around the back of her shoulder.

Harthouse: Please talk to me. Tell me about your feelings for me.

Louisa: *(Whispering.)* Not here.

Narrator 3: Louisa and Harthouse both jump nervously when they hear a sudden noise. A moment later, they realize it's only the sound of raindrops hitting the trees.

Harthouse: We have so little time to make so much of, my darling. I have been living these past weeks only in anticipation of seeing your sweet smile.

Louisa: This garden belongs to my husband. Please go—

Harthouse: I will go, but not until you agree to meet me elsewhere. Nothing in my life is worthwhile except for you. Where shall we meet? I will not go until you name the place.

Narrator 1: Louisa stares at her hands folded in her lap. She speaks quietly.

Louisa: Your rooms then. At seven tonight.

Scene 7

Narrator 2: Mr. Gradgrind sits by the window in his study in Coketown. Outside, the rain is pouring down. Lightning splits the sky. Suddenly, the door to his study bursts open. Louisa, dressed in her outdoor clothes, bursts in.

Gradgrind: Louisa!

Louisa: Father, I want to speak with you.

Gradgrind: What's the matter? How strange you look! And good heavens! Have you come here through this storm?

Louisa: Yes.

Narrator 3: Louisa throws off her cloak, revealing her disheveled hair and pale, troubled face.

Gradgrind: What is it? Louisa, tell me what's the matter?

Narrator 1: She drops into a chair next to him and puts her cold hand on his arm.

Louisa: Father, I curse the hour in which I was born.

Gradgrind: Curse the hour? What are you talking about?

Louisa: How could you give me life, yet take from me all the things that make it better than death? If I had been born blind and deaf, I might still have been better off than I am now, if only I had been allowed to exercise my imagination.

Narrator 2: She puts her head in her hands.

Louisa: If I had been allowed to have feelings and to act on them, I would have been a million times wiser, happier, more loving, more contented than I am now.

Gradgrind: I never knew you were unhappy, my child.

Louisa: Father, I always knew it. It was only because my mind and heart had been so deadened that I did as you counseled and married Bounderby. I knew that I did not love him, but I thought it made no difference. But then, soon after I was married, something inside me started to rebel.

Gradgrind: Louisa, my poor child. What have I done?

Louisa: Let me finish my tale, father. I had thought my heart was completely cold, but not too long ago, fate threw a man into my path. I had had no experience of this sort of man before. He had an easy, polished way. And almost immediately, he began to make me think he understood me and could read my thoughts. There seemed to be a real connection between us—

Gradgrind: Louisa! What are you telling me?

Louisa: Don't worry father. I have not disgraced you. But if you ask me whether I have loved this man or do love him, I tell you plainly, Father, that it may be so. I don't know!

Narrator 3: A crack of thunder shakes the house.

Louisa: This afternoon, when my husband was out, this man, James Harthouse, came to see me and declared his love for me. He expects me this minute to be meeting with him.

Narrator 1: She stands up looking extremely pale. Her hands shake wildly.

Louisa: Father, your philosophy and teaching have brought me to this end. Find some way to help me now—please!

Narrator 2: She faints, collapsing on the floor at her father's feet.

Scene 8

Narrator 3: Louisa wakes up the next morning in her old bed in her old room at home. It seems to her, at first, as if the last few years were merely a bad dream. Her sister Jane is standing next to the bed. Jane reaches down and takes Louisa's hand.

Louisa: When was I brought to this room?

Jane: Last night, Louisa. You collapsed in Father's study.

Louisa: Who brought me here?

Jane: Sissy, I believe. I found her here this morning, taking care of you.

Narrator 1: Jane smiles at Louisa, then bends down to kiss her cheek.

Jane: Will you see Father? Sissy said I was to tell him when you woke.

Louisa: What a bright, happy face you have, Jane!

Jane: Have I? I am very glad you think so. I am sure it must be Sissy's doing.

Louisa: This room looks so cheerful and welcoming. Did you do that, Jane?

Jane: Oh no, Louisa. That was Sissy.

Louisa: You can tell father I'm awake.

Narrator 2: A little later, Louisa's father enters.

Gradgrind: I can't tell you how overwhelmed I still am by what I heard last night.

Louisa: I'm sorry, Father. I know you only ever intended to make me happy.

Narrator 3: She offers him her hand. He takes it.

Gradgrind: My dear, I remained all night in my study, thinking over what passed between us. I am beginning to think that I am a terrible parent and shouldn't be trusted with anyone's welfare.

Narrator 1: She is silent. He looks uncomfortable, but continues.

Gradgrind: Some people believe that there is a wisdom of the head, and that there is a wisdom of the heart. I have not believed this to be the case. I have supposed the head to be all important. But now I think that perhaps I have been wrong. I have done my children a terrible disservice.

Louisa: Jane seems to have turned out very well, Father.

Gradgrind: If that is so, it is probably because I have been absent from here a good deal of late. And though your sister's training has been carried out according to my system, she has also had other influences from a very early age.

Narrator 2: Louisa knows that her father is talking about Sissy, Jane's constant companion and caretaker for the last several years. Louisa glances around the cozy bedroom and notes the fresh flowers on the dressing table. Mr. Gradgrind follows her gaze.

Gradgrind: I have a feeling that some change has been slowly happening in this house. What the head left undone and could not do, the heart may have been doing silently. Can it be so?

Scene 9

Narrator 3: Trying to do his best to fix a bad situation, Louisa's father writes a letter to Mr. Bounderby. As gently as he can, Gradgrind suggests that his daughter might benefit from an extended stay with her family.

Narrator 1: The idea that Louisa might need time away from her husband does not sit well with Bounderby. He insists that Louisa return by noon the following day and threatens that he will have nothing more to do with her if she does not show up on time.

Narrator 2: When Louisa has not arrived by five minutes after twelve the following day, Bounderby has her things collected and removed. Within the week, he has filed for divorce and put his country house up for sale.

Narrator 3: Bounderby moves into the bank and devotes all his attention to catching the bank robber. He has "Wanted" posters of Stephen Blackwell posted all over town.

Narrator 1: Louisa remains at home, grateful for her father's support and for the friendship of Sissy. One evening, the Gradgrind household receives some unexpected visitors.

Louisa: Sissy, who is it? Who's at the door?

Sissy: It's Mr. Bounderby, your brother Mr. Tom, and a young woman who says her name is Rachel and that you know her.

Louisa: What do they want, Sissy dear?

Sissy: They want to see you. Rachel has been crying and seems angry.

Louisa: Father, I can't refuse to see them. Shall they come in here?

Gradgrind: Certainly.

Narrator 2: Sissy escorts them in.

Mr. Bounderby: Mrs. Bounderby, I hope I don't disturb you. This is a late hour, but here is a young woman who has been making statements that make my visit necessary. Young Tom refuses for some reason or other to say anything at all about those statements, so I am obliged to confront you.

Narrator 3: Tom stands near Bounderby, staring at the floor.

Rachel: *(To Louisa.)* You have seen me once before, young lady.

Louisa: I have.

Rachel: Will you please tell Mr. Bounderby that I'm telling the truth? Tell him where you saw me and who was there.

Louisa: I went to the house where Stephen Blackpool lived, on the night of his discharge from his work, and I saw you there. He was there, too, and an old woman who did not speak and whom I could scarcely see, stood in a dark corner. My brother was with me.

Rachel: Say, young lady, if you please, why you came to Stephen's that night.

Louisa: I felt compassion for him and I wished to know what he was going to do, and I wanted to offer assistance.

Rachel: Did you offer him a sum of money?

Louisa: Yes, but he refused most of it. He would only take a few dollars as a loan.

Mr. Bounderby: Well, well. Her version of the story is the same! Who would have guessed it?

Rachel: *(To Louisa.)* Stephen Blackpool is now named as a thief in public print all over this town. Everyone is speaking out against him in the most shameful way.

Louisa: I am very, very sorry.

Rachel: When I read what's been put in print about Stephen, I went straight to the bank to say I knew where he was and to give a promise that he would be here in two days to clear his name. My letter to Stephen went out in the mail that afternoon. He wrote me back and said he was coming. He'll be here any moment now. He'll clear himself!

Scene 10

Narrator 1: Two days pass and still Stephen does not show up. Rachel receives no further letters from him, and the police do not find him.

Narrator 2: Another suspect in the bank robbery case, however, is found. Mrs. Sparsit tracks down the mysterious old woman, Mrs. Pegler, and drags her back to the bank. A crowd gathers.

Sparsit: Fetch Mr. Bounderby down. Rachel, young woman, you know who this is?

Rachel: It's Mrs. Pegler.

Sparsit: I should think it is! Fetch Mr. Bounderby.

Mrs. Pegler: Please, don't! He must not see me!

Sparsit: I will not leave until I've handed you over to him myself!

Narrator 3: Mr. Bounderby appears, accompanied by Mr. Gradgrind and Tom, with whom he's been holding conference upstairs.

Mr. Bounderby: Why, what's the matter now?

Sparsit: Sir, here is a person whom you have dearly wanted to find.

Narrator 1: Mr. Bounderby gets a good look at Mrs. Pegler for the first time.

Mr. Bounderby: *(Angrily to Mrs. Sparsit.)* Why, what do you mean by this?

Sparsit: *(Faintly.)* Sir?

Mr. Bounderby: *(To Mrs. Sparsit.)* Why don't you mind your own business ma'am? How dare you go and poke your nose into my family affairs?

Mrs. Pegler: My dear Josiah! My darling boy! I am not to blame. It's not my fault. I told this lady over and over again that I knew she was doing something you wouldn't want!

Mr. Bounderby: Why did you let her bring you? Couldn't you knock her cap off or scratch her or something?

Mrs. Pegler: She threatened me that if I resisted her, I should be brought by the police.

Narrator 2: Mrs. Pegler trails off, glancing proudly but timidly around at her surroundings.

Mrs. Pegler: Such a fine house! My dear, noble, stately boy! I have always lived a quiet, secret life, just as you wished. I have never broken the condition once. I never said I was your mother. I have admired you at a distance, and I have come to town sometimes to take a proud peep at you, but that's all!

Gradgrind: *(In a severe tone of voice.)* I am surprised, madam, that in your old age you have the nerve to face the child that you deserted so many years ago!

Mrs. Pegler: I deserted my Josiah!? The Lord forgive you for your wicked imaginations!

Gradgrind: Do you deny then, madam, that you left your son to—to be brought up in a gutter?

Mrs. Pegler: Josiah in the gutter! No such a thing, sir. Never! For shame on you! My dear boy knows, and will tell you, that though he comes from humble parents, he comes from parents who loved him dearly. His parents never thought twice about taking hardships on themselves so that he could have advantages in life like a good education.

Narrator 3: Everyone in the crowd stares at Mrs. Pegler, in amazement. They are all beginning to realize that she is telling the truth, and that all Mr. Bounderby's stories about himself have been completely untrue.

Mrs. Pegler: My son will tell you that though his mother just kept a little village shop, he never turned away from her but sent her a little money every year, enough to live on. If he didn't want his poor, old uneducated mother around, who can blame him?

Narrator 1: She gazes around again in wonder at the lovely woodwork and fine furniture.

Scene 11

Narrator 2: With one of the robbery suspects cleared, public attention shifts back to the still-missing Stephen Blackpool.

Narrator 3: Sissy befriends Rachel and tries to keep her spirits up. On a Sunday, Rachel and Sissy take a train a few miles out of town, as many Coketown residents do, to go walking in the country and escape the soot and grime of the city.

Narrator 1: The two women are careful as they walk through the fields. They know that much of the countryside has been mined for coal and is now full of hidden pits.

Sissy: It is so still here that I think we must be the first who have been here all summer.

Narrator 2: Sissy examines some rotten fragments of fence on the ground.

Sissy: And yet I don't know. This piece of fencing looks like it hasn't been broken very long. The wood is still fresh. Here are footprints, too . . . Oh, Rachel!

Rachel: What's the matter?

Sissy: There's a hat lying in the grass.

Narrator 3: Rachel picks the hat up, then breaks into sobs.

Rachel: It's Stephen's hat! Oh the poor lad! He must have been murdered!

Sissy: Maybe that's not it . . . Stay here while I go on a little way by myself.

Narrator 1: She is just in the act of stepping forward, when Rachel grabs her and screams. At the feet of the two women is a black, ragged chasm, hidden by thick grass. They both spring back and fall on their knees.

Rachel: Oh no! He's down there! Down there!

Sissy: We must run, as quickly as we can, and get help!

Narrator 2: The women dash off, running faster than they ever have before. Soon onlookers and rescue workers gather by the pit, along with a doctor. Louisa, Tom, Mr. Bounderby, and Mr. Gradgrind soon arrive as well.

Narrator 3: After what seems like endless waiting, Stephen is hoisted back to the surface.

Sissy: He's alive!

Doctor: But he's very badly hurt. I'm not sure I can help him. I'll do my best.

Narrator 1: Rachel kneels by Stephen's side.

Rachel: Stephen, can you hear me?

Narrator 2: Stephen opens his eyes.

Stephen: Rachel, my dear.

Narrator 3: Rachel takes Stephen's hand.

Stephen: Don't let go.

Rachel: Are you in great pain, my dear Stephen?

Stephen: I have been, but am not now . . .

Narrator 1: He smiles at her.

Rachel: You were trying to come back, to clear your name. But you didn't make it . . .

Stephen: When I was down there, I thought about what a muddle everything is. I thought about how people are murdered by their work. I thought about your little sister, and how she died, young and misshapen, her lungs all blackened by the poisoned air.

Narrator 2: Rachel weeps for both her long lost sister and for Stephen.

Stephen: I thought bitterly about how that young man and woman came to see me before I left, pretending to be kind but only meaning to frame me as a bank robber.

Narrator 3: Murmurs go through the crowd.

Stephen: But then I looked up at the stars and they cleared my mind. They seemed to be shining down on me. I have seen more clearly and have made it my dying prayer that the world may come together more and that people might understand each other better.

Narrator 1: Louisa comes to stand where Stephen can see her.

Stephen: I now believe that your intentions were pure and you meant no harm, dear lady. Will you take a message to your father?

Louisa: He is here. Shall I bring him to you?

Stephen: If you please.

Narrator 2: Mr. Gradgrind comes and stands beside Stephen.

Stephen: Sir, you must clear my name. This I leave to you.

Gradgrind: How can I? Tell me how.

Stephen: Sir, your son will tell you how. Ask him. I make no charges. I saw and spoke with your son one night. He remembers well. I ask no more of you than that you clear my name, and I trust you to do it.

Narrator 3: The bearers begin lifting Stephen to carry him away, since the doctor is anxious to get him to the hospital.

Stephen: Rachel, beloved lass! Don't let go of my hand. We may walk together tonight, my dear.

Rachel: I will hold your hand and stay beside you, Stephen, all the way.

Stephen: Bless you. Will somebody cover my face?

Narrator 1: They carry Stephen gently along the fields. Soon the procession becomes a funeral procession.

Epilogue

Narrator 2: By the next day, rumors of Tom's crime have been widely circulated, and the police are on the hunt. Tom explains to his father that he framed Stephen and stole the money to pay his gambling debts. Taking pity on Tom, Sissy manages to arrange for him to hide with her old circus troupe until he can leave the country. None of the Gradgrinds are ever able to see him again.

Narrator 3: In the years to come, Rachel never marries. She continues to work in the mill, always remaining sweet-tempered and serene, despite her difficult life. She is sometimes seen caring for a drunken, degraded female beggar who everyone else ignores.

Narrator 1: Bounderby dies five years later after a sudden coughing fit in the streets of Coketown. Numerous buildings, streets, churches, and bridges are named after him.

Narrator 2: Louisa never remarries or raises a family of her own, but, in later years, she enjoys spending time with Sissy's children. She learns to enjoy reading fantastic tales to them and encourages them to be sensitive and imaginative. The children grow up loving her, and she grows old surrounded by a warm family and many friends.

The End

The Luck of Roaring Camp

Bret Harte

Adapted by Suzanne I. Barchers

Summary

The men of Roaring Camp are a rough group. But when Cherokee Sal, the lone woman, dies in childbirth, they decide to raise the orphaned baby, with Stumpy as the primary caretaker. This rough group of men becomes dedicated to the child, enjoying the prosperity that seems to come with the arrival of the baby they christen "Tommy Luck." Their rude camp slowly transforms, and the men become more civilized. But the winter of 1851 brings floods, and several men—plus Tommy Luck—are swept away in a deluge.

Background Information

Bret Harte was born as Francis Brett Harte in Albany, New York, on August 25, 1839. After living in New York City and Brooklyn, he left for California with his widowed mother in 1854. He held various jobs—miner, teacher, express messenger, and printer—which prepared him for writing. While editor of the *Overland Monthly*, he published "The Luck of Roaring Camp," which brought him instant fame. He wrote many poems and stories. He also worked with Mark Twain, who is said to have credited Harte with teaching him how to write. In 1871, Harte contracted with *Atlantic Monthly* to write 12 stories a year for ten thousand dollars, the highest figure paid to an American writer up to that date. Harte retired in London in 1885. He died May 5, 1902.

Presentation Suggestions

The characters can sit casually on the floor or on stools in any order, with the narrators on either side of the stage.

Props

The students can be dressed in rugged clothes typical of men panning for gold in the mid-1800s. The stage can look like a rustic cabin, with mining artifacts.

Characters

- ❀ Narrators 1 and 2
- ❀ *Members of camp in the West:*
  - ❀ Kentuck
  - ❀ Sandy
  - ❀ Oakhurst
  - ❀ Stumpy
  - ❀ Ryder
  - ❀ Tipton

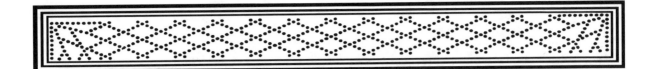

The Luck of Roaring Camp

Scene 1

Narrator 1: There is a commotion in Roaring Camp. It cannot be a fight, for in 1850 that is not novel enough to have called forth the entire settlement. The whole camp collects before a rude cabin on the outer edge of the clearing. Conversation carries on in a low tone, but the name of a woman is frequently repeated.

Kentuck: I wish we had another woman here. No matter that Cherokee Sal didn't have a husband, no woman should have to go through this alone.

Sandy: This is rough for sure, but she's surely brought it on herself.

Kentuck: That's surely true, but to give birth here in Roaring Camp all by herself? Stumpy, go in there and see what you can do. You've had experience in them things.

Narrator 2: The crowd approves the choice, and Stumpy is wise enough to bow to the majority. The door closes on the extempore surgeon and midwife, and the inhabitants of Roaring Camp sit down outside and await the new life.

Narrator 1: The camp holds about a hundred men. Some are fugitives from justice, some are criminals, and all are reckless. The men wait, talk quietly, and make wagers.

Oakhurst: I've got a gold piece that says Sal makes it through all this. Anyone want to bet against me?

Sandy: I'll take that bet. She doesn't sound good.

Kentuck: She may not make it, but I'll wager that it's a big, healthy boy.

Sandy: Nope. We need another girl for sure!

Oakhurst: Stop! Listen to that cry!

Narrator 2: The camp rises to its feet in concern. Whether owing to the rude surgery of the camp or some other reason, Cherokee Sal is sinking fast. Within an hour, she has climbed that rugged road that leads to the stars, and so passes out of Roaring Camp forever.

Narrator 1: While the men speculate as to the fate of the newborn boy, milk is found from a donkey. The men form themselves into a single line at the front door of her cabin to pay their respects.

Stumpy: Gentleman, please pass in at the front door, round the table, and out at the back door. Them that wishes to contribute anything toward the orphan will find a hat handy.

Narrator 2: The first man takes his hat off as he enters, setting an example for the rest. The men offer their comments about the babe.

Sandy: Is that him?

Kentuck: Mighty small specimen.

Oakhurst: Ain't bigger than a derringer.

Narrator 1: The contributions are characteristic: a silver tobacco box, a doubloon, a navy revolver, a diamond breastpin, a Bible, a golden spur, a silver teaspoon. The initials on the teaspoon are not the giver's.

Narrator 2: Other gifts included a pair of surgeon's shears, a Bank of England five pound note and about two hundred dollars in loose gold and silver coin.

Narrator 1: As Kentuck bends over the baby, the child catches his finger and holds it fast for a moment. Something like a blush appears on his weather-beaten cheek.

Kentuck: The darned little cuss! He rastled with my finger, the darned little cuss.

Narrator 2: Stumpy and Kentuck sit up that night, and Kentuck relates with great gusto his experience, ending with his calling the baby *the darned little cuss*. This seems to relieve him of any unjust implication of sentiment. Later he takes a walk down to the river. Then he returns to the cabin and knocks on the door. When Stumpy opens the door, Kentuck looks past him toward the baby.

Kentuck: How goes it?

Stumpy: All serene!

Kentuck: Anything up?

Stumpy: Nothing.

Narrator 1: The men pause for a moment.

Kentuck: Rastled with it—the darned little cuss.

Scene 2

Narrator 2: After Cherokee Sal is buried the next day, the camp meets to discuss what should be done with her infant. A resolution to adopt it is unanimous and enthusiastic.

Ryder: But how shall we care for it?

Tipton: Let's send the child to Red Dog. That's only 40 miles away and they have women there.

Stumpy, Kentuck, Sandy, Oakhurst: No, no!

Ryder: Besides, them fellows at Red Dog would take it over from us. They can't be trusted.

Oakhurst: What about bringing in someone to nurse it?

Ryder: What decent woman is going to want to come here?

Tipton: What about you, Stumpy? Could you take care of him?

Stumpy: Well, I've got my donkey for milk. And we can send to Sacramento for supplies.

Tipton: Everyone agrees?

Narrator 1: The men like the original and heroic plan and get the best they can afford for the baby. Strange to say, the child thrives. Perhaps it's the invigorating climate of the mountain camp, but Stumpy likes to claim credit.

Stumpy: Me and that donkey have been father and mother to him.

Narrator 2: By the time the baby is a month old, he has been known as *The Kid, Stumpy's Boy, The Coyote,* and even Kentuck's endearment, *the darned little cuss.* But the men decide it's time to give him a name.

Sandy: You know, this baby seems to have brought luck to us. How about Luck for his name?

Ryder: Sounds fine with me. Any objections?

Tipton: Let's give him a first name too. How about Tommy?

Oakhurst: Tommy Luck. That's good. Gives him a fresh start all around.

Narrator 1: Some of the men plan a christening, but it promises to be a satirical treatment of this usually serious church service. The men march to the grove with music and banners, expecting a grand revelry. They deposit the child before a mock altar, and Stumpy steps in front of the expectant crowd.

Stumpy: It ain't my style to spoil the fun, boys. But it strikes me that this thing ain't exactly on the square. It's playing it pretty low down on this here baby to make fun that he ain't going to understand. And if there's going to be any godfathers round, I'd like to see who's got better rights than me.

Oakhurst: You're right, Stumpy.

Stumpy: But we're here for a christening, and we'll have it. I proclaim you Thomas Luck, according to the laws of the United States and the state of California, so help me God.

Narrator 2: This is the first time that the name of the deity has been uttered other than profanely in the camp. Tommy is christened as seriously as he would have been under a Christian roof. He cries and is comforted in normal fashion.

Narrator 1: Almost imperceptibly, a change comes over the settlement. The cabin assigned to Tommy Luck, or "The Luck," is the first to change. Stumpy keeps it scrupulously clean, and the men appreciate the change. Tuttle's grocery imports a carpet and mirrors. Personal cleanliness improves. Even Kentuck starts wearing a clean shirt each afternoon.

Narrator 2: The men begin conversing in whispers and give up profanity. Music is acceptable, and the men rock Luck to a variety of songs. On long summer days the men take Luck to the gulch where he naps while they work.

Scene 3

Narrator 1: The summer is a time of prosperity, but the winter of 1851 brings deep snow in the Sierras. Every gorge and gulch becomes a tumultuous watercourse that descends the hillsides and tears down giant trees.

Stumpy: We've been under water before. Water put the gold into the gulches.

Oakhurst: You're right, Stumpy. The water's been here once and will be here again!

Narrator 2: However, one wet night the North Fork leaps over its banks and sweeps toward Roaring Camp. Little can be done to clear out the camp. The next morning, those fortunate to be on high ground when the floods came look for survivors.

Oakhurst: Well, boys, Stumpy is gone. Tommy Luck must be gone with him.

Narrator 1: Just then, they hear a shout. A relief boat from down-river has brought a man and an infant.

Tipton: Hey, fellas! It's Kentuck and the Luck!

Narrator 2: Kentuck, cruelly crushed and bruised, still holds the Luck of Roaring Camp in his arms. The child is cold and lifeless.

Tipton: He's dead.

Narrator 1: Kentuck opens his eyes.

Kentuck: Dead?

Ryder: Yes, my man, and you are dying too.

Narrator 2: A smile lights Kentuck's eyes.

Kentuck: Dying! He's a-taking me with him. Tell the boys I've got the Luck with me now.

Narrator 1: Kentuck, clinging to the babe, drifts away into the shadowy river that flows forever to the unknown sea.

The End

Rappaccini's Daughter

Nathaniel Hawthorne

Adapted by Jennifer L. Kroll

Summary

A young man named Giovanni moves to a distant city to attend college. He rents a room there. The window of the room looks out on a strange and magnificent garden. From his window, Giovanni watches and then befriends a beautiful young woman who is often in the garden. He later learns that the garden belongs to a famous medical researcher named Doctor Rappaccini and that the young woman in the garden is Rappaccini's equally famed daughter, Beatrice. As Giovanni and Beatrice grow closer, it becomes clear that Beatrice has a terrible secret. Through her father's experimentation, she has become poisonous. Eventually, Giovanni begins to wonder if he, too, has become part of Rappaccini's evil experiment.

Background Information

Nathaniel Hawthorne was an American author who lived from 1804 to 1864. He was a native of New England, where many of his works are set. His most famous novels are *The Scarlet Letter*, published in 1850, and *The House of Seven Gables*, published in 1851. The story "Rappaccini's Daughter" first appeared in the volume *Mosses from an Old Manse*, published in 1854. The story, like many others of its time, reveals a distrust for science and the scientific. It also, like other Hawthorne works, raises questions about the nature of good and evil.

Presentation Suggestions

In the center of the room, place Beatrice on a low chair, stool, or mat. Seat Giovanni near her on a higher stool, or have him stand near her behind a podium. To the side of Giovanni, seat Lisabetta and Baglioni. To the side of Beatrice, seat Doctor Rappaccini. Place Narrators in any convenient location.

Props

Beatrice can dress in purple. Baglioni and Rappaccini can wear lab coats or smocks. Lisabetta can wear an apron. You may wish to place a plant or flower arrangement on a table or desk near Beatrice or between Beatrice and Giovanni. Giovanni can handle a bouquet of flowers during scenes 3 and 7. Beatrice can hold a flower blossom and arrange it in her hair during scene 3. Lisabetta can hold a key and give it to Giovanni during scene 5. Baglioni can pass a vial or test tube to Giovanni during scene 6.

Characters

- ❀ Narrators 1, 2, and 3
- ❀ Lisabetta, *Giovanni's landlady*
- ❀ Giovanni Guasconti, *a university student in his late teens*
- ❀ Giacomo Rappaccini, *a noted scientist*
- ❀ Beatrice Rappaccini, *a young woman in her late teens, Rappaccini's daughter*
- ❀ Professor Pietro Baglioni, *a scientist and professional rival of Giacomo Rappaccini*

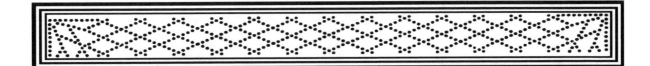

Rappaccini's Daughter

Scene 1

Lisabetta: You will take the room then, Signor? Very good.

Giovanni: Yes, I'll take it.

Narrator 1: Giovanni Guasconti has just moved from Naples, in southern Italy, to Padua, in Northern Italy, in order to attend the university of Padua. Because he has little money, he is forced to take a small room in a gloomy old house.

Narrator 2: On his own for the first time, Giovanni feels a little lonely and depressed. He knows almost no one in Padua. Looking around at his dismal room, he becomes even more downhearted. He sighs.

Lisabetta: Well! That was quite a sigh to come from one so young! I guess you probably are finding this old mansion gloomy. Cheer up. Come and put your head out the window, and you will see that the sun shines just as brightly here as it does in Naples.

Narrator 3: Giovanni puts his head out the window and sees that beneath his window is an exquisite garden.

Giovanni: Does this garden belong to the house?

Lisabetta: Heaven forbid! No—that garden is owned and cultivated by Signor Giacomo Rappaccini, the famous doctor whom I'm sure you must have heard of, even in Naples. It is said that he uses these plants to make medicines. Often you may see the doctor at work. Sometimes, you might also see his daughter gathering plants.

Narrator 1: Lisabetta straightens up the room a bit and then departs. After unpacking his things, Giovanni finds himself with nothing to do. He gazes out the window at the garden once more.

Narrator 2: He is struck by both the beauty and strangeness of the flowers and plants that he sees. Almost none of them look familiar. One shrub in particular catches his eye. Its long green and brown tendrils and many purple blossoms cascade from out of a large marble vase that stands near a fountain and pool in the center of the garden.

Narrator 3: As Giovanni is staring down at the garden, a gray-haired man in a white lab coat emerges from the opposite doorway and begins to examine the flowers. With thick gloves on his hands, he plucks away dried leaves. As he approaches the purple-flowered shrub in the center of the garden, he puts a mask over his nose and mouth. He seems reluctant to approach the plant too closely or to breathe the air around it. Suddenly, he backs up a little, takes off the mask, and calls out.

101

Giacomo Rappaccini: Beatrice! Beatrice!

Beatrice Rappaccini: Here I am, Father! What do you need? Are you in the garden?

Rappaccini: Yes, I am, and I need your help.

Narrator 1: Giovanni watches as a young woman emerges from out of the building across the way. He is immediately struck by her intense beauty. With her violet clothing and her long ropes of chestnut colored hair, she reminds him of the plant growing in the center of the garden, the one toward which she strides.

Rappaccini: Our treasure here needs some tending. I don't think it's safe for me to approach this one closely anymore. I'm afraid you'll have to be its sole caretaker from now on.

Beatrice: I'm happy to look after it.

Narrator 2: Beatrice walks right up to the purple-flowered plant and opens her arms as if to embrace it.

Beatrice: Hello, my sister! Yes, of course I'll take good care of you! And for my reward, I get to breathe your sweet perfume.

Narrator 3: Giovanni watches the father and daughter in the garden for a little while longer, until it begins to get dark. Then he closes the window and goes to bed.

Scene 2

Narrator 1: The next day, while at the university, Giovanni stops in to visit Professor Pietro Baglioni, an old friend of his father's and one of his only acquaintances in Padua. Professor Baglioni is a medical researcher who teaches classes in science and medicine.

Narrator 2: In the course of their conversation, Giovanni asks Baglioni about Giacomo Rappaccini and his plant research.

Pietro Baglioni: Well, Giovanni, since I'm a medical researcher myself, it wouldn't seem right for me to fail to say something complimentary about a famous doctor like Rappaccini. At the same time, though, I don't want to give you any wrong ideas about the man. You're the son of my friend, and I feel responsible for you, so let me just say this about Rappaccini: He is probably a greater scientist than almost anyone in Italy, but I have my doubts about his personal and professional character.

Giovanni: Doubts? What are they?

Baglioni: Do you have some kind of disease, my young friend, that you are so interested in physicians?

Narrator 3: The professor smiles.

Baglioni: I am only teasing.

Narrator 1: Baglioni pauses and becomes serious.

Baglioni: Rappaccini, it has always seemed to me, cares much more for science than for human beings. He would sacrifice human life, even his own life, I think, for the sake of adding so much as a tiny little seed to the world's store of scientific knowledge.

Giovanni: When I saw him, I thought he seemed like a terrible man—very cold. And yet, Professor, don't you think there's something noble in dedicating oneself completely to science? Such a pure love of knowledge seems like it must be a rare thing.

Baglioni: Rappaccini's a rarity alright—fortunately for us. We can only hope that other doctors have sounder views of health and healing than that man does!

Giovanni: What do you mean?

Baglioni: It is Rappaccini's theory that the medicines needed for curing every human illness can be extracted from poisonous plants. He grows every variety of poisonous plant that he can get his hands on, and he crossbreeds various plants to create new species, more poisonous than the old. His creations, it seems to me, are far more horrible than anything nature could dream up on its own.

Giovanni: Has he cured many people?

Baglioni: Now and then, I must admit, he has worked some totally marvelous cure. But I don't think he should receive much credit for his successes. I think they are just the products of chance. Now his failures—those he should be held accountable for!

Giovanni: I'm sure you're right about how much Rappaccini loves his work. Surely, though, there is something more dear to him. He has a daughter.

Baglioni: Aha! So now our friend Giovanni's secret is out! You have heard of this daughter, whom all the young men in Padua are wild about, though not half a dozen have ever had the luck to see her face. I know little of the lady Beatrice, except that Rappaccini is reported to have instructed her deeply in science. People say she is already qualified to fill a professor's chair. Perhaps her father destines her for mine!

Scene 3

Narrator 2: As Giovanni walks home from his meeting with Professor Baglioni, thoughts of the beautiful Beatrice fill his mind. In a dreamy, romantic mood, he stops in at a florist's and buys a fresh bouquet of flowers.

Narrator 3: Back in his room, Giovanni seats himself beside the window overlooking Rappaccini's garden. He stares down at the strange plants basking in the sun. For a while, the garden remains empty. Then a door opens and the lady Beatrice enters. Giovanni's heart skips a beat.

Narrator 1: Once again, Beatrice is wearing shades of purple, colors similar to those of the flowers hanging from the magnificent shrub in the center of the garden. Beatrice walks straight to this plant and throws her arms open.

Beatrice: Give me your breath, my sister, for I have grown faint from breathing common air. And, if you don't mind, I'll take one of your lovely flowers as well.

Narrator 2: Beatrice plucks one of the purple blossoms and tucks it into her hair. As she arranges the flower, a petal and a couple of leaves float down to the walkway.

Narrator 3: As he watches this scene, Giovanni notices something strange. He sees a brightly colored lizard or chameleon walking toward Beatrice and the fountain. As it crosses the fallen petal and leaves on the walkway, it suddenly, stops in its tracks and begins to thrash wildly. The animal contorts into a strange shape, and then lies still.

Narrator 1: Beatrice notices the dying creature. She makes the sign of the cross on herself, then returns to the task of arranging the flower. A sudden movement from Giovanni at his window causes her to look up. The two young people see each other. Giovanni is seized with a sudden impulse.

Giovanni: Signorina! These are pure and healthful flowers. Please accept them as a gift from Giovanni Guasconti.

Narrator 2: Giovanni throws down the bouquet that he purchased at the florist's. Beatrice walks over and picks up the flowers.

Beatrice: Thank you, Signor. I accept your gift. I would love to be able to give you, in return, this purple flower I'm wearing. Unfortunately, however, if I toss it in the air, it will never reach your window.

Narrator 3: Beatrice seems suddenly awkward and shy. She turns and hurries back toward her own home, clutching Giovanni's flowers to her chest.

Narrator 1: As he watches her run, he thinks he sees the flowers wilting in her hands. He rubs his eyes, wondering if the light is playing tricks on them.

Scene 4

Narrator 2: Although he is not certain whether he actually saw flowers wither in her hands, Giovanni decides that in the future it might be best to avoid the strange and beautiful Beatrice and her poisonous garden.

Narrator 3: For the next week or so, he stays away from the garden window, away from the eyes of Beatrice. And yet, he cannot get her out of his mind. His feelings about her become a mixture of fear and desire, with each feeling seeming to make its opposite stronger.

Narrator 1: To calm himself and remove himself from temptation, Giovanni begins to take lengthy walks through and around the city of Padua. As he is deep in tortured thought during one of these walks, he finds his arm suddenly grabbed by a panting Professor Baglioni.

Baglioni: Signor Giovanni! Stop, my young friend! I have been calling your name for blocks! Have you forgotten who I am?

Narrator 2: Baglioni studies the dark look on Giovanni's face.

Baglioni: You seem so different today than when I last saw you!

Giovanni: I have much on my mind, Professor Baglioni. Now, let me pass!

Baglioni: What? I grew up side by side with your father, and now you wish to pass me like a stranger in the street? I will not let you pass until we've at least had words.

Giovanni: Be quick then, Professor. Can't you see that I'm in a hurry?

Narrator 3: As they are speaking, a man dressed in black comes up the street toward them. He is stooped and moves feebly, as if he is in poor health. His face looks pale and sickly.

Narrator 1: And yet, his eyes seem very lively and his expression is one of great intelligence and energy. As he passes, he exchanges cold and distant greetings with Professor Baglioni.

Rappaccini: *(Nodding.)* Baglioni.

Baglioni: *(Nodding back.)* Rappaccini.

Narrator 2: Whereas the old man scarcely looks at Professor Baglioni, he fixes his eyes on Giovanni with great intensity. There is a look of intellectual curiosity in his face. He continues making his way up the street.

Baglioni: *(Whispering.)* That was Dr. Rappaccini! Has he ever seen your face before?

Giovanni: Not that I know.

Baglioni: He *has* seen you! He must have seen you! For some purpose or other, he is studying you! I know that look of his! He gets the same look on his face when bending over a bird, mouse, or butterfly that he has killed as part of some experiment. I would stake my life on it: you are the subject of one of Rappaccini's experiments!

Giovanni: That's foolishness! I don't even know the man.

Baglioni: I tell you, poor Giovanni—Rappaccini has a scientific interest in you. You have fallen into terrible hands! And the Signorina Beatrice—what part does she play in all this?

Narrator 3: Unable to stand any more of the conversation, Giovanni breaks free and hurries up the street.

Giovanni: Let me go!

Narrator 1: Baglioni looks after Giovanni, shaking his head.

Baglioni: This can't be happening! I must not let this happen. The youth is the son of my old friend and should not come to harm here in my city!

Narrator 2: Baglioni turns and begins heading home, still muttering to himself.

Baglioni: The nerve of that detestable Rappaccini! Snatching the lad out of my own hands to use him for devilish experiments! And this daughter of Rappaccini! Someone must find out her secret!

Narrator 3: Baglioni suddenly smiles to himself.

Baglioni: I may foil you yet, Rappaccini! If not professionally, perhaps in a way you never dreamed possible!

Scene 5

Narrator 1: Giovanni wanders home. When he reaches the front hallway of the gloomy old house, Lisabetta, his landlady, meets him. She smirks.

Lisabetta: Giovanni . . . there is a little secret that I want to share with you.

Giovanni: I'm busy right now.

Narrator 2: Giovanni tries to walk past Lisabetta, but she grabs the sleeve of his cloak and begins to whisper her secret.

Lisabetta: Signor! Signor! Listen! There is a private entrance to the garden!

Giovanni: What's that you say? A private entrance into Dr. Rappaccini's garden?

Lisabetta: Hush! Hush! Not so loud! Yes—into the great doctor's garden, where you may see all his fine shrubbery. Many a young man of Padua would give gold to be allowed among those flowers.

Narrator 3: Giovanni puts a piece of gold into her hand.

Giovanni: Show me the way.

Narrator 1: As Giovanni follows Lisabetta through several passageways and watches her unlock a door, he can't help but think back to the conversation that he's just had with Professor Baglioni. Lisabetta's behavior seems so odd. He suspects that she has been instructed by someone—perhaps Dr. Rappaccini—to lead him into the garden. Still, he does not turn back.

Narrator 2: As Lisabetta departs, Giovanni begins to wander around the empty garden. He examines the strange, often sinister looking plants and flowers. The few plants Giovanni recognizes are ones he knows to be extremely poisonous.

Narrator 3: After a while, Giovanni looks up and sees Beatrice walking toward him down the garden path.

Beatrice: I know, from our last meeting, that you are a connoisseur of flowers. Therefore, I'm not surprised to find that the sight of my father's rare collection has tempted you to come and take a closer look. If my father were here, he could tell you many strange and interesting facts about these plants. He has spent his lifetime studying them.

Giovanni: If what they say is true, you yourself know much about the science of these plants also. Will you be my instructor? I promise to be a diligent student.

Beatrice: Are there really such rumors about me? Do people say I'm skilled in my father's science? That's a laugh! No—though I've grown up among these flowers, I only know their colors and perfumes. And sometimes I wish I didn't even have that knowledge! Please, sir, don't believe what people say about me. Just believe what you see with your own eyes.

Giovanni: I will do one better than that. From now on, I will believe not even my own eyes, but only the words from your lips.

Narrator 1: Giovanni and Beatrice spend the next hour walking through the garden together. Giovanni is charmed by the sweetness of the lovely young woman. At the same time, though, he is frequently amazed by her incredible innocence and naïveté. She seems to know almost nothing of the world beyond her garden.

Narrator 2: As the strolling couple approaches the purple flowered plant in the center of the garden, Beatrice seems startled. She speaks to the shrub.

Beatrice: For the first time in my life, sister, I had forgotten you!

Giovanni: I remember, Signorina, that you once promised to reward me with one of the flowers of this shrub in exchange for the bouquet that I threw down to you.

Narrator 3: Giovanni steps forward and reaches out to pluck a blossom. Beatrice grabs his hand.

Beatrice: Don't touch that plant! It's fatal!

Narrator 1: She hides her face in her hands and runs from the garden. As Giovanni watches her flee, he sees the pale, thin figure of Dr. Rappaccini standing in the shadow of the garden entrance. He wonders how long Rappaccini has been watching the scene.

Scene 6

Narrator 2: That night, Giovanni cannot sleep because his mind is so filled with thoughts of—and love for—Beatrice. By the time he dozes off, it is nearly daybreak.

Narrator 3: When Giovanni wakes in the late morning, he feels a burning, tingling pain in his hand. Examining the back of his hand, he finds four purple prints that look like fingerprints and another similar print on his wrist. Shuddering, he realizes that the prints are located precisely where Beatrice grabbed his hand to prevent him from plucking the poisonous flower.

Narrator 1: This incident, however, is not enough to prevent Giovanni from furthering his relationship with Beatrice. Soon, Beatrice and Giovanni are in the habit of taking daily strolls together, laughing and talking in the garden. As soon as Giovanni returns from his last class of the day, he rushes down to see her. And if he is late for some reason, he hears her voice through the window, calling.

Beatrice: Giovanni! Giovanni! What's keeping you? Come down!

Narrator 2: Beatrice seems as smitten with Giovanni as he is with her. Yet for some reason, the two sweethearts never kiss or hold hands. They never touch each other in any way. Beatrice's reluctance to touch Giovanni concerns him, but he is so happy otherwise that it's easy to overlook this one small issue.

Narrator 3: Things continue as they are for some time, until one morning Giovanni receives a visit from Professor Baglioni. Baglioni chats about city and university gossip for a while, then takes up another topic.

Baglioni: I have been reading an old classic author lately and came across a story that interested me. You might possibly remember it. It is of an Indian prince, who sent a beautiful woman as a present to Alexander the Great. The woman was fabulously attractive, but what especially set her apart from all others was a rich perfume on her breath. Alexander, of course, fell in love with her at first sight. But then a certain wise doctor, who just happened to be present, discovered a terrible secret about her.

Giovanni: And what was that?

Baglioni: That this lovely woman had been fed with poisons from birth onward, until her whole being was so full of them that she herself had become the deadliest poison in the world. With her perfumed breath, she poisoned the very air around her. Her love would have been poison, her embrace death. Isn't this a marvelous tale?

Giovanni: It's just a childish fable. I can hardly believe that you find the time to read such nonsense along with your other, more serious studies.

Baglioni: By the way, what is that fragrance I'm smelling in your apartment? It is faint, but very sweet. It's not a very wholesome smell. I think if I were to smell it very long, it might make me sick. Where is that smell coming from? I can't see any flowers in your chamber.

Giovanni: That's because there aren't any. I'm afraid, Professor, that it's all your imagination. If one thinks about an odor long enough, one's almost certain to start smelling it.

Baglioni: My imagination doesn't usually play such tricks. And if I were to imagine any sort of an odor, it would probably be that of some nasty smelling drug that I've been working with in the laboratory. The drugs I give my patients have no floral scents—not like those administered by Dr. Rappaccini. No doubt, the learned Beatrice Rappaccini would also give each of her patients a potion smelling as sweet as her own breath. But woe to him who swallowed it!

Narrator 1: Giovanni's face becomes red as he listens to Professor Baglioni speaking this way about Beatrice. Although he tries hard to suppress his anger, he finally can't hold back.

Giovanni: Professor, you were my father's friend. No doubt, you have only the best intentions toward his son. With all due respect, though, I have to ask you not to continue speaking this way about the lady Beatrice. You don't know her. Therefore, you can't estimate just how incredibly wrong you are, how blasphemous your words about her are!

Baglioni: Giovanni! Poor Giovanni! I know this poor girl far better than you do. The time has come to hear the truth about the poisoner Rappaccini and his poisonous daughter. She is as poisonous as she is beautiful.

Giovanni: It isn't true!

Baglioni: It is! That old fable of the Indian woman has come true because of the deep and deadly science of Rappaccini, and it has come true in the person of Beatrice.

Narrator 2: Giovanni groans and hides his face.

Baglioni: Her father was not held back by natural fatherly affection. He offered his own child up as the victim of his insane zeal for science. What, then, will your fate be? Beyond a doubt, you have been selected as the subject of some new experiment. Perhaps the result will be death, perhaps a fate more awful still. Rappaccini will hesitate at nothing if he thinks it's in the interest of science.

Giovanni: *(To himself.)* This is a dream. It's got to be. Surely this all is a dream. . . .

Baglioni: But be of good cheer, son of my friend. It is not yet too late for rescue. Possibly we may even succeed in saving this miserable girl doomed by her father's madness. Look here!

Narrator 3: Baglioni holds out a little silver vial.

Baglioni: This vial was made by a famous craftsman, but its contents are more valuable still. This vase contains an antidote for poison. One little sip, and the effects of even the most horrible poison will be undone. Have Beatrice drink this potion and she may be restored to normal health.

Narrator 1: Giovanni speechlessly takes the vial from the hands of his friend. Baglioni excuses himself and leaves the boarding house. As he walks back to the university, he mutters to himself.

Baglioni: Rappaccini! I'll thwart you yet! You don't obey the laws of our profession! You must be taught a lesson!

Scene 7

Narrator 2: Giovanni is in agony. He doesn't want to believe anything negative about his beloved Beatrice. Still, he can't help but have his doubts. He thinks back to the day he threw his bouquet down to Beatrice. He remembers how the flowers seemed to wither in her hands.

Narrator 3: Giovanni decides to test Beatrice with another bouquet. He walks to the florist.

Narrator 1: As he reenters his room holding the new bouquet, Giovanni catches a glimpse of himself in the mirror. He notes with satisfaction that he is looking particularly healthy. His skin is full of color and his eyes full of life.

Giovanni: At least her poison hasn't gotten to me. At least I'm no flower that will simply wither in her hands!

Narrator 2: Giovanni suddenly notices the bouquet that he's holding. Although the flowers looked fresh only moments earlier, they now look days old and close to death.

Giovanni: *(In terror.)* Oh no! It can't be!

Narrator 3: Giovanni remembers Baglioni's comment about the strange, sweet fragrance in the room.

Giovanni: What if he was smelling my breath?! Am I becoming poisonous?

Narrator 1: Giovanni spots a spider dangling in a corner of the window. He runs toward the spider and breathes on it. The spider convulses wildly and then hangs dead.

Giovanni: I'm cursed! Doomed!

Narrator 2: All of a sudden, Giovanni hears a rich, sweet, familiar voice floating up from the garden.

Beatrice: Giovanni! Giovanni! You're late! What's keeping you? Come down and see me!

Giovanni: *(Muttering to himself.)* There she is—the only creature that my breath won't kill. I wish that it could!

Narrator 3: Giovanni rushes down into the garden and in a moment is standing facing Beatrice. Although he is wild with anger and desperation, the very sight and presence of Beatrice quiets him. Beatrice and Giovanni begin their usual rounds, walking through the garden. When they reach the purple shrub in the center, Giovanni stops.

Giovanni: Beatrice, where did this shrub come from?

Beatrice: My father created it.

Giovanni: Created it!? What do you mean? Speak clearly.

Beatrice: My father has great power over the secrets of nature. At the hour when I was born, this plant sprang from the soil. It was the offspring of his mind, while I am his natural born child. The plant and I have been like sisters ever since that day. We blossomed together. But alas! With this sisterly love came an awful doom.

Giovanni: Doom? What doom?

Beatrice: My father's love of science has estranged me from all friendships and associations with my own kind. Until heaven sent me you, I was terribly lonely.

Giovanni: Has it been hard on you being all alone?

Beatrice: Until lately, I had no idea just how lonely I was.

Narrator 1: Giovanni suddenly erupts with rage.

Giovanni: So—because you were tired of being alone, you have lured me into your world! Now I too am cut off from all the warmth of life and am trapped in this horrible nightmare!

Beatrice: Giovanni!

Giovanni: Yes—you've done that! You poisonous thing! You've filled my veins with poison! Now I am just as hateful, as ugly, as deadly a creature as you are! Both of our breaths are fatal! Maybe we should just kiss each other and die from the poison in each other's breath!

Beatrice: What's happened? Heaven have mercy upon me!

Giovanni: You dare to pray? What a concept! Maybe we should just go to the nearest church and dip our fingers in the holy water by the door. Then all the people who come in after us will die when they touch it!

Beatrice: Giovanni, why are you speaking these horrible words to me? It's true that I am the terrible thing you think I am. But you! You can simply leave this garden any time you please, go on with your life, and forget all about the poor, monstrous Beatrice.

Giovanni: Stop pretending to be so innocent! Stop pretending you don't know what's going on! Would you like to see the fabulous talent that I have gained from Rappaccini's pure, innocent daughter?

Narrator 2: A swarm of summer insects is flitting through the air. They circle around Giovanni's head, evidently attracted to the sweet smell coming from him. Giovanni lets out a stream of breath aimed at the insects and at least a dozen fall to the ground dead.

Beatrice: Oh no! It's my father's fatal science! But, please, Giovanni! You must believe that I'm not responsible for this. I had no idea. None! I dreamed only of having someone to love for a little while, someone to spend a little time with. I wanted someone wonderful to remember later in my life. Although I may seem like a horrible, evil creature to you, I am just like anyone else. My spirit craves companionship. My heart craves love. You must believe that I never, never intended any harm to come to you!

Narrator 3: Giovanni's anger has worn itself out. He realizes that he and Beatrice are both cut off from all other human relationships. They may as well at least be kind to one another. Suddenly, he also remembers the vial full of antidote that Baglioni gave him.

Giovanni: I'm sorry, Beatrice. I'm so sorry that I spoke so harshly to you! But listen—all is not lost! I have some medicine that I was given by a brilliant, respected doctor. He assures me that it is quite powerful. It's composed of ingredients that are the opposite of the poisons with which we are infected. Let's drink it together and be purified!

Beatrice: Give it to me! Let me drink first. You wait and see what happens before you try it.

Narrator 1: Giovanni reaches in his pocket for the vial of antidote. Beatrice snatches it from his hand and puts the little vial to her lips. Just then, Dr. Rappaccini emerges from the far doorway of the garden. He makes his way toward Beatrice and Giovanni with a look of satisfaction on his face. He raises his hands to them as if to bless them.

Rappaccini: My daughter! Now you are no longer lonely in the world. Pluck one of the precious flowers of your sister shrub and give it to your bridegroom. He now stands apart from other men just as you stand apart from other women. The two of you are my pride and triumph!

Beatrice: *(Weakly.)* My father—why did you inflict this miserable doom on your own child?

Rappaccini: Miserable? What do you mean, foolish girl? You find it misery to have such marvelous gifts, such power? Is it misery to be able to conquer your mightiest enemy with just a breath? Is it misery to be as terrible as you are beautiful? Would you rather be like other weak people who are exposed to all evil and are capable of none?

Beatrice: I would have liked to be loved rather than feared.

Narrator 2: She sinks down to the ground.

Beatrice: But it doesn't matter now. The poison that you've put in my breath and blood will exist no more where I am going. Farewell, Giovanni! Your words of hatred are like a poison in my heart, but it, too will soon be gone. Was there not, from the first, more poison in your nature than in mine?

Narrator 3: Beatrice swallows the antidote, knowing full well what the result will be. Because her whole life and existence has been made up of poison, the only possible antidote is death.

Narrator 1: As Beatrice takes the fatal drink, Professor Pietro Baglioni sticks his head out of a window and calls out in a tone of horror mixed with triumph.

Baglioni: Rappaccini! Rappaccini! So *this* is the result of your experiment!

The End

A Retrieved Reformation

O. Henry

Adapted by Suzanne I. Barchers

Summary

When Jimmy Valentine leaves prison, he resumes his safe-cracking career, intriguing detective Ben Price, who recognizes Valentine's methods. Valentine settles in a small town, where—to his surprise—he falls in love with the daughter of the bank's owner. He decides to go straight and give his burglary tools to an old friend. Meanwhile, Ben Price has tracked him and appears at the bank just when Valentine must decide if he is willing to risk exposure to save a child who has been locked in the bank vault.

Background Information

O. Henry was the pen name of William Sydney Porter (1862–1910). After growing up in Greensboro, North Carolina, O. Henry moved to Texas to work on a ranch. He had a variety of jobs, eventually developing a newspaper, *The Rolling Stone*. He was charged with embezzlement, jumped bail, and hid in Honduras. When he returned to Texas to visit his dying wife, he was arrested. During his three years in jail he met a character who inspired this story, which appeared on Broadway as *Alias Jimmy Valentine*. O. Henry's stories are noted for having a surprise ending.

Presentation Suggestions

Arrange the characters in the following order: Narrator 1, Narrator 2, Warden, Mike, Boy, Valentine, Price, Johnson, Annabel, Clerk, Mr. Adams, Agatha's Mother. The following can leave the stage after reading their parts: Warden, Mike, and Boy.

Props

The characters can be well dressed, in clothes typical of the late 1800s. A suitcase can be on stage. Tables and chairs can be set up to look like the inside of a bank.

Characters

- ❀ Narrators 1 and 2
- ❀ Warden
- ❀ Jimmy Valentine, *former burglar*
- ❀ Mike Dolan, *friend of Valentine*
- ❀ Luke Johnson, *detective*
- ❀ Ben Price, *detective*
- ❀ Boy
- ❀ Clerk
- ❀ Annabel, *fiancée of Valentine*
- ❀ Mr. Adams, *Annabel's father*
- ❀ Agatha's Mother

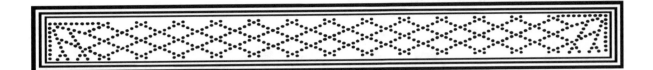

A Retrieved Reformation

Scene 1

Narrator 1: A guard comes to the prison shoe shop, where Jimmy Valentine assiduously stitches uppers. The guard escorts Jimmy to the front office to meet with the warden.

Warden: Here is your pardon, Valentine. The governor signed it this morning.

Narrator 2: Jimmy takes the papers. He has served nearly ten months of a four-year sentence. He had expected to stay only three months, at the longest. When a man like Jimmy Valentine, who has so many friends on the outside, is imprisoned, it's hardly worthwhile to cut his hair.

Warden: Now, Valentine, you'll go out in the morning. Make a man of yourself. You're not bad at heart, but you need to stop cracking safes and live straight.

Valentine: Me? Why I never cracked a safe in my life.

Warden: Oh, no. Of course not. Let's see, now. How was it you happened to get sent up on that Springfield job? Was it because an alibi would have compromised someone in high society? Or was it simply a case of a mean old jury that had it in for you? It's always one or the other with you innocent victims.

Valentine: Me? Why, Warden, I never was in Springfield in my life!

Narrator 1: The warden turns to his assistant.

Warden: Take him back and fix him with street clothes. Unlock him at seven in the morning, and let him come to the bullpen.

Narrator 2: The warden bids Valentine goodbye with a final warning.

Warden: You'd better think over my advice, Valentine.

Scene 2

Narrator 1: The next morning Jimmy stands in the warden's outer office. He has on a suit of the readymade clothes and a pair of the stiff, squeaky shoes that the state furnishes to its discharged compulsory guests.

Narrator 2: The clerk hands him a railroad ticket and a five-dollar bill with which the law expects him to rehabilitate himself into good, prosperous citizenship. The warden gives him a cigar and shakes his hand. Mr. James Valentine walks out into the sunshine.

115

Narrator 1: Jimmy heads straight for a restaurant. After a lunch, he proceeds at a leisurely pace to the depot. Three hours later, he arrives at Mike Dolan's café in a little town near the state line.

Valentine: Hello, Mike.

Mike: Sorry we couldn't make it sooner, Jimmy, my boy. But the governor was slow to issue this pardon. Feeling all right?

Valentine: Fine. Got my key?

Mike: Sure. Here it is.

Narrator 2: Jim goes upstairs, finding his room just as he had left it. Pulling the folding bed out from the wall, Jimmy slides back a panel and drags out a dust-covered suitcase. He gazes fondly at the finest set of burglar's tools in the East. It is a complete set, made of specially tempered steel, and includes two or three novelties he invented himself.

Narrator 1: In half an hour, Jimmy goes downstairs and through the café. He is dressed in tasteful and well-fitting clothes and carries his dusted and cleaned suitcase in his hand.

Mike: Got anything on?

Valentine: *(Puzzled.)* Me? I don't understand. I'm representing the Amalgamated Short Snap Biscuit Cracker and Frazzled Wheat Company.

Mike: *(Laughing.)* Jimmy, you are something, that's for sure. Good luck!

Scene 3

Narrator 2: A month later, Ben Price and Luke Johnson, both detectives, are looking at a series of reports about recent burglaries.

Johnson: Ben, did you read this report about the safe job in Richmond, Indiana, a month ago?

Price: No, Luke. What was taken?

Johnson: Just eight hundred dollars. Not much, but there wasn't a clue as to who took it.

Price: This report is about a safe in Logansport that was opened like a cheese a few weeks ago.

Johnson: How much was taken that time?

Price: The burglar took all the currency—$1,500. But he left behind securities and silver—and a rose.

Johnson: A rose? Could be Jimmy Valentine. Here's another report. A bank in Jefferson City had five thousand dollars stolen. It's getting serious now.

Price: Let's take a look at some of these bank safes.

Narrator 1: Price and Johnson investigate the scenes of the robberies.

Price: That's Dandy Jim Valentine's work. He's resumed business. Look at that combination knob—jerked out as easy as pulling up a radish in wet weather. He's got the only clamps that can do it.

Johnson: And look how clean those tumblers were punched out! Jimmy never has to drill but one hole.

Price: I'm going to get Mr. Valentine this time. I know his habits—long jumps, quick getaways, no accomplices, and a taste for good society. I'm going after him, Luke. He'll do his bit next time without any pardons if I have anything to say about it.

Scene 4

Narrator 2: One afternoon, Jimmy Valentine climbs out of a mail hack in Elmore, a little town five miles off the railroad down in the blackjack country of Arkansas. Jimmy, looking like an athletic young senior just home from college, walks down the board sidewalk toward the hotel.

Narrator 1: A young lady crosses the street, passes him at the corner, and enters a door under a sign that reads "The Elmore Bank." Jimmy looks into her eyes, forgets what he was, and becomes another man. She lowers her eyes and blushes slightly. Jimmy collars a boy who is loafing on the steps of the bank. He feeds him dimes and asks him questions about the town, while watching for the young lady to come back. By and by, she does and walks past Jimmy without paying any attention to him.

Valentine: Isn't that young lady Miss Polly Simpson?

Boy: Naw. She's Annabel Adams. Her pa owns the bank.

Valentine: Is that right?

Boy: What did you come to Elmore for? Is that a gold watch chain? I'm going to get a bulldog. Got any more dimes?

Narrator 2: Jimmy takes his leave, goes to Planters' Hotel, and speaks to the clerk.

Valentine: Good afternoon, my good man.

Clerk: Good afternoon, sir. How can I help you?

Valentine: I'd like a room.

Clerk: We can take care of that for you. Are you here on business?

Valentine: I'm looking for a location for a business.

Clerk: What kind of business?

Valentine: I'd thought of the shoe business. Is there an opening for that kind of business?

Clerk: Yes, there ought to be a good opening in the shoe line. There isn't an exclusive shoe store in the town.

Valentine: Is that right?

Clerk: Everyone buys their shoes at the dry goods and general stores now, so a shoe store would be welcome. I think you'd find this a pleasant town to live in. The people are very sociable.

Valentine: Thanks, I think I'll stay a while and look over the possibilities.

Clerk: Can I call the bellhop for your suitcase?

Valentine: No, it's rather heavy. I'll carry it up myself.

Narrator 1: The phoenix of ancient Greek and Roman mythology is a bird that is reborn after death, arising from its own ashes. Like a phoenix, Jimmy Valentine becomes Mr. Ralph Spencer. He remains in Elmore and prospers. He opens a shoe store and secures a good run of trade.

Narrator 2: He is also a social success and makes many friends. He meets Miss Annabel Adams and becomes more and more captivated by her charms. At the end of a year, the situation of the reinvented Ralph Spencer is this: he has won the respect of the community, his shoe store is flourishing, and he and Annabel are engaged to be married in two weeks.

Narrator 1: Annabel's father, the typical, plodding country banker, approves of his daughter's fiancé. Annabel's pride in Jimmy almost equals her affection. Jimmy is ready to put away his past and writes to one of his old friends in St. Louis.

Valentine: *(Reading aloud as he writes.)*

> Dear Old Pal:
>
> I want you to be at Sullivan's place in Little Rock, next Wednesday night, at nine o'clock. I want you to wind up some little matters for me. And, also, I want to make you a present of my little kit of tools. I know you'll be glad to get them—you couldn't duplicate the lot for a thousand dollars. Say, Billy, I've quit the old business—a year ago. I've got a nice store. I'm making an honest living, and I'm going to marry the finest girl on earth two weeks from now. It's the only life, Billy—the straight one. I wouldn't touch a dollar of another man's money now for a million. After I get married, I'm going to sell out and go West, where there won't be so much danger of having old scores brought up against me. I tell you, Billy, she's an angel. She believes in me; and I wouldn't do another crooked thing for the whole world. Be sure to be at Sully's, for I must see you. I'll bring along the tools with me.
>
> Your old friend,
>
> Jimmy

Scene 5

Narrator 2: The Monday night after Jimmy writes this letter, Detective Ben Price comes quietly into town in a livery buggy. He lounges about town in his quiet way, until he finds out what he wants to know. From the drugstore across the street from Spencer's shoe store, he gets a good look at Ralph D. Spencer.

Price: *(To himself.)* Going to marry the banker's daughter, are you, Jimmy? Well, I don't know.

Narrator 1: The next morning, Jimmy is going to Little Rock to order his wedding suit, buy something nice for Annabel, and see his friend, Billy. It will be the first time he has left town since he came to Elmore. He thinks it's safe to venture out.

Narrator 2: After breakfast, quite a family party goes downtown together—Mr. Adams, Annabel, Jimmy, and Annabel's married sister with her two little girls, ages five and nine. They go by the hotel where Jimmy still boards, and he comes out with his suitcase. Then they all go to the bank. There stands Jimmy's horse and buggy and driver, ready for the ride to the railroad station.

Narrator 1: All of them go inside the bank, and Jimmy sets down his suitcase. Annabel, bubbling with happiness, picks it up.

Annabel: Wouldn't I make a nice salesman? My! Ralph, how heavy it is! Feels like it's full of gold bricks.

Valentine: Lots of nickel-plated shoehorns in there that I'm going to return. Thought I'd save shipping charges by taking them up. I'm getting awfully economical.

Narrator 2: The Elmore Bank had just put in a new safe and vault. Mr. Adams is very proud of it.

Mr. Adams: Come! Come! You must take a look at our new vault. It's not very big, but it has the very best door. Look—three solid steel bolts holding the handle, plus it has a time lock.

Narrator 1: While Mr. Adams demonstrates the workings of the open safe, Ben Price saunters up to the bank counter and leans on his elbows, looking casually into the vault beyond the railings. He tells the teller that he doesn't want anything; he is just waiting for a man he knows. Meanwhile, the shining metal and clock and knobs on the new safe delight the two children, May and Agatha.

Narrator 2: Suddenly, there's a scream from the women. May has playfully shut Agatha in the vault.

Agatha's Mother: *(Agitatedly.)* Agatha is inside the vault! Get her out!

Mr. Adams: The door can't be opened! The clock hasn't been wound nor the combination set.

Narrator 1: Agatha's mother screams hysterically.

Mr. Adams: Hush! Everyone be quiet for a moment. Agatha! Listen to me.

Narrator 2: They can hear the faint sound of the child wildly shrieking in panic in the dark vault.

Agatha's Mother: My precious darling! She will die of fright! Open the door! Break it open! Can't you men do something?

Mr. Adams: *(Shakily.)* There isn't a man nearer than Little Rock who can open that door. What shall we do? That child—she can't stand it long in there. There isn't enough air, and besides, she'll go into convulsions from the fright.

Narrator 1: Agatha's mother, frantic now, beats the door of the vault with her hands. Somebody wildly suggests dynamite. Annabel turns to Jimmy, her eyes full of anguish, but not yet despairing. To a woman nothing seems quite impossible to the powers of the man she worships.

Annabel: Can't you do something, Ralph—*try*, won't you?

Valentine: Annabel, give me that rose you are wearing, will you?

Narrator 2: Hardly believing that she hears him right, she unpins the bud from her dress and places it in his hand. Jimmy stuffs it into his vest pocket, throws off his coat, and pulls up his shirtsleeves. With that act Ralph D. Spencer passes away, and Jimmy Valentine takes his place.

Valentine: Get away from the door, all of you.

Narrator 1: He sets his suitcase on the table, and opens it out flat. From that time on he seems to be unconscious of the presence of anything else. He lays out the shining implements swiftly and orderly, whistling softly as he always does when at work. In a deep silence, the others watch him as if under a spell.

Narrator 2: In a minute, Jimmy's pet drill is biting smoothly into the steel door. In ten minutes—breaking his own record—he throws back the bolts and opens the door.

Agatha's Mother: Agatha!

Narrator 1: Agatha's mother gathers Agatha into her arms. Jimmy Valentine puts on his coat, and walks outside the railings toward the front door. As he goes out, he thinks he hears a faraway voice that he once knew call, "Ralph!" But he never hesitates. A big man stands in his way at the door.

Valentine: Hello, Ben. Found me at last, have you? Well, let's go. I don't know that it makes much difference, now.

Narrator 2: And then Ben Price acts rather strangely.

Price: Guess you're mistaken, Mr. Spencer. Don't believe I recognize you. Your buggy's waiting for you, isn't it?

Narrator 1: Ben Price turns and strolls down the street.

The End

The Legend of Sleepy Hollow

Washington Irving

Adapted by Jennifer L. Kroll

Summary

In the early 1800s, a small-town school-teacher named Ichabod Crane courts a local heiress named Katrina Van Tassel. In doing so, he angers Brom Bones, a local daredevil and prankster, who also fancies Katrina. Brom begins to play pranks on Ichabod. The rivalry between the two men comes to a head one autumn evening. Ichabod and Brom both attend a party at the Van Tassel house. During the latter part of the party, they listen to and tell spooky stories. On his way home through the dark countryside, Ichabod is pursued by the Headless Horseman, one of the figures of local legend described during the party storytelling session. Ichabod disappears and is never seen again.

Background Information

Washington Irving, who lived from 1783 to 1859, is sometimes called "the first American man of letters." Along with "Rip Van Winkle," "The Legend of Sleepy Hollow" is one of Irving's most famous works. These two stories both were first published in 1819 in *The Sketch Book of Geoffrey Crayon, Gent.* Both are Americanized versions of German folktales.

Presentation Suggestions

Seat Katrina Van Tassel in the center, with Brom Bones on one side of her and Ichabod Crane on the other. Seat the Young Men to the side of Brom. Place Mrs. Von Steussel, Hendrick Von Steussel, and Mrs. Klinghoffer to the side of Ichabod. Behind this row of readers, arrange the other characters, perhaps on higher stools or chairs. Seat the Neighbors and Partygoers near each other.

Props

If costuming is available, readers might wear three-corner hats or bonnets to represent the time period. Students not reading parts can be enlisted to make clip-clop noises with pens or hands on desks during the portions of the play where Ichabod is riding his horse. The classroom lights can be dimmed and candles lit or other spooky touches added during scenes 4 and 5.

Characters

- ❀ Narrators 1, 2, and 3
- ❀ Ichabod Crane, *a country schoolteacher*
- ❀ Hendrick Von Steussel, *a ten-year-old boy*
- ❀ Mrs. Von Steussel, *Hendrick's mother, a country farmer's wife*
- ❀ Mrs. Klinghoffer, *a neighbor of the Von Steussels*
- ❀ Young Men 1 and 2, *friends of Brom Bones*
- ❀ Brom Bones, *a young man, in love with Katrina Van Tassel*
- ❀ Katrina Van Tassel, *a young heiress*
- ❀ Servant, *worker for the Van Tassel family*
- ❀ Neighbors 1 and 2
- ❀ Partygoers 1 and 2
- ❀ Balthus Van Tassel, *a wealthy local landowner and father of Katrina*

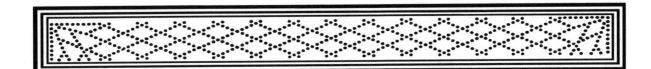

The Legend of Sleepy Hollow

Scene 1

Narrator 1: The year is 1820. Two young boys come rushing into a country farmhouse, accompanied by a tall, bony gentleman in his late twenties or early thirties.

Hendrick Von Steussel: Mother! Mother! The schoolteacher has come home with us.

Mrs. Von Steussel: It is delightful to see you again, Mr. Crane. I trust both of the boys have been behaving themselves these days.

Ichabod Crane: Of course, of course. They are among my best pupils.

Narrator 2: Crane winks at the two boys. Although he doesn't really like children, he pretends to be great friends with his students whenever it is convenient.

Mrs. Von Steussel: *(To the boys.)* Go help your father with the chores, boys. *(To Ichabod Crane.)* Come over here by the fire, sir, and warm your bones. And let me get you a slice of pumpkin pie. It's freshly made. Some say it's the best pumpkin pie in the county.

Crane: I've heard as much.

Mrs. Von Steussel: Goodness me, you are thin, sir. You need a woman to look after you and fatten you up.

Crane: I've been thinking that myself, dear lady. For years, I've given myself to learning without thought of marriage, but now I'm beginning to think I would like to marry.

Mrs. Von Steussel: Any girl would be lucky to marry an educated man like you, Mr. Crane. Most of the people around here are uneducated farmers. We do admire a gentleman of taste and accomplishments. Care for another slice of pie?

Crane: Don't mind if I do, ma'am.

Mrs. Von Steussel: You have quite an appetite, sir, for one so thin. Why don't you just stay for dinner?

Narrator 3: Ichabod smiles. He has been hoping all along for a dinner invitation.

Crane: Why, I am delighted to receive such an offer from the finest cook in Sleepy Hollow.

Mrs. Von Steussel: That is indeed great praise, coming from your lips, sir. I know that you have dined with most of the families in the county by now.

Crane: It's one of the advantages of being a country schoolmaster, I guess. I'm always getting invited to dine with one or another of my student's families.

Mrs. Von Steussel: And with the families of your choir pupils, too. I hear that you have been rather a regular visitor at the Van Tassel farm, of late.

Narrator 1: Ichabod blushes.

Crane: Why, yes, I do dine there often. The Van Tassels have been very gracious to me.

Mrs. Von Steussel: Are you a special friend of young Miss Katrina?

Narrator 2: Ichabod blushes a deeper shade of red.

Crane: She is a pupil in my choir group.

Mrs. Von Steussel: Half the young men in this county would wish to be in your shoes, Mr. Crane— dining at the Van Tassels every week. Katrina is a lovely thing. And, as her father's only child, she'll someday inherit the whole Van Tassel estate. I don't need to tell you that that's some of the best land in the county.

Crane: I've heard as much. A fine house, too. It's all worth a pretty penny, they say.

Mrs. Von Steussel: The girl knows what she's worth. The way she dresses and wears those gold bracelets! A year ago or so, she had five or six suitors pursuing her at one time. She didn't discourage any of them. Once Brom Bones got his eye on her, though, the others all began to keep their distance. With all his famous feats of strength and practical jokes, Brom Bones is something of a hero to the other young men.

Crane: Katrina could never fall for a simple country boy. She values learning and refinement far too much.

Mrs. Von Steussel: Brom Bones might not be much for manners, but he's a big, strong, handsome lad.

Crane: Forgive me for saying so, but I don't believe Miss Von Tassel would ever settle for a man like Brom Bones.

Scene 2

Narrator 3: As afternoon turns into evening, Ichabod Crane remains at the Van Steussel residence. After a filling dinner, he settles in by the fire. A neighbor of the Van Steussels, Mrs. Klinghoffer, comes in to share the local gossip with Mrs. Von Steussel.

Narrator 1: Eventually, the conversation turns to supernatural happenings, as it often does in this very superstitious community. Ichabod happily joins the discussion, repeating tales of witchcraft that he's read in books.

Crane: The haunting I've just described is discussed in a book titled *The History of New England Witchcraft* by Cotton Mather. The book is one of my favorites. I've read it a number of times. Since the event is recorded in that book, there can be no doubt that it actually happened.

Mrs. Klinghoffer: It's a blessing to have such an educated man among us.

Mrs. Von Steussel: How dreadful your tales of witchcraft are, Mr. Crane!

Mrs. Klinghoffer: Yes. Thank goodness we don't have that sort of thing around here. We do have our own worries, however, with all the ghosts and goblins about. That Galloping Hessian is especially frightening.

Crane: Galloping Hessian?

Mrs. Klinghoffer: Can it be that in all your time here, nobody in the neighborhood has told you about our most famous haunting?

Crane: Perhaps I do know the tale. Is this Galloping Hessian the same ghost that some call the Headless Horseman?

Mrs. Klinghoffer: The same. A number of folks from the county have seen this ghost. They say he's the spirit of a German mercenary soldier who lost his head during the War of Independence. Sometimes, near midnight, he can be seen on the road that passes through Sleepy Hollow and over the old covered bridge. It is said that he carries his head under his arm. Sometimes he chases travelers. They also say that he tethers his horse in the graveyard each night.

Narrator 2: Ichabod shivers.

Mrs. Von Steussel: Perhaps it is nothing but a tale. Still, I wouldn't want to be near Sleepy Hollow come midnight!

Narrator 3: Later that night, as Ichabod walks home alone, he tries not to think about the ghost stories he has recently heard and told. The harder he tries not to think about ghosts and goblins, however, the more nervous he becomes.

Crane: Who's there? Show yourself at once! Oh—it's only the shadow of a branch. Silly me.

Narrator 1: Ichabod walks on, his heart still racing. Not long later, a sudden sound from out of the woods makes him jump.

Crane: What's that? Oh—it's only a whippoorwill.

Narrator 2: He continues walking cautiously on. Suddenly, a large beetle flies into his forehead.

Crane: Augh! Help! I've been struck by a witch's token!

Narrator 3: He falls to the ground, with his hands covering his face.

Crane: Hmm. Perhaps it was merely a beetle, after all.

Narrator 1: He gets to his feet again and continues on his way home.

Crane: What a dreadfully dark and lonesome walk. I think I will sing a psalm to cheer my way.

Narrator 2: Ichabod begins to sing in a horrible, loud, nasal voice.

Scene 3

Narrator 3: Time passes, and Ichabod continues to spend a great deal of time charming free dinners out of local farmwives. Using his role as choirmaster to gain invitations, he spends an increasing amount of time dining at the Van Tassel residence.

Narrator 1: Although Ichabod does not openly court Katrina Van Tassel, his visits allow him many opportunities for quiet talks and walks with the lovely young woman. The Sleepy Hollow villagers notice that Katrina now seems to favor the schoolmaster, rather than Brom Bones.

Young Man 1: Brom, how is it that your horse is so seldom seen outside the Van Tassel house these days?

Young Man 2: The villagers are all saying that that spindly schoolteacher is winning your girl away from you.

Brom Bones: I've got a score to settle with that man.

Young Man 1: Are you going to challenge Ichabod Crane to a duel? I would love to see that fight.

Bones: I have tried to provoke that man to fight with me, but he just won't take the bait.

Young Man 2: Of course he won't. That pompous beanpole wouldn't stand a chance against you, Brom, and he knows it.

Bones: Don't underestimate Ichabod Crane. He's cowardly thing, but he's sly. He's using his position as choirmaster to wheedle his way into the Van Tassel household and into Katrina's good graces. Well, it won't be as easy as he thinks.

Young Man 1: What are you going to do, Brom? Can we help?

Bones: Gentlemen, I think perhaps tomorrow night there won't be any choir practice for the skinny schoolteacher and his favorite student.

Young Man 2: Why not?

Narrator 2: Brom Bones gets a sly smile on his face.

Bones: Because we're going to stop up the chimney at that schoolhouse. As soon as Crane lights the evening fire, the whole place will fill up with smoke.

Young Man 1: This is going to be fun! You always come up with the best pranks.

Narrator 3: Brom Bones and his pals carry off their plan without a hitch. Choir practice is totally disrupted. In the weeks to come, Brom Bones plays more pranks. On several occasions, he breaks into the schoolhouse at night and turns everything topsy-turvy.

Narrator 1: Although Ichabod tries to fasten the schoolhouse windows and doors as tightly as possible, the break-ins continue. The superstitious schoolmaster begins to fear that witches might be using his schoolhouse for their meeting place.

Narrator 2: Besides playing pranks, Brom also takes every opportunity to ridicule Ichabod in front of Katrina.

Bones: Good morning, Katrina.

Narrator 3: Brom approaches Katrina on the road in front of the local store. At his side is a mongrel dog.

Katrina: Good morning, Brom. Who's your friend?

Bones: Well, dear Katrina, I'm very concerned with the quality of the singing lessons that you've been receiving from that schoolteacher. So I've brought in a rival choirmaster. His voice is much more pleasant than that of Mr. Crane, don't you think?

Narrator 1: Brom gives the dog a cue, and it begins whining. All the townspeople gathered around laugh at the joke. Katrina looks embarrassed, but she laughs, too.

Scene 4

Narrator 2: One autumn afternoon, as Ichabod sits on a high stool at the end of his classroom, he hears the sound of hoof beats outside. Looking out the window, he sees one of the Van Tassel servants approaching. He springs to his feet and rushes to the schoolhouse door.

Servant: Mr. Crane, sir, you are invited to a merry making, that is to say a quilting frolic to be held tonight at the Van Tassel place.

Crane: Why thank you! I shall be happy to attend.

Narrator 3: The servant excuses himself with a bow. For the rest of the afternoon, Ichabod rushes his students through their lessons.

Narrator 1: He punishes the students who read, recite, or complete their arithmetic problems too slowly by slapping their hands or backsides with a birch rod. Finally, the rushed lessons are completed.

Crane: You are all free to go an hour early today.

All: Hooray!

Narrator 2: Books are flung aside without being put away on the shelves, and inkstands are overturned in haste. The students all rush out the schoolhouse door and race about the town green, shouting with joy.

Crane: *(To himself.)* I must look my best tonight.

Narrator 3: Ichabod spends a half hour arranging several locks of his hair in front of a bit of broken mirror hanging in the back of the schoolhouse.

Crane: *(To himself.)* A horse! I must come riding up on a horse. Then I'll look like a gallant gentleman. I must see if old Hans Van Ripper will let me borrow his horse.

Narrator 1: A little later, Ichabod rides through town, mounted on Van Ripper's horse, whose unlikely name is Gunpowder. Ichabod holds his head high, with pride, believing himself to look like a knight in shining armor. Unfortunately, he looks like no such thing.

Neighbor 1: Look! Here comes the schoolmaster, riding on a broken down old plow horse.

Neighbor 2: Look how its mane and tail are matted up with burs! That poor bony old thing!

Neighbor 1: Look how the schoolteacher's knees come up to his elbows! His stirrups are far too short.

Neighbor 2: It looks like he's trying to fly, with his elbows flopping up and down like that!

Narrator 2: It is nearly sundown when Ichabod arrives at the estate of Balthus Van Tassel. In the yard, Brom Bones holds the center of attention. He is busy displaying feats of horsemanship on his black steed, Daredevil, while others look on admiringly.

Partygoer 1: What a handsome horse!

Partygoer 2: They say that only Brom Bones can manage that horse. It throws all other riders.

Partygoer 1: I've heard Brom say that he doesn't like obedient, well-broken horses. He thinks any real lad of spirit should risk his neck by riding an equally spirited beast.

Narrator 3: Ichabod dismounts, stables his horse, and walks past Brom Bones' admirers into the house. He is delighted to find a large tea table heaped with platters of cakes, sliced ham, roast chicken, peach and pumpkin pies, and numerous other delicacies. Balthus Van Tassel mingles with his guests, inviting them to make themselves at home.

Balthus Van Tassel: Please, fall to and help yourselves.

Narrator 1: The guests are barely finished eating when a small orchestra strikes up a tune. Ichabod searches out Katrina.

Crane: Miss Katrina, will you do me the honor of dancing with me?

Katrina: I'd be delighted.

Narrator 2: Soon it is dark outside, and the guests from the yard come in to watch the dancing. Brom Bones sulks in a corner while the schoolteacher shares dance after dance with Katrina Van Tassel.

Narrator 3: When the dancing ends, Ichabod joins a group of older folks talking with Balthus Van Tassel at one end of the porch. The old people gossip over old times, telling long, drawn-out stories of the Revolutionary War.

Narrator 1: Eventually, these wildly exaggerated war tales give way to ghost stories. Ichabod sits for hours listening to the tales of local goblins and hauntings. Many of the storytellers return again and again to the legend of the Headless Horseman.

Balthus Van Tassel: Yes, old Doffue Martling saw the Horseman out by that old church, a few years back. His hair went gray, all at once from the fright of it.

Partygoer 2: Old Brouwer had a worse time with the Horseman, from what I've heard. He didn't believe in ghosts. Then one night, he was riding home through Sleepy Hollow, and he heard the sound of hoofs behind him. He turned around, and saw the figure of the Hessian, so he spurred his horse into a run. The Horseman started to gallop as well and got right up behind Old Brouwer.

Partygoer 1: I heard that the Horseman chased Brouwer all the way down to the covered bridge by the church then suddenly turned into a skeleton, threw old Brouwer into the brook, and sprang away over the treetops. Nobody's seen the Horseman since.

Partygoer 2: Brom Bones has. He's raced the Headless Horseman.

Partygoer 1: That can't be true.

Bones: It's true.

Narrator 2: Brom Bones seats himself with the group and joins in the discussion.

Bones: One night, on my way back from Sing Sing, I was overtaken by the Horseman, and I offered to race with him for a bowl of punch. I would have won it, too, for Daredevil was beating the goblin horse all the way through the hollow. But just as I came to the church bridge, the Hessian bolted and vanished in a flash of fire.

Scene 5

Narrator 3: It is very late before Ichabod bids goodnight to the Van Tassels and remaining guests, mounts the dilapidated Gunpowder, and heads back toward Tarrytown.

Narrator 1: As he rides though the hills, the only sounds he can hear are the occasional melancholy chirp of a cricket or the twang of a bullfrog.

Crane: *(To himself.)* It is certainly quiet out here.

Narrator 2: As he rides through the dark, quiet night, all the ghost stories he's heard play over and over in his mind.

Crane: What's that up ahead? Oh—it's Major Andre's tree—named after the famous major who was killed nearby. That tree almost looks like a creature of some kind, with all its giant gnarled limbs. I must keep my mind on cheerier things.

Narrator 3: Ichabod begins to whistle. A moment later, however, he falls silent.

Crane: I'd swear I just heard my whistle answered. But it can't have been. I must have just heard a blast sweeping sharply through the dry branches.

Narrator 1: Ichabod continues cautiously on toward Major Andre's tree. As he nears the tree, he thinks he sees something white hanging from its branches.

Crane: A ghost! Oh—it's just a place where the tree was struck by lightning.

Narrator 2: Ichabod inches closer to the imposing tree. Shadows from its gnarled branches dance in his path. Suddenly, he hears a low groan. His teeth begin to chatter wildly.

Crane: Calm, calm. Be steady. That's just the sound of two boughs rubbing against each other.

Narrator 3: Ichabod breathes a sigh of relief as he safely passes the tree. But now, he finds himself facing new danger. About two hundred yards from the tree, a small brook crosses the road.

Crane: That brook is the very spot where Major Andre was killed. The marksmen were concealed in those chestnut trees over there.

Narrator 1: As he approaches the setting of Major Andre's murder, Ichabod's heart begins to thump. He gives his horse a kick in the ribs and attempts to spur it quickly over the little bridge. The horse balks and makes a sideways movement into a fence.

Crane: Stupid old horse!

Narrator 2: Ichabod jerks the reins, startling old Gunpowder and sending him into a thicket of brambles on the opposite side of the road. The schoolmaster begins to whip and spur the horse, which finally rambles onto the little bridge and stops in the center of it.

Crane: Go on, you stupid beast!

Narrator 3: Just at this moment, the sound of a little splash draws Ichabod's attention. In the dark shadow of a grove, on the edge of the brook, he sees something huge, misshapen and towering.

Crane: It looks like . . . a horseman! *(Stammering.)* Who are you?

Narrator 1: When no answer is returned, Ichabod begins pounding on the sides of his horse with his heels. His horse finally clops forward and off of the bridge.

Narrator 2: Ichabod continues on, down the road. All the time, the towering shadow moves along beside him, just off the road. Ichabod tries to steady himself by singing a psalm tune, but his voice falters.

Crane: *(To himself.)* That horseman is keeping his distance. There's no cause for alarm.

Narrator 3: Suddenly, as Ichabod travels up a mount of rising ground, the figure of his fellow traveler becomes silhouetted against the sky. Ichabod lets out a scream.

Crane: The horseman! He's headless! Dear lord preserve me! The stories are true!

Narrator 1: The Headless Horseman's huge black steed rears up onto his massive back legs. Ichabod notices that the horseman is not only headless, but is carrying his head on the pommel of his saddle.

Crane: Go! Go! You stupid horse! To the covered bridge!

Narrator 2: Gunpowder finally begins to run. As he makes a mad dash toward the covered bridge up ahead, the straps holding Ichabod's saddle break. Ichabod just barely hangs on as the saddle clatters off onto the road.

Crane: Hans Van Ripper will be angry about that broken saddle, but never mind that. I've got to make it to that bridge. Brom said the horseman disappeared there.

Narrator 3: After moments that seem like hours, Gunpowder goes clattering onto and over the covered bridge. As his mount clears the bridge, Ichabod looks over his shoulder. He does so just in time to see the headless rider rising up in his stirrups.

Crane: His horrible head! He's hurling it at me! Augh!

Narrator 1: Ichabod tries to duck, but it's too late. The ghost's missile hits Ichabod in the head with a tremendous crash. He finds himself tumbling headlong into the dust, as Gunpowder and the goblin rider gallop past him and off into the distance.

Epilogue

Narrator 2: The next morning, the old horse was found without his saddle, soberly chomping on grass at his master's gate. The children assembled at the schoolhouse, but no schoolmaster arrived. By afternoon, Hans Van Ripper, concerned about the fate of both the schoolmaster and his missing saddle, set out with a search party.

Narrator 3: The investigators found no Ichabod. All that they found was a trampled saddle, lots of deep hoof prints on the road, and, at the end of the covered bridge, the hat of the unfortunate Ichabod. Close beside the hat lay a shattered pumpkin.

Narrator 1: The schoolteacher's mysterious disappearance became the subject of many local stories. Years later, a traveler brought news that Ichabod was still alive and living in a distant part of the country. There, it was said, he had studied the law, become a politician, written for newspapers, and finally had been made a justice of the local small claims court. To this day, however, the old country wives living near Sleepy Hollow maintain that Ichabod Crane was spirited away by supernatural means.

Narrator 2: And Katrina Van Tassel—what became of her? Shortly after Ichabod's disappearance, she married Brom Bones, a young man who always was observed to look exceedingly knowing whenever the story of Ichabod's disappearance was related.

The End

Captains Courageous

Rudyard Kipling

Adapted by Suzanne I. Barchers

Summary

Harvey, an arrogant, rich young man, is crossing the Atlantic on a steamer near the Newfoundland Banks with his mother. During the passage, he suddenly falls overboard. He is rescued by a fisherman in a dory and is taken to the schooner. When Harvey insists that he is rich and that the captain should abandon his fishing and return him to New York at once, the captain assumes Harvey has been rendered crazy by his near drowning. He puts Harvey to work, who soon realizes he has no choice but to cooperate. Harvey and the captain's son become close friends, and Harvey learns how to work. After an eventful summer of fishing, Harvey, mature and much wiser, is reunited with his grateful family.

Background Information

Rudyard Kipling was born on December 30, 1865, in Bombay, India, where his father directed an art school. In this faraway land, young Rudyard's nurse taught him Hindi and told stories of jungle animals. The Kiplings moved back to England when Rudyard was six years old, but in 1882 he returned to India, where he worked as a journalist and wrote stories and poems about the Indian culture he so loved. He returned to England in 1889, by which time people were already familiar with his writing. In 1892, he moved to the United States, where he lived with his American wife until 1896. There he wrote two of his most famous works, *The Jungle Book* and *Captains Courageous*, the latter of which he wrote at age thirty-one. Kipling's work was praised for its precise technical detail, for example, the accurate description of life on a schooner in *Captains Courageous*. Rudyard Kipling received the prestigious Nobel Prize for literature in 1907. He died on January 18, 1936.

Presentation Suggestions

The narrators can sit on stools on the side. The three gentlemen can stand to one side and exit the stage after scene 1. Harvey, Dan, Captain Troop, and the other fisherman can stand in the center of the stage. Mr. and Mrs. Cheyne can enter the stage for scene 9.

Props

The gentlemen, Harvey, and Mr. and Mrs. Cheyne can be dressed in fine clothing. The rest of the characters can be dressed in casual fishing clothing.

Characters

- Narrators 1 and 2
- Gentlemen 1, 2, and 3
- Harvey, *wealthy young man*
- Manuel, *fisherman*
- Dan, *captain's son*
- Captain
- Platt, *fisherman*
- Long Jack, *fisherman*
- Cook
- Olley, *fisherman*
- Mr. Cheyne, *Harvey's father*
- Mrs. Cheyne, *Harvey's mother*

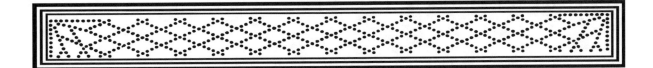

Captains Courageous

Scene 1

Narrator 1: A steamer bound for Europe moves through the North Atlantic fog somewhere off the Grand Banks of Newfoundland. The steamer rolls and lifts, whistling to warn the fishing fleet of its presence. A gentleman enters the liner's smoking room, joining three other men.

Gentleman 1: That Harvey Cheyne is the biggest nuisance aboard. He's too fresh.

Gentleman 2: I know the kind. America is full of that kind.

Gentleman 3: There isn't any harm to him. He's more to be pitied than anything. They've dragged him around from hotel to hotel ever since he was a kid. I was talking to his mother this morning. She's a lovely lady, but she doesn't pretend to manage him. He's going to Europe to finish his education.

Gentleman 1: His education hasn't begun yet. That boy gets two hundred a month pocket money, he told me. He isn't even sixteen.

Gentleman 2: Railroads, isn't that his father's business?

Gentleman 1: Yes. That, and mines, lumber, and shipping. Built one place at San Diego and another at Los Angeles. Owns half a dozen railroads, half the lumber on the Pacific slope, and lets his wife spend the money. The West doesn't suit her, so she just tracks around with the boy, trying to find what will amuse him, I guess.

Gentleman 2: Why doesn't the old man attend to him?

Gentleman 3: He doesn't want to be bothered it seems. Pity, because I suspect there's a heap of good in the boy if you could get at it.

Narrator 2: The door bangs, and a slim-built boy, 15 years old, a half-smoked cigarette hanging from one corner of his mouth, leans in over the high footway. His look is a mixture of irresolution, bravado, and cheap smartness. He is dressed in a cherry-colored blazer, knickerbockers, and red stockings, with a red flannel cap at the back of his head.

Harvey: (*In a high, loud voice.*) Say, it's thick outside. You can hear the fish boats squawking all around us. Say, wouldn't it be great if we ran one down?

Gentleman 1: Shut the door and stay outside.

Harvey: Who'll stop me? Did *you* pay for my passage? Guess I've as good right here as the next man.

Narrator 1: Harvey picks up some dice and begins throwing them from hand to hand.

Harvey: Say, gentlemen, can't we make a game of poker between us?

Narrator 2: No one answers.

Gentleman 3: How's your mother? I didn't see her at lunch.

Harvey: She's in her stateroom I guess. She's almost always sick on the ocean. I'm going to give the stewardess fifteen dollars for looking after her. I don't go down more than I have to. This is my first time on the ocean, but I haven't been sick since the first day! Say, my cigarette's out. Any one of you have a cigarette on him?

Narrator 1: One of the men opens his cigar case and hands a shiny black cigar to Harvey who lights it with a flourish. Harvey doesn't realize he's lighting a terrible "stogie" as he inhales deeply.

Gentleman 2: How do like my cigar?

Narrator 2: Harvey's eyes are full of tears. He answers through shut teeth.

Harvey: Fine, full flavor. *(Pausing.)* Guess we've slowed down a little. I'll skip out and see what the log says.

Narrator 1: Harry staggers over the wet decks to the nearest rail. Since he had boasted that he was never seasick, his pride makes him go aft to the deck at the stern. The deck is deserted, and he crawls to the end, near the flagpole. Harvey doubles up in agony. The stogie plus the surge of the seas makes him faint from seasickness. As he gives in to a faint, a roll of the ship lifts him over the rail. Another wave pulls him off, closing over him. Harvey blanks out.

Scene 2

Narrator 2: Harvey rouses to the sound of a dinner-horn such as they used to blow at a summer school he once attended. Slowly he understands that he has fallen overboard and is perhaps about to drown in mid-ocean. Then he realizes he is lying on a pile of half-dead fish, looking at a broad human back clothed in a blue jersey.

Harvey: *(To himself.)* It's no good. I'm dead.

Manuel: Aha! You feel well now? Fine good job that I catch you. How did you come to fall out?

Harvey: I was sick and couldn't help it.

Manuel: Just in time I blew my horn and your boat she yaw a little. Then I see you come down. I think you are to be cut into fish bait by the screw, but you drift to me. I pull you in like a big fish. So you shall not die this time.

Harvey: Where am I?

Manuel: You're with me in the dory. Manuel's my name, and I come from the schooner *We're Here* of Gloucester.

Narrator 1: Harvey looks up, terrified at the swells of the sea around the small dory. He thinks he hears a gun and shouting. Then something looms alongside, and he is lifted up and seemingly dropped into a dark hole. Someone gives him a hot drink, and he falls asleep.

Narrator 2: Some time later, Harvey wakes facing a boy about his own age dressed in a blue jersey and high rubber boots. The boat is neither sliding nor rolling, but is rather wriggling herself about through the water. He groans in despair, thinking of his mother.

Dan: Feeling better? Have some coffee?

Harvey: Isn't there milk?

Dan: Well, no. There won't be likely till mid-September. It's not bad. I made it.

Narrator 1: Harvey drinks in silence and ravenously eats some pieces of crisp fried pork.

Dan: I've dried your clothes. Guess they've shrunk some. They ain't our style much. Are you hurt?

Narrator 2: Harvey stretches but can't find any injuries. He shakes his head, indicating that he's fine.

Dan: That's good. Go on deck. Dad wants to see you. I'm his son, Dan. I'm cook's helper and do everything else aboard that's too dirty for the men. There hasn't been a boy here except me since Otto went overboard. How'd you come to fall off in a dead flat calm?

Harvey: It wasn't a calm. It was a gale, and I was seasick.

Dan: If that's your notion of a gale . . . well, anyway, hurry! Dad's waiting.

Narrator 1: Harvey, like many other young men of his background, has never received a direct order.

Harvey: Your dad can come down here if he's so anxious to talk to me. I want him to take me to New York right away. I'll pay him.

Dan: (*Shouting.*) Say, Dad! He says you can slip down to see him if you are anxious that way. Hear, Dad?

Captain: Quit fooling, Dan, and send him to me.

Narrator 2: Dan sniggers and throws Harvey his shoes. Something in the captain's tones makes him hoist himself up a ladder to the deck. Dan follows.

Captain: Morning—good afternoon, I should say. I'm Captain Disko Troop. You've nearly slept the clock around.

Harvey: Morning.

Captain: Now, let's hear all about it. What might be your name? Where from and where are you bound?

Narrator 1: Harvey shares a short history of the accident and demands to be taken immediately to New York, claiming his father will pay for his return.

Captain: Hmm. I can't say we think much of someone who falls overboard from that kind of ship in a flat calm.

Harvey: Do you think I'd fall into your dirty little boat for fun?

Captain: I don't know what your notion of fun is. But if I was *you*, I wouldn't call the boat that saved you names.

Harvey: I'm grateful for being saved, but the sooner you take me to New York, the better it'll pay you.

Captain: How?

Harvey: Dollars and cents! You've done the best day's work you ever did. I'm all the son Harvey Cheyne has. And if you don't know who Harvey Cheyne is, you don't know much. Now turn her around and let's hurry.

Captain: I don't see New York any more. Nor Boston. We may see Eastern Point in September. Then your pa may give me ten dollars. Then of course maybe he won't.

Harvey: Ten dollars! Why see here . . . Wait! I had $134! All stolen!

Captain: What might *you* have been doing at your age with $134?

Harvey: It was part of my pocket money—for a month.

Captain: *(To Dan.)* Oh! That is only part of his pocket money—for one month only. *(To Harvey.)* You don't remember hitting anything when you fell over do you? I remember when old man Hasken tripped on a hatch and butted the mainmast with his head. About three weeks later, he declared war on Sable Island! Now he's home playing with little rag dolls. Well, we're sorry for you—and so young. We won't say no more about the money.

Harvey: Of course you won't! You stole it!

Captain: Suit yourself. We stole it if that's any comfort to you. Now about going back. If we could do it, which we can't, you're in no fit state to go back to your home. We've just come on to the Banks, working for our bread. *We* don't see half of a hundred dollars a month, let alone pocket money. With good luck we'll be ashore again the first week of September.

Harvey: But it's May now, and I can't stay here doing nothing just because you want to fish.

Captain: Right and just. No one asks you to do nothing. There's a heap you *can* do since we lost one of our men, Otto, overboard. You've turned up, though there are rather few things you can do, I imagine. Except talk. And you won't need to talk here. I'll give you ten and a half dollars a month, say thirty-five at the end of the trip. You can tell us about your dad and your ma later.

Harvey: She's on the steamer! Take me to New York at once!

Captain: Poor woman. When she has you back, she'll forget it all, though. We can't go back. There's only eight of us and we'd lose the season.

Harvey: But my father would make it all right!

Captain: He'd try. I don't doubt he'd try. But a whole season is eight men's bread. You'll be in better health in the fall. Go help Dan.

Harvey: Do you mean I'm to *help* Dan?

Captain: And other things.

Narrator 2: Harvey stamps the deck.

Harvey: I won't! My father will give you enough to buy this dirty little fish kettle ten times over. I tell you I won't do menial work!

Captain: Hush now. It's ten and a half and I'll teach you what you need to know.

Harvey: No!

Narrator 1: Harvey doesn't remember exactly what follows. Suddenly, he is lying on his back, with a bleeding nose.

Captain: Dan, I was set against this young fellow when I saw him. Now I'm sorry for him. He's not responsible for his talk. Be gentle with him, but see to it that he works.

Narrator 2: The captain goes into the cabin, leaving Dan to comfort the luckless heir to 30 million dollars.

Scene 3

Narrator 1: While Dan comforts him, Harvey tries to recover from the humiliation of being struck by Captain Troop.

Dan: I know the feeling, Harvey. First time Dad laid me out was the last—and that was my first trip. Makes you feel sick *and* lonesome.

Harvey: It does.

Narrator 2: Harvey shoulders rise and fall with spasms of dry sobbing. Then he tells Dan his story. He regales Dan with tales of life as the son of a multimillionaire.

Dan: Hold on. Before you tell me any more, I want you to say "hope you may die" if you're lying.

Harvey: Of course. Hope I may die right here if every word I've spoken isn't the cold truth.

Narrator 1: Dan is a shrewd young man and ten minutes' questioning convinces him that Harvey isn't lying—much.

Dan: Your dad really has a private car?

Harvey: Actually, he has two private cars.

Dan: Gosh! I believe you, Harvey. Dad's made a mistake for once in his life! He thinks his judgment is perfect! He'll be mad clear through! He hates to be mistaken. Harvey, don't let on that's he's wrong!

Harvey: I don't want to get knocked down again.

Dan: No, you'll have to take right hold and pitch in alongside of me. Dad always gives me double since I'm his son. He doesn't want to seem to be favoring me. But he's a just man. All the men say so. And about that money in your pocket? Neither me nor Dad knows anything about that money. We were the only two who touched you after you were brought aboard. That's my say!

Harvey: Seems to me, I haven't been very grateful about being saved from drowning. I could have lost the bills in the sea. Where's your father?

Dan: In the cabin. Why do you want him again?

Harvey: I have something to say to him.

Narrator 2: Harvey finds the captain, busy with a notebook.

Harvey: I'm here to take things back. When a man's saved from drowning, he shouldn't call people names.

Captain: Right and just.

Harvey: So I'm here to say I'm sorry.

Captain: I thought this would be good for you. I'm seldom wrong in my judgment. You weren't responsible for what you did. Go about your business.

Narrator 1: Harvey returns to Dan, and they begin preparing for the return of the men who have been fishing. Soon they see the first dory, heavy with a full load of fish, returning. Dan explains the job ahead. Soon, the dory is secured to the ship and Manuel, Harvey's rescuer, is coming aboard.

Manuel: *(To Harvey.)* Aha! You are well now? This time last night the fish, they fish for you! Now you fish for fish!

Harvey: I'm ever so grateful.

Narrator 2: Harvey reaches in his pockets out of habit, forgetting that he can't reward Manuel with money.

Manuel: There's nothing to thank me for. How shall I leave you adrift? Now you are a fisherman! Dan, I haven't cleaned the boat today. Too busy. Clean it for me, Dan.

Narrator 1: Harvey and Dan begin to clean out the boat. As other dories come in, they stow their catch in a pen on board and clean the boats. After dinner, the men fall into the rhythm of cleaning the fish and moving the freshly cleaned cod to the hold below. Harvey pitches the fish by twos and threes down the hatch. Manuel stands among the fish, salting them thoroughly.

Narrator 2: After an hour, Harvey would have given the world to rest. Fresh, wet cod weigh more than you would think. But he feels for the first time in his life that he is one of the working gang of men. He takes pride in the thought and holds on. Finally, they have disposed of the fish.

Dan: Tired, Harvey?

Harvey: Dead sleepy.

Dan: We have first watch. Mustn't sleep on watch.

Harvey: But the moon is so bright. Bright as day. What can happen?

Narrator 1: Harvey begins to fall asleep.

Dan: Harvey! That's when things *do* happen. I've taken a liking to you, Harve, but I'll lay into you with a rope's end if you nod off once more.

Narrator 2: The moon looks down on a slim youth in knickerbockers and a red jersey, staggering around the cluttered decks of a schooner, while behind him, waving a knotted rope, walks a boy who yawns and nods. At last the clock strikes ten. The two boys are asleep as one of the fishermen rolls them into their berths.

Scene 4

Narrator 1: The next morning, the long blue seas are full of sails and dories. The smoke of some liner appears far away on the horizon. Captain Troop stares at the craft all around. Dan explains his father's behavior to Harvey.

Dan: Dad's doing some thinking on the cod, and the other captains know that Dad knows where to find the fish. See them acting like they're looking for nothing? They're really watching to see what Dad will do. Don't speak to him now—he'll just get mad.

Narrator 2: After some time, Troop looks down and removes the pipe from his teeth.

Dan: Dad, we've done our chores. Can we fish for a while?

Captain: Not in those cherry-colored clothes. Give him something to wear. But if anyone asks you what I'm calculating to do, speak the truth—that you don't know.

Dan: Come on, Harve.

Narrator 1: A little red dory, the *Hattie S.*, lays astern of the schooner. The boys drop in, and Dan begins instructing Harvey on the fine points of rowing and fishing. After a while, Harvey feels a tug and pulls up zealously.

Harvey: Why these are strawberries! Look!

Narrator 2: Harvey pulls up a perfect reproduction of the fruit found on land, except that there are no leaves and the stem is slimy.

Dan: Don't touch them! Don't—

Narrator 1: The warning comes too late. Harvey picks them off the hook and admires them. Then his fingers throb as though he had grasped many nettles.

Harvey: Ouch!

Dan: Now you've learned that you should touch only fish with your naked fingers. Bait up again, Harve. Earn your wages.

Narrator 2: Harvey smiles at the thought of his ten and a half dollars a month and wonders what his mother would say if she could see him hanging over the edge of a fishing dory in mid-ocean. Suddenly, his line flashes through his hand.

Dan: Give him room! I'll help you.

Harvey: No you won't! It's my first fish . . . is it a whale?

Dan: Halibut, maybe. He's big. Are you sure you want to land it alone?

Narrator 1: For the next twenty minutes Harvey battles the fish. The boys are both exhausted by the time they bring it in.

Dan: Beginner's luck! He's all of one hundred pounds!

Narrator 2: The boys hear a gun fired off the schooner and row back. None of the other fishermen have brought anything more than 15 pounds. After dinner, a fog rolls in and the captain seizes this opportunity to slip away from the other schooners. Harvey watches Tom Platt weigh anchor.

Platt: Never seen the anchor weighed before?

Harvey: No, where are we going?

Platt: To fish and make berth. It's all new to you, but we never know what may come either.

Narrator 1: Tom Platt and Long Jack take over Harvey's education while the ships moves along.

Long Jack: Now, Harvey, how do you reef the foresail? Take your time answering.

Narrator 2: Harvey points to leeward.

Harvey: Haul that in.

Long Jack: Haul what in? The North Atlantic?

Harvey: No, the boom. Then run that rope you showed me back there.

Platt: That's no way!

Long Jack: Quiet! He's learning and he doesn't have the names yet. Go on, Harve.

Harvey: Oh, it's the reef pennant. I'd hook the tack on to the reef pennant and then let down—

Platt: Lower the sail, child!

Harvey: Lower the throat and peak halyards.

Narrator 1: The men continue with Harvey's training.

Long Jack: Very good, Harvey. You're learning.

Narrator 2: Soon the men are called back to work, pulling crab-covered cod up and over the sides of the schooner. At first Harvey thinks that fishing over the sides is preferable to unloading the dories. Then his back aches at the pull of the cod up and over the high sides. The evening passes, and the boys fall into bed.

Scene 5

Narrator 1: The next morning Harvey wakes to a surging sea. The *We're Here* groans as she pitches through the heavy seas.

Long Jack: Now ashore, we'd have chores. We're well clear of the fleet, and in this weather, we've no chores.

Harvey: *(To Manuel.)* For how long?

Manuel: Till she gets a little quiet and we can row to fish. You do not like?

Harvey: I would have been sick a week ago, but it doesn't seem to upset me now—much.

Manuel: That's because me make you a fisherman!

Narrator 2: The men begin to sing songs and tell stories of the sea. Suddenly, Tom Platt stops Dan from starting a song.

Platt: Hold on! That's a Jonah for sure.

Harvey: What a Jonah?

Platt: A Jonah's anything that spoils the luck.

Dan: At least we know Harve's no Jonah. We had a good catch the day after we caught him.

Narrator 1: The cook throws up his head and laughs in a strange way.

Long Jack: Don't do that! We ain't used to it.

Dan: *(To the cook.)* What's wrong? Isn't Harve our mascot? Wasn't our catch good?

Cook: Oh! Yes! I know that, but the catch is not finished yet.

Dan: He ain't going to do us any harm. What are you hinting at?

Cook: No harm. No. But one day, he will be your master, Danny.

Dan: *(Placidly.)* That all? Humph. Not by a jugful.

Cook: *(To Harvey.)* Master! *(To Dan.)* Man!

Dan: That's news! How soon?

Cook: In some years, and I shall see it. Master and man—man and master.

Platt: How in thunder did you work that out?

Cook: In my head, where I can see.

Long Jack: How?

Cook: I don't know, but so it will be.

Narrator 2: Cook went back to peeling potatoes and will not say another word.

Dan: Well, a heap of things have to come about before Harve's any master of mine. But I'm glad he's no Jonah.

Scene 6

Narrator 1: Harvey enjoys many long talks with Dan, who tells Harvey what he would do if he had the ship of his dreams, a new haddocker.

Dan: Those new haddockers are as fine as a yacht forward. Dad's set against them, but there's heaps of money in them. Dad can find fish, but he's not progressive. Ever see the *Elector* of Gloucester? She's a daisy!

Harvey: What do they cost, Dan?

Dan: Piles of money. Fifteen thousand, maybe more. There's gold-leaf and everything. Guess I'd call her the *Hattie S.,* just like the dory.

Narrator 2: In one of their late night talks on deck, Dan reveals that Hattie is a girl who had sat in front of him in school. The boys become firm friends who rarely disagree.

Narrator 1: Because of his youth and his many chores, Harvey doesn't wonder too much about how his mother is bearing up under the shock of his supposed death. One day, however, it occurs to him that his new life is better than being snubbed by strangers in the smoking room of a hired liner.

Narrator 2: The others are always ready to listen to what they call his "fairy tales" of life ashore. Because no one but Dan will believe the stories to be about himself, Harvey invents a friend who has a rich, amazing lifestyle.

Narrator 1: For days, Captain moves them through the fog along the Grand Bank, in a triangle of 250 miles on each side. The fish are biting, and everyone works in spite of the fog. Harvey becomes adept at many of the tasks, and the men notice.

Platt: *(To Captain Troop.)* See how Harvey takes on the very walk of a mariner? Guess you were mistaken in your judgments. What made you think he was crazy?

Captain: He was. Crazy as a loon when he came aboard. But I cured him.

Platt: He tells good yarns. The other night he told us about a kid his own size steering a cunning little rig with four ponies. Curious kind of fairy tale, but interesting.

Captain: Guess he makes them up out of his head. But I know Dan believes him at times.

Narrator 2: They never work on Sundays, but shave and wash themselves. The captain begins to teach Harvey the meaning of the chart, and Harvey catches on quickly. The men share tales of their adventures on other ships—rounding the Horn, being part of a blockade, surviving gales and cold that kept men pounding and chopping at ice all over the ship, and seeing pretty girls in Madeira washing clothes in streams under the moonlight.

Narrator 1: During the week, Captain Troop directs them to the best fishing, while other crews try their best to follow them. On occasion, a ship pulls alongside and the men barter or exchange news or insults. Most ships move on in search of fish.

Scene 7

Narrator 2: Early one foggy morning, Dan and Harvey tumble out of bed, sneak fried pies from the kitchen, and go on deck to enjoy them. They find the captain ringing the bell.

Captain: Harvey, take over the bell. Keep it going. I seem to hear something.

Narrator 1: Harvey rings the forlorn bell and in the pauses hears the muffled shriek of a liner's siren. He remembers how he once thought it would be "great" if a steamer ran down a fishing boat. That boy now rings a bell for his life while a thirty-foot steel stem storms along at twenty miles an hour! Harvey rings the bell while Dan blows on a conch.

Dan: All they do is slow down their propellers a bit to be within the law. That's not much consolation when we're at the bottom. Hark!

Narrator 2: Harvey finds himself looking up and up at the wet edge of a clifflike bow, leaping, it seemed, directly over the schooner. Suddenly he hears a voice shouting.

Olley: Heave to! You've sunk us!

Harvey: What?

Dan: It's a boat out yonder. Ring! We're going to look.

Narrator 1: In a few minutes, most of the men are in dories, looking for the boat.

Dan: Look! There's a foremast. And there's an empty dory.

Narrator 2: Then the men see something face down, in a blue jersey—part of what was once a man. Harvey pounds at the bell, fearing they will be sunk at any minute.

Dan: It's the *Jennie Cushman!* They've cut her clean in half. Here's Dad—he's got the old man, Jason Olley. That must have been his son's body we saw. Oh, Harve.

Narrator 1: Captain Troop hauls the gray-headed man aboard.

Olley: Disko, what did you pick me up for?

Narrator 2: Troop drops a heavy hand on his shoulder.

Olley: My son is gone and my nine-thousand-dollar boat. If you'd left me alone my widow could have gone and worked for her keep and never known for sure what happened. Now I'll have to tell her.

Captain: Better lie down a bit, Jason.

Narrator 1: One of the men leads the grieving father below. The men sorrowfully resume their work. Hours drift by. Then a schooner bell strikes nearby and a voice calls out.

Sailor: Have you heard about the *Jennie Cushman*?

Captain: We've got Jason aboard here. Anyone else survive?

Sailor: We found one. He was snarled up in a mess of lumber. His head's cut some.

Captain: Who is he?

Sailor: Guess it's the young Olley. We were kind of drifting when we found him. Why don't you send the old man aboard? We're short-handed, and we'll take care of him.

Captain: I'll send him over and anything else you might need!

Sailor: Sure could use an anchor that will hold. Say! Young Olley's getting excited. Send the old man along.

Narrator 2: A happy reunion follows, and the men make their departure. The fog continues for days, and the captain keeps them busy around the ship. Finally, the fog lifts and Troop shouts to the crew.

Captain: Hurry, boys! We're in town!

Scene 8

Narrator 1: To the end of his days, Harvey will never forget the sight of the town. The sun, which they have not seen for nearly a week, is just clear of the horizon. The low red light falls onto the sails of three fleets of anchored schooners. There are nearly a hundred of them. Men hail, whistle, cat-call, and sing.

Harvey: The captain is right! It's a town!

Captain: There's about a thousand men here.

Narrator 2: The *We're Here* skirts around the northern squadron, and the men greet friends. They all seem to know about Harvey's rescue and ask if he's worth his salt yet. After they tie up to a buoy, the men scatter from the ship in the dories to visit old friends and warn old enemies.

Narrator 1: Later the men begin fishing, competing for the cod that are swimming in droves, biting as steadily as they swim. The fishing is wonderful, but lines tangle among the fishermen, even though they stay around their own ships.

Narrator 2: After a week of fishing, long deep swells begin. The ships separate to save their sides. Then the storm grows quickly one evening, and the crew members play host to wet strangers unable to return to their ships in their dories. After the storm, there is a general sorting out among the fleet. Only a few men died, but many are cut or bruised. Tom Platt hears of an acquaintance's death and attends the usual auction of the Frenchman's goods. Dan goes along and buys a knife with a brass handle.

Narrator 1: Fog settles in again. Harvey and Dan return to fishing in the dory. Dan pulls out his new knife and tests the edge on the gunwale.

Harvey: That's a great knife. How'd you get it?

Dan: At that auction. Cheap.

Harvey: Why was it so cheap?

Dan: Superstition. Some don't fancy taking iron off a dead man.

Harvey: But it's business at an auction.

Dan: We know it, but some folks believe in superstition, not reason. I was told the knife had been used to kill a man. Course when I heard that, I was keener than ever to get it!

Harvey: I'll give you a dollar for it when I get my wages. Say, I'll give you two dollars!

Dan: Honest? You like as much as all that? Well, to tell the truth, I kind-of got it for you—to give. But I didn't let on till I saw how you'd take it. It's yours and welcome, Harve, because we're dory-mates, and so on and so forth. Catch it!

Harvey: But look, Dan, I don't see—

Dan: Take it. Ain't no use to me. I wish you to have it.

Harvey: Dan, I'll keep it as long as I live.

Dan: *(Laughing.)* That's good to hear. Look—your line is fastened to something.

Narrator 2: Harvey buckles the belt that holds the knife at his waist. Then he pulls at the line.

Harvey: She acts as if she were on strawberry bottom, but it's sand here, right?

Dan: We'd better haul it up and make certain.

Narrator 1: They pull together. Then they give a shrill, double shriek of horror, for out of the sea comes the body of the dead Frenchman buried two days before. The hook had caught him under the right armpit, and he sways, erect and horrible, head and shoulders above water. His arms had been tied to his side—and he has no face. The boys fall over each other in a heap at the bottom of the dory while the body bobs alongside, held on by the shortened line.

Harvey: The tide brought him!

Dan: Oh, Lord. He's come for the knife. Take it off!

Harvey: I don't want it! I can't find the buckle!

Narrator 2: Harvey sits up to unfasten the belt, facing the head with no face under its streaming hair. Dan cuts the line as Harvey flings the belt far over the side. The body shoots down with a plop.

Dan: He come for it—on your line.

Harvey: I wish I hadn't taken the knife. Then he'd have come on *your* line.

Dan: I don't know if that would have made any difference. We're *both* scared out of ten years growth.

Harvey: I know, but look here. It couldn't have been *meant.* It was only the tide.

Dan: Tide! They sunk him six miles to the south of the fleet and we're another two miles away from that.

Harvey: Wonder what he did with that knife. Well, I'm heaving my catch overboard too.

Dan: Why? *We* won't be eating them.

Harvey: I don't care. I had to look at his face while I was taking the belt off. You can keep your catch if you like.

Narrator 1: Dan throws his fish over, too.

Dan: Wish we were back at the ship. This fog . . . I'd give a month's pay if this fog would lift. They'll be looking for us at the ship soon.

Narrator 2: Within a few minutes, the cook rows up in a dory, looking for the boys. The men listen in awe to their story, following it with ghost stories until nearly midnight. The next morning, the men race against other fishermen, gathering their last loads. Finally, the ship is full, and Captain Troop proudly begins maneuvering his ship among the others, preparing to begin the journey home.

Narrator 1: As the days pass, Harvey has more time to appreciate the finer points of a proud ship moving through the seas. The best fun is when the boys are put on the wheel together.

Dan: Next week you'll be home and wanting to hire a boy to throw water on the windows so you can sleep. Do you know the best part of getting ashore again?

Harvey: A hot bath?

Dan: That's good, but a nightshirt's better. Ma will have a new one for me, all washed soft. It's home, Harve! You can sense it in the air.

Narrator 2: And before long, land is in plain sight. In honor of Otto, who had fallen overboard early in the journey, they lower the flag of the *We're Here* to half-mast. They make their way to a wharf and silently throw down a rope.

Narrator 1: Harvey sits down by the wheel and sobs as if his heart would break. Dan's mother, who had seen the ship approach, comes aboard the schooner and kisses Dan on the cheek. No one thinks the worse of Harvey for crying, and soon they make their way to the captain's house.

Narrator 2: The next morning, Troop sends a telegram to Harvey's family. When Harvey gets a response, he shows it to Dan, swearing him to secrecy. The crew, including the captain, assumes that no one has heard from Harvey's family, confirming their belief that Harvey's stories were indeed fairy tales.

Scene 9

Narrator 1: Harvey Cheyne, Senior, had spoken little of his sorrow, devoting himself to Mrs. Cheyne who talked incessantly about their son. They had no hope, and Mr. Cheyne's dreams of Harvey becoming his companion, partner, and ally had died. He had taken his wife to San Diego, where he coped with business as best he could. He is considering dropping out of the business altogether when a white-faced secretary hands him a telegram.

Mr. Cheyne: *(Reading.)* Picked up by fishing schooner *We're Here* having fallen off boat great times on Banks fishing all well waiting Gloucester Mass care Disko Troop for money or orders wire what shall do and how is Mama Harvey N. Cheyne.

Narrator 2: The father lets it fall, his head down on the rolltop of the shut desk, breathing heavily. The secretary runs for Mrs. Cheyne's doctor, who returns to find Cheyne pacing to and fro. He reassures Cheyne that the telegram must be true and they proceed to Mrs. Cheyne's room and tell her the news. Her shriek echoes through the house.

Narrator 1: Mr. Cheyne returns to his usual efficient style and begins to make plans to cross the country. Within minutes he has devised a schedule on his trains, ensuring that they and their private car will arrive out east as quickly as possible. Eighty-seven hours and thirty-five minutes after they begin their journey, they complete the run from tidewater to tidewater. And Harvey is waiting for them.

Narrator 2: The family feasts the returned prodigal in private, enjoying tales of Harvey's adventures. His mother fondles his hand, rough and hard from his work. Mr. Cheyne, well used to judging men, sees that his son is no longer the dough-faced youth who would insult his father and reduce his mother to tears. His son now has eyes that are steady and clear, unflinching, and a voice that is distinct and respectful.

Mrs. Cheyne: Why didn't you tell the captain to put you ashore? You know Papa would have made it up to him ten times over.

Harvey: I know it. But he thought I was crazy. I'm afraid I called him a thief because I couldn't find the bills in my pocket.

Mrs. Cheyne: A sailor found them by the flagstaff that night.

Harvey: That explains it then. I don't blame Troop any. I just said I wouldn't work, and he hit me on the nose!

Mrs. Cheyne: My poor darling! They must have abused you horribly.

Harvey: Well, after that, I saw the light. The captain gave me ten and a half dollars a month. He's paid me half now. I took on with Dan, his son, and pitched right in. I can't do a man's work yet. But I can handle a dory almost as well as Dan. And I don't get rattled in a fog—much. I know my ropes and can fish till the cows come home. Say, you've no notion what a heap of work there is in ten and a half a month!

Cheyne: I began with eight and a half, my son.

Harvey: That so? You never told me, sir.

Cheyne: You never asked. I'll tell you about it some time.

Harvey: Troop says the most interesting thing in the word is to find out how the next man gets his vittles. It's great to have a good meal again, though we were well fed. You have to meet Tom Platt, Long Jack, Cook, and Manuel. Manuel saved my life. He found me adrift and hauled me in.

Mrs. Cheyne: It's a wonder your nervous system isn't completely wrecked.

Harvey: What for, Mama? I worked like a horse, ate like a hog, and slept like a dead man.

Narrator 1: This is too much for Mrs. Cheyne, and she retires to her stateroom.

Cheyne: You can depend on me to do everything I can for the crew, Harve. They seem to be good men on your showing.

Harvey: Best in the fleet. Troop thinks he's cured me of being crazy. Dan's the only one who knows about you, the private cars, and all the rest of it. I'm not *quite* sure Dan believes. I want to paralyze them tomorrow. I need to be back to finish cleaning out.

Cheyne: You need to work?

Harvey: I told Troop I would.

Cheyne: Hire a substitute.

Harvey: Can't sir. I record the weights of the fish for the catch. Troop says I have a good head for figures.

Narrator 2: Mr. Cheyne, grateful that Harvey intends to follow through with his obligation, discusses their plans for the next day, and they go to sleep.

Scene 10

Narrator 1: The next morning, Harvey has left before his parents. They arrive at the wharf where the *We're Here* rides high. All hands are busy, with Harvey recording the weights while the others unload the fish. Mr. and Mrs. Cheyne approaches Dan. The crew, used to questions from summer boarders, continues with their work.

Cheyne: Who's that boy?

Dan: Well, he's kind of supercargo. We picked him up adrift off the Banks. Fell overboard from a liner, he says. He's a fisherman now.

Cheyne: Is he worth his keep?

Dan: Dad! This man wants to know if Harve's worth his keep? *(To Mr. Cheyne.)* Say, would you two like to come aboard? We'll fix a ladder for you.

Narrator 2: Mr. and Mrs. Cheyne go aboard. Mrs. Cheyne stands aghast amid the mess and tangle on the deck.

Captain: Are you interested in Harve?

Cheyne: Well, yes.

Captain: He's a good boy and catches right on. You heard how we found him. He was suffering from nervous prostration when we found him, I guess, or his head had hit something. He's all over that now. You're welcome to look around.

Narrator 1: Meanwhile, Dan dances around the deck, whispering to the crew that this is Harve's folks and that his dad hasn't caught on yet. They all gather, anxious to see their captain discover the truth. They arrive just in time.

Cheyne: I'm glad he has a good character, because—he's my son.

Narrator 2: Later, Long Jack vows that he heard the captain's jaw click as it fell open.

Cheyne: I got this telegram four days ago, and we came over.

Dan: In a private car?

Cheyne: Of course.

Long Jack: There was a tale he told us of driving four little ponies in a rig of his own. Was that true?

Mrs. Cheyne: He had a little rig in Toledo.

Narrator 1: Long Jack whistles and looks at the captain.

Captain: I was—I am mistaken in my judgment. I don't mind telling you, Mr. Cheyne, that I mistrusted the boy. I thought he was crazy with all his talk about money.

Cheyne: So he told me.

Captain: Did he tell you something else? 'Cause I pounded him once.

Cheyne: Oh, yes. I should say it probably did him more good than anything else in the world.

Captain: I thought it was necessary, or I wouldn't have done it. I don't want you to think we abuse our boys.

Cheyne: I don't think you do, Mr. Troop.

Mrs. Cheyne: Tell me, who is who. I want to thank you and bless you—all of you.

Narrator 2: Mrs. Cheyne nearly throws herself at Manuel, thanking him for saving her son. She kisses Dan on both cheeks. Then they show her where Harvey slept and ate, all the while explaining the boat's daily life. Finally, Harvey appears.

Captain: *(To Harvey.)* I was mistaken, Harve. I was mistaken in my judgment. You needn't rub it in.

Dan: *(To himself.)* I'll take care of that!

Captain: You'll be going off now, won't you?

Harvey: Not without the balance of my wages, unless you want to have the *We're Here* attached.

Captain: That's so. I'd clean forgot. Here you are. You done all you contracted to do, and you done it about as well as if you'd been brought up—

Dan: Outside a private car?

Harvey: Come on, and I'll show it to you.

Narrator 1: They all marvel at the stamped leather, silver door handles, cut velvet, and rare inlaid woods. Harvey enjoys this moment the most. Mrs. Cheyne decrees that a meal is in order and practically waits on them herself. Later, Mr. Cheyne and Captain Troop enjoy cigars in the *We're Here* cabin. Cheyne knows he is dealing with a man to whom he cannot offer money. He also knows that no money can repay Troop. He waits for an opening.

Captain: I haven't done anything *to* or *for* your boy except make him work and learn. He has twice my boy's head for figures.

Cheyne: What do you plan to make of your boy?

Captain: Dan's just a plain boy, and he doesn't allow me to do any of his thinking. He'll have this ship one day. I know he isn't anxious to leave the business.

Cheyne: Ever been west, Mr. Troop?

Captain: Been as far as New York in a boat. No use for railroads. Salt water's good enough for the Troops.

Cheyne: I can give him all the salt water he's likely to need—till he's a skipper.

Captain: How's that? I thought you were a railroad king.

Cheyne: I also own a line of tea-clippers that travel from San Francisco to Yokohama. Six of them, iron built, about seventeen hundred and eighty tons apiece.

Captain: That boy never told!

Cheyne: He didn't know. I only took over the Blue M freighters this summer.

Captain: The Blue M! I know Phil Airheart—he's a mate on the *San José* and his sister lives right here. If I'd known that, I'd have jerked the *We're Here* back to port at once.

Cheyne: That might not have been so good for Harvey. Now what I was getting at is to know if you'd lend me Dan for a year or two. Airheart is skipper now. Would you trust him to Airheart? We'll see if we can make him a mate.

Captain: Look, Banks ways aren't clipper ways. He can steer, but he's weak on navigation.

Cheyne: Airheart will attend to that. He'll ship as boy for a voyage or two and then we'll move him along. Suppose you take him in hand this winter, and I'll send for him early in the spring. And any time you want to see him, I'll take care of his transportation.

Captain: If you'll walk with me, we'll go to my house and talk this over with my wife. I've been crazy with my judgment. Let's see what she says about all of this.

Narrator 2: Mrs. Troop knows that Dan is bound for the sea and approves. Dan is delighted to accept the offer, knowing that this will be the road to a fine life.

Narrator 1: The Cheyne family makes a holiday of their stay among their new friends. While Mrs. Cheyne regains her health, father and son enjoy long walks, each sharing stories of their lives. They plan for Harvey's college education, and Mr. Cheyne agrees that one day he'll sign over his line to Harvey.

Narrator 2: Finally, the holiday comes to a close, the *We're Here* is ready for its next journey, and everyone makes their farewells.

Scene 11

Narrator 1: A few years later, on the other edge of America, a young man comes through the clammy sea fog up a windy street flanked with expensive houses. He meets another young man and dismounts from his horse.

Harvey: Hello, Dan!

Dan: Hello, Harve!

Harvey: What's the best with you?

Dan: Well, I'm to be second mate this trip. Ain't you almost through with that expensive college of yours?

Harvey: Getting there. I'm coming into the business for keeps next fall.

Dan: Our ships?

Harvey: Nothing else. You just wait until I get my knife into you, Dan. I'm going to make the old line lie down and cry when I take hold.

Dan: *(Chuckling.)* I'll risk it.

Narrator 2: Harve peers through the fog as he holds the reins of his horse.

Harvey: Where's that man, anyway?

Narrator 1: The old cook of the *We're Here,* who had insisted on staying with Harvey, comes forward to take the horse's bridle. He allows no one else to attend to any of Harvey's wants.

Dan: *(To the cook.)* Thick as the fog on the Banks, ain't it?

Narrator 2: The old man doesn't reply at first. Then he taps Dan on the shoulder.

Cook: Master—man. Man—master. You remember, Dan Troop, what I said? On the *We're Here*?

Dan: Well, I won't go so far as to deny that it does look like it as things stand at present. The *We're Here* was a noble packet, and one way and another, I owe her a heap—her and Dad.

Harvey: Me, too!

The End

Zorro!
Or
The Curse of Capistrano

Johnston McCulley

Adapted by Jennifer L. Kroll

Summary

In colonial California, a rich landowner named Don Diego Vega seeks to marry a young woman of good family named Lolita Pulida. Lolita's parents are poor because a corrupt governor and government have cheated them out of much of their fortune. Even though marriage with Don Diego would be advantageous from a financial standpoint, Lolita refuses Don Diego's offer. Diego is too bookish, unromantic, and without spirit, Lolita thinks. Lolita is far more interested in the dangerous, mysterious outlaw, Zorro, who shows up one day in her family's home. As the story of *Zorro* unfolds, this mysterious highwayman appears repeatedly, and always at just the right moment to save Lolita's honor, life, and her family's name. His secret identity is only revealed and his mask removed at the end of the play.

Background Information

Johnston McCulley was an American author who wrote primarily for popular or "pulp" magazines during the first half of the 1900s. He continued writing for such publications until his death in 1959. McCulley's most enduring creation was the hero Zorro. His first Zorro story appeared in installments in the *All-Star Weekly* between August and September of 1919. That story, the basis for this play, was titled *The Curse of Capistrano*. McCulley was inspired to create the fictional Zorro after reading about an historical bandito named Joaquin Murieta. Over the years, McCulley's character, Zorro has been the subject of many novels and movies, as well as a television series.

Presentation Suggestions

Seat Don Diego Vega and Zorro together front and center. If possible, place them on higher seats than other readers. Seat the Pulidos together, in front of or near Don Diego and Zorro. Seat the Tavern Keeper, Jailer, army members and Governor to one side of the central characters. Seat Juanita, the young ranchers, and Don Alejandro to the other side of the central characters. Place the Narrators in any suitable location.

Props

The student reading Don Diego's part might wear glasses, a bow tie, or other items to make him appear bookish or nerdy. Zorro can wear a mask over his eyes, a cowboy hat, and a bandana around his neck. Army members can wear camouflage clothing to signify their army status. Don Alejandro and the Pulidos can be dressed in nice clothing.

Characters

❀ Narrators 1, 2, and 3

❀ Tavern Keeper

❀ Pedro Gonzales, *a sergeant in the army*

❀ Don Diego Vega, *a twenty-five-year-old man*

❀ Don Carlos Pulido, *a nobleman*

❀ Doña Catalina Pulido, *a noblewoman*

❀ Señorita Lolita Pulido, *the Pulidos' eighteen-year-old daughter*

❀ Zorro, *a notorious bandit*

❀ Captain Ramon, *an army captain*

❀ Juanita, *a maid*

❀ Juan, *a young gentleman rancher*

❀ Don Alejandro Vega, *an elderly man*

❀ Victor, *a young gentleman rancher*

❀ Martin, *a young gentleman rancher*

❀ Officer

❀ Jailer

❀ Governor

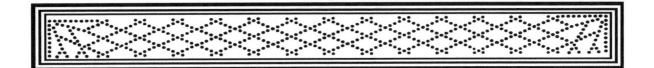

Zorro!
Or
The Curse of Capistrano

Scene 1

Narrator 1: During the early 1800s, a corrupt governor controls the Mexican territory of California. Those who do favors for him receive high places in his army.

Narrator 2: In a tavern in the little town of Reina de Los Angeles, Sergeant Pedro Gonzales sits with soldiers clustered around him. The tavern's owner approaches their table, carrying mugs of wine.

Tavern Keeper: They are saying in the town that Señor Zorro is abroad again.

Pedro Gonzales: Señor Zorro, eh? Is it my fate always to hear that name? Mr. Fox, in other words.

Tavern Keeper: Yes, and he has proved as difficult as a fox to catch.

Gonzales: He wears a mask, and he flashes a pretty blade, they tell me. Of course, I have yet to see the man. He carries out his deeds far from wherever my troops may be.

Tavern Keeper: There is a reward.

Gonzales: I know it! A pretty reward it is, too, offered by the governor for Zorro's capture. But what good does that do me? When I am away on duty at San Juan Capistrano, Zorro shows up at Santa Barbara. I dine at San Gabriel, and he robs at San Diego de Alcala!

Tavern Keeper: Well, he never has visited us here.

Narrator 3: The tavern door opens, and the men look up. Along with a gust of wind and rain, Don Diego Vega enters.

Don Diego Vega: Did I startle you somewhat, señores?

Gonzales: You, my friend, are so mild mannered and soft-spoken that you are unlikely to startle anyone.

Diego: It is true that I do not have a reputation for riding like a fool, fighting like an idiot, and playing the guitar under every pretty woman's window. Yet I do not wish to be mocked.

Gonzales: Your pardon, my very good friend! Please join us! We have been speaking of the notorious Señor Zorro.

Diego: More talk of violence! Is it even possible in these times for a man to hold conversation about music or the poets?

Gonzales: You are unlikely to find anyone speaking of poetry these days. Zorro, the famous thief and cutthroat, is the talk of the town!

Diego: From what I hear, he is no cutthroat. And he has robbed none except officials who have stolen from the poor. He has punished none except brutes who mistreat others. Let him have his little day in the public eye.

Gonzales: I would rather see him dead and have the reward!

Scene 2

Narrator 1: The next morning, Don Diego rides to the ranch of Don Carlos Pulido.

Don Carlos Pulido: *(To his wife, Catalina.)* My dear, do you see that rider in the distance?

Doña Catalina Pulido: Yes, but I can't make out his features.

Carlos: I pray that he is not another of the governor's tax collectors. They have taken a fortune from us already. We are nearly penniless now.

Catalina: Could it be Don Diego Vega?

Carlos: It is Don Diego! Perhaps this is a stroke of good fortune at last! Let us make him as welcome as possible. Don Diego is a very rich and powerful man.

Catalina: If the governor's men find out that we are on close terms with Don Diego, surely they will think twice before harassing us further.

Narrator 2: A servant hurries out and helps Don Diego from his horse.

Carlos: I am glad to have you as a visitor at my poor hacienda, Don Diego.

Diego: It is a long, dusty road. It tires me to ride a horse this distance.

Carlos: How are things in Reina de Los Angeles?

Diego: Everything is the same, except that Señor Zorro is all the talk.

Carlos: At least I have nothing to fear from that highwayman. Everyone knows that I've been stripped of almost everything the governor's men could carry away. They'll take the house next.

Diego: Such a thing must be stopped. Anyhow, I did not ride through the terrible sun and dust to talk with you about such gloomy subjects.

Carlos: Whatever your errand, I am glad to welcome you to my home.

Diego: Yesterday, I had a talk with my father. He doesn't think I'm accepting my responsibilities as I should. He wishes me to take a wife.

Carlos: It is something every man should do.

Diego: And so I have come to see you about it.

Carlos: To see me about it?

Diego: I wish to court your daughter. May I have your permission?

Carlos: Of course you may court Lolita! *(To his wife.)* Catalina, do you hear what our visitor is saying?

Catalina: *(Smiling.)* I do. *(To Diego.)* An alliance between our families would bring us much joy. I do hope that you may win her heart with your courtship.

Diego: As to the courtship, I must make it clear that there will be no undue nonsense. Either the lady wants me, or she doesn't. I don't intend to play a guitar beneath her window or any other such foolishness.

Narrator 3: Señorita Lolita Pulido comes onto the porch to join her parents.

Señorita Lolita Pulido: I am happy to see you again, Don Diego.

Diego: Señorita, I have asked for permission to seek your hand in marriage. Do you think I'd make a proper husband?

Lolita: *(Taken aback.)* Why, I—that is—

Diego: Just say the word, señorita, and your family can make arrangements for the ceremony. They can send word to me, so I don't have to make the trip here again. Do you want to marry me?

Lolita: *(Angrily.)* Don Diego Vega, is this your idea of courtship and romance? You're not even willing to ride four miles on a smooth road to see a woman whom you wish to wed?

Narrator 1: Lolita storms back into the house. Don Carlos looks anxiously after her.

Diego: I fear that I have displeased her.

Carlos: Well, maybe she will change her mind later.

Diego: I hope so. I will take my leave now and call again another day.

Scene 3

Narrator 2: Hours later, the same day, Lolita is dozing on the patio. She is awakened by a touch on her arm and sits up quickly. Before her stands a man in a long cloak, whose face is covered with a black mask. She gasps.

Zorro: Silence, and no harm will come to you, señorita.

Lolita: You—you are—

Zorro: You have guessed it, my charming señorita. I am known as Señor Zorro.

Lolita: And you are here—

Zorro: I mean no harm to you or any in this house, señorita. I punish those who are unjust, and your father is not. Rather would I punish those who do him evil.

Lolita: I—I thank you.

Zorro: I am simply weary, and your hacienda is an excellent place to rest. I'm sorry to awaken you, señorita, but I felt that I must speak. You are so beautiful, I just had to sing your praises!

Lolita: I wish my appearance had this effect on some other men I know!

Zorro: And does it not? Impossible!

Narrator 3: Suddenly, Don Carlos rushes onto the patio, alarmed.

Carlos: It's the bandit! Zorro! *(To Zorro.)* Get away from my daughter!

Zorro: *(To Carlos.)* Do not be frightened. I mean no harm.

Carlos: Scoundrel! How dare you enter an honest man's house?

Zorro: I am no enemy of yours, Don Carlos. In fact, I have done some things that should appeal to a man who has been persecuted.

Carlos: What do you want here?

Zorro: I crave your hospitality, señor. I would like to eat and drink.

Carlos: A thief and highwayman has no claim upon the hospitality of this house!

Zorro: I take it that you fear to feed me, since the governor may hear of it. Don't worry. You can always say that you were forced to do it.

Narrator 1: The Pulidos reluctantly serve Zorro dinner but secretly send their servant to alert the authorities.

Lolita: *(Whispering to Zorro.)* You must go—at once. I am afraid that my father has sent for the soldiers.

Zorro: *(To Carlos and Catalina.)* I must go now. Thank you for your hospitality. I promise that it shall be repaid.

Narrator 2: The hooves of the approaching army can be heard approaching outside.

Narrator 3: Grasping his sword, Zorro runs from the room and out to the patio. He throws the candles to the floor and extinguishes them as he goes. The Pulidos hear the masked man call his horse. Then they hear the sound of hooves tearing off into the distance. A split second later, soldiers rush in.

Gonzales: The fiend escapes! To horse and after him!

Carlos: Lights! Lights!

Narrator 1: A servant relights the candles as the soldiers dash back out to their horses and depart. A few minutes later, another horse can be heard approaching the house.

Carlos: Someone else is coming!

Narrator 2: Captain Ramon enters.

Captain Ramon: Where are my men?

Carlos: Gone, señor! Gone after that highwayman!

Ramon: He escaped?

Carlos: He did, with your men surrounding the house.

Ramon: The men took after him?

Carlos: They are upon his heels, señor.

Ramon: Ladies, you must pardon my bold entrance.

Catalina: The pardon is granted freely. You have met my daughter?

Ramon: I have not had the honor.

Narrator 3: Ramon takes a good look at Lolita and seems to like what he sees.

Ramon: It's too dark to find my men out there. If it's no bother for you, I'll stay here and await their return.

Carlos: By all means. Be seated, señor, and I'll have a servant fetch wine.

Ramon: I think Señor Zorro must be avoiding me. Whenever he strikes, I am always far away. Just tonight, when the alarm came, I was not at headquarters, but at a friend's home. That's why I didn't ride out with the soldiers. If only I could get my hands on him!

Catalina: You think you could conquer him, señor?

Ramon: Undoubtedly! I understand he really is not much of a swordsman.

Narrator 1: Suddenly, a closet door flies open, and Zorro steps into the room.

Zorro: I shall take you to task for that statement, señor, because it is a falsehood.

Catalina: Oh, my!

Carlos: I—I thought you had escaped!

Zorro: Ha! It was a trick! My horse escaped—but I did not!

Ramon: Then there shall be no escape for you now!

Zorro: Back, señor! I shall fight you gladly. Señor Carlos, please move your family to the corner of the room while I cross blades with this teller of lies!

Narrator 2: Zorro and Ramon begin to fence. Their blades flash back and forth.

Zorro: Ha! I almost had you there, my captain. Where do you prefer to be cut, on your left or right shoulder?

Ramon: If you are so certain of your ability, cut my right shoulder!

Narrator 3: Zorro obliges Ramon by making a cut in his right shoulder. Ramon drops to the floor in pain.

Zorro: I ask your pardon, ladies and gentlemen, for this scene. And now I must be going. *Buenos noches!*

Narrator 1: Zorro dashes through the kitchen and onto the patio, where his horse awaits him. He gallops off.

Narrator 2: Carlos and Catalina bandage Ramon and bring him a mug of wine.

Catalina: You must stay until you are feeling quite well, señor.

Ramon: It's only a scratch.

Narrator 3: Ramon spends the next few hours chatting with the Pulido family. As Lolita leaves the room, Ramon turns to Carlos.

Ramon: Don Carlos, I come from a good family, and the governor is friendly toward me, as no doubt you have heard. My future is assured.

Carlos: I am glad to hear it, señor.

Ramon: I never set eyes upon your daughter until this evening, but she has captivated me. I ask permission to court your daughter.

Carlos: I must tell you that just this morning Don Diego Vega asked me the same question.

Ramon: He did? Ha! That sickly, lifeless shell of a man!

Carlos: Don Diego Vega is from a very noble family, so of course I didn't refuse him. But I must tell you—the señorita weds nobody unless it is her wish, and I am not sure that she is at all interested in Don Diego.

Ramon: Then I may try for her hand?

Carlos: You have my permission.

Scene 4

Narrator 1: Two days later, Carlos, Catalina, and Lolita are on their way to Don Diego Vega's house in Reina de Los Angeles. As their carriage bumps along, Carlos rereads an invitation letter from Don Diego.

Carlos: *(Reading.)* The soldiers are pursuing this Señor Zorro, and it has been reported that the high-wayman has a band of rogues under his command. There is no telling what may happen next. Moreover, I have heard that the bandit has visited your daughter, and he may seek to see her again.

Catalina: *(Interrupting.)* It frightens me to think of it!

Carlos: *(Continuing to read.)* I therefore beg of you to come at once to my house in Reina de Los Angeles and make it your home for a day or two. I will be away at my ranch, but I have left orders with my servants to cater to you. I hope to see you when I return in three days.

Lolita: I'm sure nothing bad would have happened if we had stayed at home.

Catalina: But, my dear! This is a wonderful opportunity for you to see everything that could be yours if you would only agree to marry Don Diego.

Lolita: I'm sorry, Mother, but I can't marry him. I do not love him.

Carlos: It is within your power to save us all from financial ruin. Remember that, and don't be too hasty about your decision. You might find that you like him more after you know him better.

Lolita: I'll do my best to like him, but I can't promise that I will be his wife.

Catalina: Well, Captain Ramon also has asked permission to court you. He is a dashing gentleman, don't you think?

Lolita: He is handsome enough, but I do not like the look in his eyes.

Catalina: *(Sighing.)* You are too particular.

Scene 5

Narrator 2: Lolita stands in the library of Don Diego's house, browsing through his books.

Lolita: How strange! Volume after volume of love poetry! So many books on horsemanship and fencing! Tales of great generals and warriors! I would never have guessed that such books would be favorites of Don Diego!

Narrator 3: The sound of pounding can be heard in the hall. Juanita, one of Don Diego's servants, hurries to the door. She opens it and sees Captain Ramon.

Juanita: Don Diego is not at home, señor. He has gone up to the ranch.

Ramon: But Don Carlos and his wife and daughter are here, are they not?

Juanita: Don Carlos and his wife are out on a visit this evening, señor.

Ramon: The señorita? Is she here?

Juanita: She is, but—

Ramon: In that case, I shall pay my respects to the señorita.

Juanita: Señor! I don't think her parents would approve of you visiting while they are away.

Ramon: Out of the way!

Narrator 1: Ramon shoves Juanita aside. In moments, he appears at the library door.

Ramon: Ah, señorita! I felt that I must have a few words with you.

Lolita: What are you doing here? My parents would be very upset!

Ramon: There is something I need to say to you.

Lolita: What can that be, señor?

Ramon: Your beauty has inflamed my heart, and I would have you for my wife. Don Diego Vega is not worthy of you. He has no courage, no spirit.

Lolita: *(Outraged.)* You speak ill of him in his own house! That seems wrong. You should leave now, I must insist.

Ramon: But I must have an answer. Am I not the man for you?

Narrator 2: Ramon tries to put his arms around Lolita. She backs away.

Lolita: My father will hear of your behavior!

Ramon: Your father! A man who is being robbed because he has no political sense! I do not fear your father! He should be proud of the fact that Captain Ramon looks at his daughter.

Lolita: Señor!

Ramon: I have done you a great honor by asking you to be my wife!

Lolita: *(Angrily.)* Done *me* an honor! You horrible man!

Ramon: You are so pretty, even when you are angry.

Narrator 3: Ramon corners Lolita and puts his arms around her. She pushes him away and slaps his face.

Lolita: You are no gentleman! I wouldn't marry you if you were the last man alive!

Narrator 1: Lolita and Ramon suddenly become aware of Zorro's presence in the room.

Zorro: *(Angrily, to Ramon.)* I may be an outlaw, but at least I respect women! On your knees, Ramon! Ask the lady's forgiveness! And then you will slink from this house like the dog you are, or I will soil my blade with your blood!

Ramon: Ha! I'll never—

Zorro: On your knees!

Narrator 2: Zorro springs forward and throws Ramon to the floor.

Zorro: Now tell the señorita you are sorry!

Ramon: *(Muttering.)* Sorry.

Narrator 3: Zorro picks Ramon up, propels him to the door, and pitches him out into the darkness.

Lolita: *(To Zorro.)* Thank you!

Narrator 1: She kisses him on his masked cheek. He gazes into her eyes.

Lolita: You are the very opposite of that horrible Ramon.

Zorro: I would do anything for you, dear lady.

Lolita: I feel the same, señor. Ever since we met the other day, I can't stop thinking of you.

Zorro: But you don't even know what I look like without my mask. I could be hideous, disfigured.

Lolita: It wouldn't matter to me. I can see what kind of man you are plainly enough.

Narrator 2: When Lolita's parents return later that evening, Señor Zorro is gone. Lolita tells them about the evening's events, but she does not reveal her growing feelings for Señor Zorro.

Scene 6

Narrator 3: During the following week, the Pulidos return to their home, and Zorro makes a number of appearances around Reina de Los Angeles. Each time the soldiers pursue him, he gets away.

Narrator 1: When he rescues a monk who is being unjustly whipped, Zorro is again pursued by soldiers on horses. A group of wealthy young gentlemen join in the hunt. These riders gain on the masked bandit, then suddenly lose his trail near the home of Don Diego Vega's father, Don Alejandro Vega. Don Alejandro opens the door when the gentlemen knock.

Juan: Don Alejandro! We have been riding hard and are tired. May we come inside for food and drink?

Don Alejandro Vega: Of course! What brings you out this way?

Juan: We pursue Señor Zorro, the highwayman. Has he been in this neighborhood?

Alejandro: I don't think so. My son rode in safely just a short time ago.

Narrator 2: The men step inside and join Don Diego at a table.

Juan: You did not see the bandit, Don Diego?

Diego: I did not. That is one stroke of good fortune.

Narrator 3: Food and wine are brought. The men continue to speak of Zorro.

Victor: It is lucky for Señor Zorro that we did not catch up with him.

Martin: Any one of us is a match for the fellow.

Diego: Señores, you will pardon me if I retire. I am weary from my journey.

Juan: Of course, Don Diego. Join us again when you are rested.

Narrator 1: Don Diego leaves the room. The men continue drinking, boasting, and speaking of Zorro.

Martin: Just give me the chance to cross blades with him!

Victor: If only this Señor Zorro were here now!

Narrator 2: Zorro suddenly appears, standing in the doorway to the house.

Zorro: Señores, he is here!

Martin: It's him! It's him!

Zorro: So these are the sort of men who hope to take Señor Zorro! What idle boasts!

Victor: Come Zorro! I'll fight you!

Zorro: You have drunk too much wine, señor, as have you all. Not one of you can handle a blade right now.

Alejandro: There is one who can!

Narrator 3: Don Alejandro springs to his feet.

Alejandro: *(To Zorro.)* I openly say that I have admired some of the things you have done, señor. But now you have entered my house and are abusing my guests. I must challenge you!

Zorro: I have no quarrel with you. Don Alejandro, and you have none with me. I refuse to cross blades with you.

Alejandro: You will fight!

Zorro: Señores, you will not allow this aged gentleman to fight me, will you?

Juan: No! Of course not!

Narrator 1: The men quiet Don Alejandro and urge him to sit down again.

Zorro: What a bunch you all are! You drink wine and make merry while injustice is all about you. Why don't you take up your swords and attack oppression? Live up to your noble names! Be men, not fashion plates!

Narrator 2: Angry at Zorro's insulting words, Martin jumps to his feet.

Zorro: Sit down. I have not come here to fight you. I have come to tell you the truth concerning yourselves. The truth is that your families can make or break a governor. You could all band together and make some use of yourselves. You seek adventure? There is adventure aplenty, fighting injustice.

Victor: But the politicians—

Zorro: Do you really think that the politicians would dare stand against you, sons of the region's most powerful families? Band together and give yourselves a name!

Martin: But what you're suggesting is treason!

Zorro: It is not treason to bring down a tyrant. Are you afraid?

Juan: No! We're not afraid!

Zorro: Then make your stand!

Victor: You would lead us?

Zorro: Most certainly, señores.

Narrator 3: For the next several hours, the men debate Zorro's proposition. In the end, they agree to band together with him.

Martin: Señor Zorro, you have a bargain.

Scene 7

Narrator 1: While the young noblemen form a league with Zorro, Captain Ramon plots his revenge against Lolita. He visits the governor and convinces him that the Pulido family is in league with Zorro. The governor sends his soldiers to their home to make arrests.

Officer: You are Don Carlos Pulido?

Carlos: I have that honor, señor.

Officer: I have orders to place you under military arrest.

Carlos: Arrest! Who gave you such orders?

Officer: His Excellency, the governor.

Carlos: And what's the charge?

Officer: Treason and aiding enemies of the state!

Carlos: But that's preposterous!

Officer: You and your daughter and wife are all to accompany me.

Carlos: What? My whole family! Are we to go to army headquarters?

Officer: No, to the jail.

Scene 8

Narrator 2: Zorro and his band meet at midnight to discuss plans for rescuing the Pulido family from the jail.

Zorro: Are we all here?

Juan: All except Don Diego Vega. He is ill with a fever.

Narrator 3: The men decide on a plan. A little later, at the jail, the keeper is going about his nightly duties when he suddenly feels a pistol on his temple.

Zorro: Open, if you value you life!

Jailer: What—what is this?

Zorro: Señor Zorro is talking to you!

Jailer: By the saints—

Zorro: Open, fool, or you die instantly!

Jailer: I . . . I'll open the door. Only spare me!

Narrator 1: The guard opens the door, and Zorro's troop rushes in.

Zorro: Where are the keys to the prison rooms?

Jailer: On . . . on that table, señor.

Zorro: Lie down! On your face! And remain exactly as you are! . . . Now, which cell holds the Pulido family?

Jailer: *(In a muffled voice.)* The second one.

Narrator 2: The rescuers rush to the second cell, where they find the Pulidos.

Catalina: Señor Zorro!

Zorro: I have come with some friends to rescue you!

Carlos: We cannot go with you, señor. How would it look? We are already accused of being in league with you.

Zorro: There's no time to argue with me. *(To his men.)* Escort these fine people from this wretched place.

Narrator 3: Two of the men lead Carlos out. Two others escort Catalina. Zorro extends his arm to Lolita.

Zorro: You must trust me, señorita!

Lolita: *(Warmly.)* I trust you completely.

Scene 9

Narrator 1: The rescuers split up to make pursuit more difficult. Don Carlos and Doña Catalina are successfully carried to safety.

Narrator 2: For a while, it looks as if Zorro and Lolita will also make their escape. Then, as they round a bend in the road, they run head-on into a band of troopers. The two turn their horses and gallop back into Reina de Los Angeles with bullets whizzing all around them.

Lolita: Señor! My mount is stumbling terribly! I don't think he can go much further!

Narrator 3: Lolita's horse starts to fall. Just before she crashes, Zorro catches Lolita in his arms. The two jump to the ground and rush into a nearby tavern with Zorro waving his pistol.

Zorro: Out, everyone!

Narrator 1: The tavern owner and his staff all hurry out into the street. Lolita slams the door shut and bolts it, while Zorro tips over a large table. They push the table up against the door.

Zorro: I fear this may be our end.

Lolita: Surely the saints will save us!

Gonzales: *(Calling from outside, where he stands with the governor.)* I have an offer from His Excellency, the governor. He has no wish to cause your death or to injure the señorita. He asks only that you come out with the lady.

Zorro: Why should we come out?

Gonzales: He says that you shall be given a fair trial—and the Señorita also.

Zorro: Ha! I have seen samples of His Excellency's fair trials.

Gonzales: His Excellency bids me to say that this is your last chance.

Zorro: Tell His Excellency not to waste his breath.

Gonzales: We can batter down the door and take you.

Zorro: Yes, but we may take you down in the process. Who will be the first to try his luck?

Narrator 2: The door begins to shake, as officers throw their bodies against it and strike at it with heavy objects. Soon there is a large crack in the wood.

Narrator 3: Lolita grabs a sharp kitchen knife and thrusts it through the crack. A cry of pain is heard from the other side. Zorro joins in with his sword. Eventually, though, a volley of pistol balls pierces the door, and Lolita and Zorro are forced to back away.

Lolita: It is almost the end, señor.

Zorro: I know, señorita.

Scene 10

Narrator 1: Just then, the other members of Zorro's band ride up to the tavern.

Governor: Ah look! Young men from all the wealthiest families in the area have come to show their loyalty. Thank you, men! But please, just move to the side, and let my troopers deal with this.

Juan: We represent power in this region, do we not?

Governor: Yes, of course.

Martin: You would not wish to stand against us, would you?

Governor: Of course not! But, I pray you, let the troopers get this fellow.

Juan: You don't understand. In recent years, the people of these parts have been robbed, harassed, and imprisoned, simply because they are not friendly to the ruling powers. This must stop.

Martin: And so we have banded together to make sure it stops. You should know that we ourselves rode with Señor Zorro when he invaded the jail and rescued the prisoners.

Governor: *(In a placating tone of voice.)* Gentlemen, gentlemen. Just let me say—

Martin: Silence, until I am done! We stand together, and the strength of our united families is behind us. Command your soldiers to attack us, if you dare.

Governor: Good sirs, of course not! Perhaps I was hasty in the matter of the Pulido family. I promise now that they will receive pardon.

Martin: No, you misunderstand. We also want a complete pardon for Señor Zorro, who has done nothing wrong. And, finally, we ask you to give up your office and title, since your governance is no longer desired in this region.

Narrator 2: The governor pauses for a moment to assess the situation. He realizes that he cannot rule without the support of the influential families represented before him.

Governor: *(Sighing.)* I suppose I have no choice but to submit to your wishes.

Victor: Señor Zorro, Señorita Lolita! Do you hear this man? Open the door and come out.

Narrator 3: Zorro and Lolita cautiously push away the table, pry open the door, and step out to face the crowd.

Governor: Take your mask off, man! I wish to see the face of the man who has cost me so much.

Zorro: Well, all right. But I fear that you will be disappointed when you see my poor features.

Narrator 1: Señor Zorro removes his mask. The crowd gasps. Standing before them is none other than Don Diego Vega. Lolita looks at Don Diego. She laughs and takes his hand in hers.

Lolita: How I misjudged you! How we have all misjudged you! You have revealed your true self to us only when wearing a mask!

The End

The Oblong Box

Edgar Allan Poe

Adapted by Suzanne I. Barchers

Summary

A gentleman books passage on a ship bound for New York City. He is delighted to learn that a college friend, newly married, will be on board. After a delay, the ship departs. The gentleman tries to renew his acquaintance with Mr. Wyatt, privately wondering at the plainness of the bride and speculating on the contents of a long, oblong box Mr. Wyatt keeps in his room. The ship must be abandoned during a storm, and Mr. Wyatt drowns trying to save the oblong box. The gentleman later meets with the captain, who reveals the mystery behind Mr. Wyatt and the oblong box.

Background Information

Edgar Allan Poe was born in Boston on January 19, 1809. His parents were actors, and his father deserted his mother shortly before his birth. Poe's mother died when he was two years old, and the Allans of Richmond, Virginia, adopted him. He traveled with them to England, where they lived for a number of years, returning to America when Poe was eleven. He was a brilliant, defiant student of great athletic and acting ability. He attended the University of Virginia at age seventeen, but by age eighteen he had left school for Boston, where he published his first book of poems. By 1830, he had entered the army, was attending West Point, and had published another collection of verse. After the death of his adoptive mother and his father's remarriage, his relationship with Mr. Allan soured. His writing career blossomed. At twenty-six, he married his fourteen-year-old cousin, Virginia Clemm. In 1842, she nearly died from a burst blood vessel, recovered, but then had repeated similar episodes until she died in 1847. Poe began to drink heavily, finding occasional solace in his work. He died on October 7, 1849. "The Oblong Box" was written in 1844.

Presentation Suggestions

The narrators, the gentleman, and Captain Hardy have primary roles. Consider placing these readers to one side or having the narrators on one side and the gentleman and Captain Hardy on the other side. Marian, Mrs. Wyatt, and Mr. Wyatt can be grouped together. The three ladies can be grouped together.

Props

The stage can have a nautical theme. The characters can dress in clothing appropriate for affluent people of the 1800s.

Characters

- ❀ Narrators 1 and 2
- ❀ Gentleman
- ❀ Hardy, *captain*
- ❀ Marian, *Wyatt's sister*
- ❀ Mrs. Wyatt
- ❀ Ladies 1, 2, and 3
- ❀ Mr. Wyatt

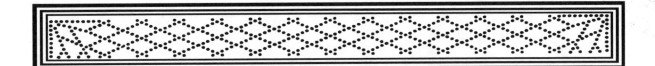

The Oblong Box

Scene 1

Narrator 1: A gentleman engages passage from Charleston, South Carolina, to the city of New York on the *Independence.* The ship is set to sail on the fifteenth of June, weather permitting. On the fourteenth, the gentleman boards the ship to arrange some matters in his stateroom.

Narrator 2: He discovers that among the names of the passenger list there includes Mr. Cornelius Wyatt, a friend and former fellow student at the university. He recalls Cornelius as a moody artist, but one with a warm heart. Mr. Wyatt, traveling with his new wife and two sisters, has reserved three staterooms. The gentleman speculates to himself that the third stateroom must be for excess baggage, and eagerly anticipates meeting Mr. Wyatt's wife, whose beauty and wit Mr. Wyatt has often described. The gentleman speaks to the captain about the Wyatt party.

Gentleman: Good morning, Captain Hardy.

Hardy: Good morning, sir.

Gentleman: I see that Mr. and Mrs. Wyatt will be making the journey with us. I am acquainted with Mr. Wyatt and most anxious to meet his bride.

Hardy: Ah, yes. They were to visit today as well, but Mrs. Wyatt was a little indisposed. They will not board until tomorrow, at our time of sailing.

Gentleman: Then, in that event, I shall see you on the morrow.

Narrator 1: The gentleman returns to his hotel. The next morning as he is leaving the hotel, he happens upon Captain Hardy, who greets him with unwelcome news.

Hardy: Owing to unforeseen circumstances, I'm afraid we won't be sailing this morning, sir.

Gentleman: What circumstances? The weather seems fine. Indeed, there is a stiff southerly breeze.

Hardy: I'm sorry for the inconvenience. I'm not at liberty to discuss the circumstances. I will send word when we are ready to depart. Good day, sir.

Scene 2

Narrator 2: For nearly a week, the gentleman waits impatiently for word. Finally, he is summoned, and he immediately boards the ship. There he finds Mr. Wyatt, who seems distracted and moody. Mr. Wyatt's sister, Marian, introduces the gentleman to Mr. Wyatt's wife.

Marian: If you please, let me introduce you to my new sister-in-law.

Mrs. Wyatt: I am delighted to meet you, sir. Please excuse me, sir. I am going to my stateroom.

Narrator 1: The gentleman watches the party depart, talking quietly to himself.

Gentleman: I am astonished! This bride is quite plain, not the beauty Cornelius led me to expect. She is dressed exquisitely, however. No doubt she has the intelligence and grace to match and that is what captured my friend's heart.

Narrator 2: While the gentleman watches, a cart arrives at the wharf. The cart holds an oblong pine box, about six feet long.

Gentleman: *(To himself.)* That explains the third stateroom. I've heard rumors that Cornelius has been conferring with the Nicolino about acquiring some art. I'll wager he has obtained Nicolino's copy of Leonardo's *Last Supper,* done by Rubini the younger. He's smuggling it to New York, under my very nose! I'll quiz him well on this matter! He can't think he can get away with such a secret!

Narrator 1: The gentleman notes in surprise that the box emits a strong, disagreeable odor and that it is inscribed with the address of Mrs. Adelaide Curtis, who he knows to be the artist's wife's mother. His surprise turns to astonishment when he sees the box delivered to Mr. Wyatt's stateroom instead of to the third stateroom.

Gentleman: *(To himself.)* Perhaps the address is part of the ruse—Cornelius can't bear to have the art out of his sight. Ah, Cornelius.

Narrator 2: The first three or four days of the journey bring fine weather. The passengers are social, except for Mr. Wyatt and his sisters, who behave stiffly. Mr. Wyatt seems morose, and the sisters rarely leave their stateroom. In contrast, Mrs. Wyatt becomes excessively intimate with ladies and amuses the men as well. The ladies find her wanting, however, and soon fall to gossiping about her.

Lady 1: She seems a good-hearted thing, but she is rather plain.

Lady 2: She doesn't seem to have much education. And she is just a bit too flirtatious with the men, for a bride!

Lady 3: Well, *I* think she's vulgar!

Lady 1: *I* heard that she had no dowry.

Lady 2: What could he have seen in her? He seems to be an accomplished gentleman.

Lady 3: Perhaps he has been trapped. She seems just the sort.

Lady 1: Well, there's no doubt that he's her husband. I am so weary of hearing her say "my beloved husband"!

Lady 2: But he hardly acts the husband. He rarely leaves his room, and he seems so sad.

Lady 3: Something isn't right. I can tell.

Narrator 1: The gentleman overhears the gossip and wonders to himself how his friend could have made such a poor match. He also wonders why his friend doesn't tell him about his acquisition of the painting and vows to get his revenge. One day he encounters Mr. Wyatt on deck and seizes the opportunity to visit with him.

Gentleman: *(Jovially.)* Cornelius! Let's walk the deck for a bit. It's a beautiful day at sea, isn't it?

Mr. Wyatt: *(Quietly.)* Yes.

Gentleman: Of course it is. Why, we'll be in New York before we know it! You'll have time to enjoy your new marriage.

Mr. Wyatt: Yes.

Gentleman: And of course you have the *box.* Such a peculiar shape, that box.

Narrator 2: The gentleman winks, smiles knowingly and gently pokes Mr. Wyatt in the ribs. Mr. Wyatt stares at him as if he can't comprehend the gentleman's witticism. Slowly he seems to understand the jest. His eyes grow large, and his face turns red and then pale. He begins to laugh almost hysterically, finally falling in a faint upon the deck.

Narrator 1: The gentleman summons help, and Mr. Wyatt is revived and put to bed. Perplexed, the gentleman resolves to avoid Mr. Wyatt for the rest of the voyage. But sleeplessness keeps him awake for two nights, and he notes Mrs. Wyatt entering the third stateroom alone. He speculates that a divorce may be imminent.

Narrator 2: The gentleman also hears sounds of the lid of the box being disengaged, followed by low sobbing. Some time later, the lid seems to be replaced, with the sounds of nails being forced into their old places.

Scene 3

Narrator 1: The gentleman's speculation on the nature of these events disappears, however, with the onset of a furious gale. On the third day, the storm begins to let up, but the ship has become too damaged to stay afloat.

Narrator 2: The captain loads the crew and passengers into a crowded longboat, preparing to make for shore. Mr. Wyatt boards with his family.

Mr. Wyatt: Captain, you must wait while I get the box.

Hardy: Mr. Wyatt, you can see there is no room.

Mr. Wyatt: I insist! I must have it!

Hardy: Sit down, Mr. Wyatt. You will capsize us if you do not sit quite still.

Mr. Wyatt: The box! The box, I say! Captain Hardy, you cannot, you *will* not refuse me. Its weight will be but a trifle—it is nothing—mere nothing. By the mother who bore you—by your hope of salvation, I *implore* you to go back for the box!

Hardy: Mr. Wyatt, you are mad. I cannot listen to you. Sit down, I say, or you will swamp the boat. Stay—hold him—seize him! He is about to go overboard! There! I knew it! He is over!

Narrator 1: Mr. Wyatt manages to board the wreck and rushes to his cabin. Meanwhile, the heavy seas sweep the longboat away from the ship. The passengers watch as Mr. Wyatt drags the oblong box on deck. He takes a rope, passes it around the box and then around his body. In an instant, both body and box are in the sea, disappearing suddenly, at once and forever. Everyone is silent for a moment. Then the gentleman speaks.

Gentleman: Did you observe, Captain, how suddenly they sank? I confess that I entertained some feeble hope of his final deliverance.

Hardy: They sank like a shot, but they will soon rise again—but not till the salt melts.

Gentleman: The salt!

Hardy: Hush!

Narrator 2: The captain points to the wife and sisters of the deceased.

Hardy: We must talk of these things at some more appropriate time.

Narrator 1: The survivors suffer during four days of intense distress, finally landing upon the beach opposite Roanoke Island. At length they obtain passage to New York.

Scene 4

Narrator 2: A month later, the gentleman happens to meet Captain Hardy on Broadway. Their conversation turns to the disaster.

Gentleman: Captain, can you tell me now about Mr. Wyatt?

Hardy: Yes, I suppose it's time. Tell me what you have deduced.

Gentleman: Wyatt had told me that the woman he was marrying was beautiful. This woman was merely plain, almost common. I couldn't help but notice that she did not stay in his stateroom, but occupied the third one. I thought perhaps a divorce was imminent.

Hardy: Wyatt was telling you the truth. His wife was lovely, and most accomplished. Mr. Wyatt had obtained three rooms—for himself and Mrs. Wyatt, for her two sisters, and for Mrs. Wyatt's lady's maid. The day you visited the ship, June 14, she suddenly sickened and died. The husband was frantic with grief—but circumstances forbade deferring his voyage to New York. It was necessary to take the corpse of his adored wife to her mother. Yet he knew that the passengers would abandon a ship if they knew there was a dead body aboard.

Gentleman: That explains the delay! You were concocting a scheme to get the body on board.

Hardy: Yes, I arranged for the partially embalmed corpse to be packed in a large quantity of salt and to be shipped as merchandise.

Gentleman: So the woman with him was an impersonator.

Hardy: Yes, the third stateroom was for his wife's lady's maid. Wyatt prevailed upon her to act as Mrs. Wyatt, but of course she kept her room, where she slept every night.

Narrator 1: After Captain Hardy leaves, the gentleman ponders the fate of Mr. Wyatt and his oblong box. He recalls his walk on deck with Mr. Wyatt, regretting his inquisitive, impulsive temperament about the contents of the oblong box.

Narrator 2: Years later the gentleman continues to regret his action. He rarely sleeps soundly at night. A countenance haunts him, no matter how he turns in his bed. And an hysterical laugh forever rings in his ears.

The End

Frankenstein

Mary Wollstonecraft Shelley

Adapted by Jennifer L. Kroll

Summary

Captain Robert Walton and his ship's crew are on an expedition to the North Pole, when they spot a huge humanlike creature traveling north on a dogsled. Shortly thereafter, they pull a second sled driver, a sick and dying man, into their ship. This man, Victor Frankenstein, explains that he was pursuing the huge sled driver seen earlier. Captain Walton befriends Frankenstein, who tells his incredible story. The sled driver he has been chasing is actually a monster that Frankenstein created out of reanimated human body parts stolen from graves. Angry with its creator, this monster became dangerous and now must be caught and killed. This script is divided into two parts, which can be performed in two sittings.

Background Information

Frankenstein, or the Modern Prometheus is the most famous novel by English writer Mary Wollstonecraft Shelley, who lived from 1797 to 1851. Shelley was the only child of famous feminist writer Mary Wollstonecraft and William Godwin, a novelist and philosopher. At age sixteen, Mary caused a great scandal when she ran off to live with the twenty-one-year-old poet Percy Bysshe Shelley, who was, at that time, married to another woman. Mary conceived Frankenstein during a famous house party that took place at Lake Geneva in Switzerland. She was only nineteen at the time. Mary and Percy were staying with Lord Byron, the English poet, and some other friends. They all decided to create horror tales and share them with one another. Frankenstein was Mary's tale. After Percy Shelley's early death at age twenty-four, Mary supported herself and their only surviving child by writing. Her later novels include Valpurga (1823) and The Last Man (1826).

Presentation Suggestions

Seat Victor Frankenstein and the Monster in the center. Seat Walton, the Crew Members, and the Narrators in an angled line to one side of them. Seat Henry Clerval, Elizabeth Lavenza, Mr. Frankenstein, Ernest Frankenstein, and the Irish Villager in an angled line to the other side. You may wish to have characters stand when they are interacting. You may wish to have a table set up to one side that can serve as Victor's laboratory table during the laboratory scenes.

Props

Captain Walton and the Crew Members can wear sailor caps. Victor can wear a laboratory coat or handle laboratory equipment such as beakers, vials, and wires—possibly also rubber body parts—during the laboratory scenes. The monster can wear a scary mask of some kind and remove it while speaking.

Characters

- ❀ Narrators 1, 2, and 3
- ❀ Crew Members 1 and 2
- ❀ Robert Walton, a ship captain
- ❀ Victor Frankenstein, a Swiss man of about twenty-four
- ❀ Henry Clerval, Victor Frankenstein's best friend
- ❀ Mr. Frankenstein, Victor's father
- ❀ Ernest Frankenstein, Victor's young brother
- ❀ Elizabeth Lavenza, Victor Frankenstein's fiancée
- ❀ The Monster
- ❀ Irish Villager

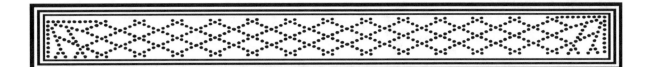

Frankenstein

PART I

Scene 1

Narrator 1: Captain Robert Walton is on his way to explore the North Pole, when his ship becomes surrounded by ice. For days, it scarcely has room to float. The crew members become anxious and frightened. They keep a close lookout for any signs that the ice might be breaking. One day, as Walton and some of his men look out over the frozen plains of ice, they see a strange sight.

Crew Member 1: Look! What's that over there?

Crew Member 2: It looks like someone driving a team of sled dogs.

Crew Member 1: Impossible! We're near the North Pole! Nobody could survive out here.

Crew Member 2: That driver doesn't look like an ordinary man. He's huge!

Crew Member 1: He seems to be traveling north. He's crazy! If we ever get out of this ice, I say we head south immediately.

Crew Member 2: And give up our goal of exploring the North Pole?

Captain Robert Walton: Gentlemen, let me have a look through that telescope.

Narrator 2: As Walton looks through the telescope, the huge sled driver disappears into the distance.

Narrator 3: About two hours later, a loud crunching and cracking noise shakes the boat.

Crew Member 1: Captain! Captain! The ice is breaking! We're free! Should we get the ship moving?

Walton: No. Not yet. It's best to wait until the ice has had a chance to disperse. Tomorrow morning, we'll set off. For now, let's just count our blessings and get some rest.

Narrator 1: The next morning, when Walton goes up on deck, he is surprised to find his crewmen pulling someone into the boat.

Crew Member 2: Look, Captain! It's another sled driver. All his dogs have died, and he's been stranded on a piece of floating ice since yesterday.

Narrator 2: Captain Walton looks at the man being pulled into the boat. Unlike the other driver seen through the telescope, this one seems to be an ordinary man of normal size. He looks to be more dead than alive.

Victor Frankenstein: *(Weakly.)* Before I come on board, you must tell me where you're bound. I'm following someone headed north. Are you going that way? If not, I cannot accept your hospitality.

Walton: Yes, we are headed north. But, sir, I fear you are delirious from cold and hunger, or you wouldn't even consider rejecting our help. You are not likely to find any other help in these parts. *(To the crew.)* Make up a bed for this man immediately!

Scene 2

Narrator 3: In the days to come, Captain Walton befriends the stranger, whose name, it turns out, is Victor Frankenstein. Even after he is warmed, fed, and rested, the stranger remains ill. While lying on his sickbed, he gradually tells Walton his life story.

Victor Frankenstein: I was born in Geneva, Switzerland, and spent my happy childhood in the mountains. Until the age of five, I was an only child. Then, on a trip to Italy, my parents adopted an orphan girl named Elizabeth Lavenza. I loved Elizabeth from the first moment I saw her. It was always understood, within our family, that Elizabeth and I would marry one day.

Walton: And did you?

Victor Frankenstein: That, my friend, is a later chapter in my story. I must tell you first about the events that sealed my fate and made me the most unfortunate of men alive. Mine is a long and horrifying tale. Are you sure you wish to hear it?

Walton: My friend, I am most curious to learn about the events leading up to our strange meeting. Please continue, if you are feeling strong enough.

Victor Frankenstein: Very well, then. When I was seventeen, my parents decided to send me to a university in Germany. Just before I was to leave, the first great catastrophe of my life occurred. My mother died of scarlet fever. On her deathbed, she joined my hand in Elizabeth's and reminded us that it was her dearest wish for us to marry. She begged Elizabeth to look after my father and two younger brothers.

Narrator 1: Frankenstein reaches weakly for a drink of water, takes a sip, and continues.

Victor Frankenstein: So, with a heart full of sorrow, I left for Germany and the university. I was sad, yet happy to go. I was still mourning the death of my mother and found it difficult to leave behind Elizabeth, my father, brothers, and my best friend, Henry Clerval. Yet I had always been highly interested in science, and I was excited about the opportunity to pursue my studies in depth.

Walton: What area of science was your special interest?

Victor Frankenstein: I was fascinated by the workings of the body, and my dearest wish was to someday fully understand the source of human life—an ambitious goal! For my first two years at the university, I attended lectures and met with professors. It eventually became clear to me that this approach was not helping me to gain the knowledge I sought. So I stopped attending lectures and meeting with my professors.

Walton: Did you leave the university?

Victor Frankenstein: Not officially, but I isolated myself from everyone there and continued my studies and experiments on my own. I was determined to achieve my goal—to gain an understanding of the very cause of life. I tried to learn everything that I could about the physical body. I studied bone structure, the internal organs, and the human brain. In fact, I even went to graveyards at night in order to examine the corpses. I sneaked into the mortuary to look at the corpses of the newly dead. I watched the changes a body goes through as life seeps out of it.

Narrator 2: Walton shivers in horror.

Walton: Weren't you afraid to go to cemeteries and mortuaries at night?

Victor Frankenstein: As children, our father did not let us hear tales of the supernatural. He tried to keep us from becoming superstitious. So you see, dead bodies were not frightening to me—merely interesting. I was full of enthusiasm for my studies and obsessed with the thought of attaining my goal. Nothing could hold me back.

Walton: Did you learn anything from your studies of the dead?

Victor Frankenstein: I did. In fact, I discovered the very thing I sought. I came eventually to understand the secret of life and death.

Narrator 3: Walton looks at Frankenstein with an expression of disbelief.

Victor Frankenstein: You think I am mad! But what I'm telling you is true! After days and nights of incredible labor and sleeplessness, I discovered the source of life. In fact, I became capable of giving life to lifeless matter.

Walton: How? What—

Victor Frankenstein: I will not tell you in detail just what my discovery was. As I relate the rest of my tale, it will become obvious to you why I am taking that secret to my grave. I will only tell you what I did, not how I did it. What I did was this: I set out to create a human form out of dead body parts, and to reanimate that form . . .

Narrator 1: As Victor Frankenstein tells his tale of horror, its scenes come to life for Captain Walton.

Scene 3

Narrator 2: It is a rainy night. Twenty-year-old Victor Frankenstein stands in his dimly lit laboratory an apartment on the top floor of an old house in Germany. Around him are electrical instruments, beakers of chemicals, and containers filled with various body parts. More body parts are strewn around the room. Frankenstein looks pale and thin. Dark circles ring his eyes.

Victor Frankenstein: The time has come. My creation is ready to come to life.

Narrator 3: On the table in the center of the laboratory lies a body. It is actually not one body, but a collection of parts from different bodies all assembled together. Frankenstein gathers his electrical instruments around himself and begins to perform a procedure. He stares down at the unmoving body.

Victor Frankenstein: Nothing! He's not moving. What am I doing wrong?

Narrator 1: Suddenly, Frankenstein sees one dull yellow eye of the creature open. He notices that the creature has begun to breathe. Its limbs twitch.

Victor Frankenstein: He's alive! I've done it!

Narrator 2: Frankenstein looks down again at the body on the table—now a living, breathing thing. He suddenly feels repulsed by it. He sees how its yellow skin barely covers the muscles and veins underneath.

Narrator 3: The creature stares up at its creator with watery yellow eyes. It reaches a hand toward Frankenstein. With a gasp of horror, Frankenstein runs from the laboratory and out of the house. Shaking uncontrollably with fright, he wanders the town all night, trying to avoid returning home.

Scene 4

Narrator 1: The next morning, as Frankenstein is walking the streets, he chances upon the familiar figure of his best friend from home, Henry Clerval.

Henry Clerval: My friend! How lucky to bump into you! I've only just arrived in town.

Narrator 2: Clerval notices that Frankenstein looks pale and ill and shaky.

Henry: For heaven's sake, what's the matter? What's happened to you? I suspected that something was wrong when no letters came from you in such a long time. We've all been very worried—especially Elizabeth. She misses you terribly.

Victor Frankenstein: I'm sorry not to have written more often. The truth is that lately I've been so deeply engrossed in a project that I haven't allowed myself much sleep. I have no intention of working on that project any more, however.

Henry: You look like you're about to collapse. Why don't we go back to your apartment?

Narrator 3: Victor begins leading his friend back to the building where he lives. When they reach the stairs, he suddenly thinks of the monster and panics.

Victor Frankenstein: Wait here. Don't come up for a moment, Henry. I have to check on something.

Narrator 1: Victor dashes up the stairs. His heart races as he slowly turns the knob to his apartment door.

Narrator 2: Nothing happens. The apartment is empty. Frankenstein rushes around checking every corner but can find no sign of the monster. He is overwhelmed with relief and darts back down the stairs with a crazed smile on his face.

Victor Frankenstein: *(Excitedly.)* Come up, my friend! Come in!

Narrator 3: Once in his apartment, he begins leaping around wildly. He laughs strangely.

Henry: What's gotten into you? You're scaring me, Victor.

Narrator 1: Suddenly, glancing out the window, he thinks he catches a glimpse of the monster. He sinks to the ground, shaking in fear and covering his eyes.

Victor Frankenstein: Save me, Henry! Save me!

Narrator 2: Frankenstein passes out on the floor, ill and exhausted. Several weeks go by before he is fully aware of his surroundings again. In the meantime, Henry cares for his sick friend.

Scene 5

Narrator 3: Once Frankenstein is again well, the two old friends enjoy the rest of their year together at the university. They attend lectures, talk about books, and hike in the nearby fields and forests.

Narrator 1: Frankenstein abandons his scientific studies. Instead, he takes courses on subjects of interest to Henry, like languages and literature. For a while, Victor is happy. Then, in late spring, he receives terrible news in a letter from home.

Mr. Frankenstein: My dear Victor, I am so sorry that I must write you with this terrible news. Your little brother William is dead. He has been murdered. Last Thursday evening, Elizabeth, the boys, and myself all went out for a picnic near the woods. The two boys ran off to play together, but at the end of the day, only Ernest returned. He told us that William had gone to hide during a game of hide-and-seek but then hadn't come back. We searched all night by the light of torches. At about five the next morning, I found William's body down by the river's edge. He was stretched out on the grass, dead. The bruises of his murderer's fingers were on his neck. Please come home, Victor! Elizabeth is in agony. Only you can comfort her. We all need you right now.

Narrator 2: The letter is signed "Your loving father." Frankenstein immediately packs his bags and sets off on a journey home to the Swiss Alps. As he nears his father's house, he stops off at the spot where he knows his brother to have been murdered.

Narrator 3: It is a stormy night. Lightning flashes across the sky, and thunder echoes through the mountains. At the riverbank where his dead brother once lay, Frankenstein breaks down in tears.

Victor Frankenstein: William, my brother. You were an angel! Who could have done such a thing?

Narrator 1: As he speaks these words aloud, Frankenstein sees a huge, twisted figure moving among the trees nearby. He stands frozen in terror. A sudden flash of lightning reveals the identity of the figure. It is the monster.

Narrator 2: When the next lightning flash comes, the monster has disappeared.

Victor Frankenstein: *(To himself.)* I see it now! William's death is my own fault! I have loosed an evil creature into the world, and it has murdered my brother!

Narrator 3: Feeling total horror, Frankenstein turns away from the river and heads home. It's early morning before he reaches the door of his father's house. Ernest, Frankenstein's younger brother, opens the door.

Ernest Frankenstein: Victor! You're here! Thank goodness!

Narrator 1: The two brothers hug each other.

Ernest: I have more news to tell you. They've found William's murderer, but the news brings us no joy.

Victor Frankenstein: Found his murderer?! Who has been able to follow him across the Alps?

Ernest: Follow him across the Alps? What are you talking about? The murderer is none other than our servant Justine.

Victor Frankenstein: Justine! No! Impossible! Who would ever believe that sweet girl to be capable of such a crime? Why is she being blamed?

Ernest: On the night of William's murder, she disappeared. She didn't come back until the next morning. Then, Mother's locket was found in her pocket. William had been wearing it when he was murdered. All the evidence seemed to point to Justine, so she was arrested. Her trial is today.

Narrator 2: Frankenstein's father enters the room.

Mr. Frankenstein: Victor! Thank goodness you are home.

Victor Frankenstein: Father!

Narrator 3: They hug each other.

Victor Frankenstein: Father, there's been a terrible mistake. Justine is not William's murderer!

Mr. Frankenstein: I wish I could believe that was true. It breaks my heart to think that Justine could have done something so horrible.

Victor Frankenstein: But she hasn't! She's innocent.

Mr. Frankenstein: If she is, as you say, let's pray that they don't convict her today. Her very life is at stake.

Narrator 1: Elizabeth Lavenza, Frankenstein's fiancée, enters the room. Victor has not seen her in a long while and rushes to embrace her.

Elizabeth Lavenza: Victor! Perhaps you can find some way to prove the innocence of poor Justine. Alas! Who is safe, if that sweet girl can be convicted of such a crime?

Victor Frankenstein: I'm sure she will be acquitted, dear Elizabeth.

Narrator 2: Unfortunately, Victor is wrong. Later that day, the court finds Justine guilty of William's murder. The turning point of the trial occurs when Justine cannot come up with an explanation for her possession of the locket. The jury gives Justine the death penalty. She is put to death the following morning.

Scene 6

Narrator 3: Elizabeth and the Frankensteins are stunned and grief-stricken. Victor, of course, is the most tormented of all.

Victor Frankenstein: *(To himself.)* That poor girl! And my darling William! I caused both of their deaths when I created that brute! I am their murderer! And where will it all stop? Who else will die at the hands of my creation? What am I going to do?

Narrator 1: Day and night, Victor weeps bitterly. He refuses to eat and grows pale and thin.

Elizabeth: Victor, you must eat something. You're wasting away! And you must stop dwelling on these horrors. Get outside. Get some sunshine. I'm very worried about you.

Victor Frankenstein: Perhaps I will go out and take a hike up the mountain. I always find that calming.

Elizabeth: Yes. That's an excellent idea.

Narrator 2: Victor heads out into the sunshine. He begins hiking up a trail that winds around Mount Blanc, the tallest peak in Europe. As the hours pass, he feels his grief and anxiety falling away. For the first time in weeks, Victor begins to feel something like joy.

Narrator 3: Then, suddenly, he catches a glimpse of a figure jumping across rocks in the distance. He notices that this person seems to be strangely tall and moving at a superhuman speed. As the figure comes closer and closer, Victor recognizes the monster.

Victor Frankenstein: *(In a raised voice, to the monster.)* Devil! How do you dare to approach me after what you've done? Aren't you afraid of what I might do to you? Be gone! Or, rather, stay, that I might stamp out your life! I only wish that by killing you I could bring back to life the victims you have murdered!

Narrator 1: The monster looks at Victor with a mocking smile.

Monster: I expected you to greet me this way. Everybody hates the miserable, and I am more ugly and lonely and miserable than any other living thing. Yet you, of all people, should treat me better. You created me—and now you say you're going to kill me. You've got such nerve, toying with life this way.

Victor Frankenstein: You horrible monster! Why are you here? What new crimes are you planning?

Monster: If you do your duty toward me, I promise to commit no more crimes. But if you refuse to agree to my conditions, I will make the rest of your life pure misery.

Victor Frankenstein: You fiend! I will take away the life I never should have given you!

Narrator 2: In a fury of hatred and anger, Frankenstein leaps toward the monster. The monster steps to one side, easily avoiding the attack.

Monster: Be calm and listen to what I have to say, before you go attacking me! It's foolishness, anyhow, to think you can hurt me. You made me bigger and stronger than yourself. I am more agile and quicker, too.

Narrator 3: Frankenstein takes another swing at the monster, who ducks out of the way.

Monster: Besides, I don't want to fight with you. You are my creator, and I would like to be able to treat you with respect. I don't want to be this horrible brute I've become. I want to be virtuous. And to make me virtuous, all you need to do is to be my friend and make me happy.

Victor Frankenstein: You and I can never be friends! We are enemies!

Narrator 1: The monster ignores Frankenstein and continues.

Monster: All around me, I see happy people, happy creatures. It seems that I alone am denied happiness. Everyone hates and fears me. They all think I'm hideous and dangerous. Frankenstein, when you made me I was good, not evil. My soul was full of love. It is loneliness and abuse that have made me as I now am. Listen to my story! I beg you! Then you will understand.

Victor Frankenstein: I curse these hands that made you!

Monster: Both of our futures are in those hands of yours. Please! Just listen to my story and my proposal.

Narrator 2: Victor gives in.

Victor Frankenstein: All right, then. I will hear your story.

Narrator 3: Victor follows the monster across ice and rocks to a cave. There the monster lights a fire and begins to tell his tale.

PART II

Scene 1

Monster: Frankenstein, what can I tell you about the early weeks and months of my existence? I put on some clothes before leaving your apartment. Still, I was cold, for the weather was harsh. And I knew nothing of the world I had entered.

Narrator 1: As Victor listens, the monster goes on to describe how he learned about day and night, hunger and thirst. He explains how he discovered that fire could keep him warm and that berries and roots could help to satisfy his hunger.

Monster: After wandering for many days, I came to a village. I smelled food cooking in a cottage. Since I was hungry, I went inside. As soon as I'd stepped through the doorway, though, the children in the cottage began to scream and one of the women fainted.

Narrator 2: The monster's eyes show great pain as he describes what happened next.

Monster: Then the rest of the villagers came running. Many of them shrieked when they saw me. Some threw rocks at me and hit me with sticks. I was forced to flee for my life.

Narrator 3: The monster explains how several days later he came upon an isolated cottage at the edge of a forest. Finding a low wooden shed at the back of a cottage, he crawled inside to escape from the cold and snow. To his delight, he discovered that a chimney made up the back wall of the shed, keeping it warm.

Monster: During all that winter, I continued to live in this shed, hiding myself from the cottage's inhabitants. Only at night did I come out to find food. During the day, I was able to watch the cottagers through cracks in the back wall of the shed. After watching these people for many weeks, they began to seem like friends to me. I started to think of the three cottagers—a blind old man and his grown son and daughter—as my family.

Narrator 1: The monster explains how he learned what a "family" is and what "love" is by watching the cottagers. After some time, he began to realize that despite their love for one another, these people were not altogether happy.

Monster: At first, I could not imagine why they weren't happy. They seemed to have everything in the world, to me. Eventually, I figured out that one of the reasons for their unhappiness was that they did not have enough food. This made me feel terrible. You see, I had been stealing part of their food during each night. After I realized that I was hurting my family, I stopped stealing their food. I vowed to live only on the berries, nuts, and roots that I could find.

Narrator 2: Victor Frankenstein listens in astonishment as the monster continues describing his experience with the cottagers.

Monster: I decided to try to help my family in another way as well. I began to cut firewood for them each night. I took the young man's tools and went into the woods. The first time I did this, my people were so surprised! The young man and woman stood staring at the giant pile of firewood. They thought they'd experienced a miracle.

Narrator 3: The monster explains how he eventually came to understand the language of the cottagers.

Monster: It didn't take me long to figure out what some words meant. I learned "fire," "milk," "bread," and "wood" very quickly. I also learned the names of the family members. The old man was always called "father." The girl's name was "sister," "daughter," or "Agatha." The man was "brother," "son," or "Felix." Most of my knowledge of their language I learned later, though, when a fourth family member arrived.

Narrator 1: The monster describes how, one day in spring, a beautiful woman rode up to the cottage on horseback. The cottager named Felix seemed overjoyed at her arrival. He hugged and kissed the woman many times.

Monster: I discovered that this new young woman's name was Safie. I also quickly figured out that the language she spoke was not the same one my family used.

Victor Frankenstein: So who was this Safie and where had she come from?

Monster: I eventually pieced together the story of Safie and her connection to the other cottagers. The cottage family had once lived in Paris. There, they had been wealthy. And there, Felix had met the visiting Arabian woman, Safie, and fallen in love with her. Political troubles had driven the family away from Paris, separating Felix and Safie.

Victor Frankenstein: How did the Arabian woman communicate with the other cottagers, if she didn't speak their language?

Monster: The night after her arrival, Felix began to teach this new woman his language. I listened very carefully. In the days that followed, I learned the language along with Safie. With her, I also learned about letters and writing.

Narrator 2: The monster explains how, as Safie learned to read books, he learned with her. Through the books Safie read, he learned all about history and geography, about kings and heroes, and about government and religion.

Monster: And the more I learned about human beings, the clearer it became just how separated I am from every other human being on Earth. I am ugly and deformed. I have no mother, no father, no friends, and no family. I never had a childhood. I had no past before you created me.

Narrator 3: Suddenly full of guilt and shame, Victor Frankenstein puts his head in his hands. The monster continues his tale.

Monster: One night while I was looking for food in the forest, I stumbled onto a suitcase that had been lost. Back in my shed, I examined its contents. I found it held some clothes and three books. I dressed in the clothes and eagerly began to read the books. Through them, I learned much about the world I lived in. I came to love goodness and hate evil.

Narrator 1: Frankenstein keeps his face buried in his hands.

Monster: Another book I found at the same time also changed my life. You see—when I took off the clothes I'd been wearing—ones I got from your apartment—I discovered a diary in the pocket of your jacket. That was your diary, Victor Frankenstein. In it you had written a day-by-day account of my creation.

Narrator 2: Victor looks up with fearful eyes.

Monster: What I read sickened me. I began to feel anger toward you, my creator, for the first time. You had made me different than all others—doomed to be alone. One day, I saw my reflection in a pool of water. I was horrified at what I saw. I understood then why people fear and hate me. But still I hoped that my cottage friends might be different. I dreamed of coming out of hiding and introducing myself to them.

Narrator 3: The monster explains how he waited for a time when the young people were all gone, and only the blind old man was sitting in the cottage.

Monster: I fearfully went to the door of the cottage and knocked. The old man came to the door. "Please," I said. "I am cold and tired. I would be grateful if you'd let me sit and rest with you for a moment." "Of course. Come in and sit by the fire," the old man said. I assured the old man that I meant no harm and only sought friendship. I explained that people often fear me, despite my gentle nature. "I believe you have a strange story to tell," the old man said to me. He asked if he could hear my story. "Maybe I can help you," he said.

Narrator 1: The monster's eyes sadden as he tells what happened next.

Monster: But before I could tell the old man my story, I heard Felix, Agatha, and Safie outside. I knew I didn't have any time to lose. I threw myself at the old man's feet. I begged him to help me, to save me. But the cottage door opened before he could reply. The young people entered.

Victor Frankenstein: What did they do?

Monster: Agatha fainted. Safie screamed and ran back out again. Felix ripped me away from the old man's knees. Somehow, he managed to throw me down to the ground. Then, he began to beat me with a stick. I ran from the cottage and hid in my shed.

Victor Frankenstein: And did you try to speak with the old man again, later?

Monster: I never had the chance. By the next morning, the family had fled from the cottage, taking all their possessions with them. I never saw my beloved family again.

Narrator 3: Victor finds himself feeling intense pity for the monster.

Monster: My heart was broken. I had no place to go and didn't know what to do. And it was then that I decided to try to find you—my creator. I decided to demand justice from you, to make you pay for what you had done to me. I decided to begin looking for you in Geneva, the city you had named as your home in your diary.

Narrator 1: The monster describes his journey to Geneva. He explains how he traveled at night, purposely staying away from all towns and people.

Monster: But, one day, as I was hiding in the woods, a girl came running past me, then slipped and fell into a raging stream. I rushed from my hiding place and jumped into the water to help her. After struggling against the current, I managed to get her safely to shore. But would I be thanked for saving her life?

Narrator 2: The monster scowls.

Monster: Of course not. As I pulled the girl out of the water, a man ran up to me. He tore the child from my arms. Then he shot me with a gun and ran off.

Victor Frankenstein: Were you badly wounded?

Monster: Yes. I was in great pain. I lay there for days, miserable and bleeding. It took weeks before I was able to walk again. During the time when I was recovering, my anger grew greater and greater. I was more determined than ever to find you.

Narrator 3: The monster describes his continued journey to Geneva.

Monster: Finally, one evening, I stood at the edge of a forest, looking down at the city of Geneva. As I stood there, a beautiful child ran out of the woods toward me. He was very young, and I thought to myself, "Perhaps this child is so young that he has not yet learned to be afraid of ugliness. Perhaps he will talk to me." I caught the boy's arm as he ran past. "Child," I said, "talk to me. I won't hurt you."

Narrator 1: Victor shudders and turns very white as he listens to what happened next.

Monster: The boy began to scream and shout. "Let me go!" he yelled. "Let me go you ugly monster!" He told me that his name was Frankenstein and that his father was an important man in Geneva. "My father will kill you!" he screamed.

Narrator 2: The monster describes how the boy struggled in his arms and called him names.

Monster: He demanded to be released. But I had found a member of the Frankenstein family, and I was not about to let him go. I grabbed the boy's throat to silence him. I hadn't meant to kill the boy, but I suddenly found him dead in my arms.

Narrator 3: Victor stares at the monster in horror.

Monster: I looked at the dead boy. And, instead of sorrow, I began to feel joy. I hoped that the death of this boy would cause you as much pain as you have caused me. Then I noticed that the boy had a locket around his neck.

Victor Frankenstein: My mother's locket! What did you do, you brute?

Monster: I left the dead boy and wandered along the river. Soon I came to a barn. A woman was sleeping on the straw. She was young and beautiful. Seeing her there made me feel angry because I knew she would run screaming from me, if she were awake. I decided to make this girl pay for all the women who had looked on my face in horror. I placed the locket in the pocket of her jacket, framing her for the murder of the Frankenstein boy. Then I fled from the barn.

Narrator 1: The monster describes how, after that time, he remained in the mountains above the Frankenstein home, waiting for the chance to meet his creator.

Monster: Now I have found you, and now I demand justice! I am lonely and miserable. No human being—or any creature—wants my company. Here is what you must do for me, Victor Frankenstein. You must make a female just as ugly and deformed as I am. I demand that you provide me with a companion. It's my right to have one!

Victor Frankenstein: Never! No amount of torture could ever make me agree to that! Am I supposed to make another monster like yourself so that both of you can run through the world together, destroying it? My final answer is no! Now be gone, murderer!

Monster: You call me a murderer. Yet, at this very moment, you wish you could kill me. If you killed me right now, would you call that murder? In killing humans, I have only done to others what they wish to do—what they try to do—to me. Make me a companion—make me happy—and I assure you that I will never kill again. But if you deny me all friendship, I promise that I will make your life as miserable as my own.

Narrator 2: Victor Frankenstein pales in terror at the monster's words.

Monster: I only want that which every other creature has. Just make me a companion, and I swear you will never see either of us again. We will go live together in the wilderness of South America.

Narrator 3: After much debate, Frankenstein finally consents to the monster's plan.

Victor Frankenstein: All right—I will make you this female companion.

Monster: Very well, then. I will stay out of sight, but I will be watching you until you finish the task. When my companion is ready, I will come to you.

Scene 2

Narrator 1: Weeks go by. Although he is afraid to face the monster's anger, he puts off creating the female companion. He thinks that before creating another creature, he had better learn more about what he's doing. He considers taking a trip to England to study some recent discoveries made there.

Narrator 2: In the meantime, Victor, Elizabeth, and the other Frankensteins take walks in the mountains and trips out onto a nearby lake in a rowboat. It seems to all the others that Victor's depression is finally lifting.

Mr. Frankenstein: Victor, it is good to see your spirits so much improved. Perhaps this would be a good time for you and Elizabeth to finally wed. It was your mother's dearest wish and now is mine as well. Seeing the two of you married will be a great comfort to me in my old age. Of course, I don't want to push you into anything that you do not wish to do.

Victor Frankenstein: Father, don't worry. Of course I still wish to marry Elizabeth. There's not another woman in the world whom I could love as I love her. But there's something I need, or rather, want to do before I marry her.

Mr. Frankenstein: And what could that be, my son?

Victor Frankenstein: I want to take a trip to England.

Mr. Frankenstein: A trip? Of course. It is good for a young man to see something of the world before he marries. But I worry about your health and state of mind. I would feel much better if somebody were to go to England with you. Perhaps your friend Henry?

Narrator 3: Victor at first argues that he must travel alone but eventually gives in and agrees to bring Henry along on his trip to England.

Scene 3

Narrator 1: Once in London, Victor studies and collects laboratory materials. Henry is usually left to tour the city alone. After several months, Victor has collected all the materials needed to begin work on the new creature.

Narrator 2: At about that time, the two men receive an invitation to visit friends in Scotland.

Victor Frankenstein: *(To himself.)* Excellent! Scotland is such a sparsely populated place. I'll be able to find just the perfect location for a new laboratory.

Narrator 3: Once the two men arrive in Scotland, Victor abandons Henry to find a new laboratory space and sets to work on the second monster.

Victor Frankenstein: I'm going to leave you for a little while, Henry. Have a good time with our friends. When I come back, I promise to do some serious sightseeing with you.

Henry: If you feel you must be alone for a while, I understand. Just make sure that you come back happy, healthy, and well rested.

Narrator 1: Victor finds the ideal spot for a new laboratory on an isolated island off the coast of Scotland. Only a few people live there. He rents a small hut, and sets to work to create a mate for his monster.

Narrator 2: He works hard day and night to complete the task. He doesn't allow himself time to think about what the consequences of his actions might be. Only when the new, female creature is nearly complete, does he finally begin to consider this.

Victor Frankenstein: *(To himself.)* What am I doing? I don't have any idea what this new creature will be like. What if she's much more evil and dangerous than the first monster? What if she hates the other monster and refuses to have anything to do with him? He's promised to take her to the wilderness of South America, but what if she refuses to go?

Narrator 3: And, finally, the worst thought of all occurs to him.

Victor Frankenstein: *(To himself.)* What if they have children? What if I'm creating a whole race of monsters that will bring destruction, pain, and terror to human beings for centuries to come? Can I possibly take this chance? Am I buying my own peace at the risk of the whole human race?

Narrator 1: Victor paces back and forth in front of his laboratory table. He debates with himself about whether to continue his work. Suddenly, glancing up and out the hut's window, he catches a glimpse of the monster, watching him and smiling. Its smile looks hideous and disgusting to Victor. He shudders.

Victor Frankenstein: *(To himself.)* It's followed me here! The disgusting brute! That smile—it looks so evil! How can I ever even consider giving life to another creature like that one?

Narrator 2: Victor looks down at the nearly completed body of the female monster lying on his laboratory table. He comes to a decision. He begins to tear the body on the table into little pieces. As he does, the door of his hut flies open and the monster rushes in, howling with rage and pain.

Monster: What are you doing? Do you dare to break your promise?

Victor Frankenstein: Yes, I do! I will never create another monster like you!

Monster: I have tried to reason with you. Now, I find that I must threaten you. I have power over you, Victor Frankenstein. I can make you so miserable that you hate the very light of day!

Victor Frankenstein: Your threats can have no effect on me. I have made my decision. I cannot turn a race of demons loose on the earth. Be gone from here!

Monster: But it's not right! Every creature has a mate. I am the only one who is forced to be completely alone! You are taking away the last possibility of my happiness. With no hope of happiness, all that remains is for me to seek revenge!

Victor Frankenstein: No matter how you threaten me, my decision is final. Be gone!

Monster: Very well. I'm going. But remember—I shall be with you on your wedding night!

Scene 4

Narrator 3: In a rush, the monster is gone. All that night, Victor Frankenstein tosses and turns, thinking about the monster's words.

Victor Frankenstein: *(To himself.)* He said that he would be with me on my wedding night. So that's when he is going to kill me. But I'll be ready for him! I'm not going to die without a struggle!

Narrator 1: In the morning, Victor abandons his laboratory hut and leaves the island in a small boat. The ocean is rough, and his boat is tossed and blown off course. Eventually, it comes to land, but in an unfamiliar place. As his boat comes ashore, a group of people rush down to the beach from a nearby village.

Victor Frankenstein: My good friends—will you be so kind as to tell me the name of this town?

Irish Villager: *(Rudely.)* You will know soon enough.

Narrator 2: Victor is surprised by the looks of anger he sees in the villager's faces. Two of the men grab him roughly by the arms and begin forcing him to walk.

Victor Frankenstein: *(Alarmed.)* Where are we going?

Villager: We are taking you to see the judge. You will tell him what you know about a man who was found murdered here last night.

Victor Frankenstein: I wasn't even here last night! This is all a big mix up. But I'm sure we will get it sorted out shortly.

Narrator 3: Victor is taken into a sort of police station. Accompanied by a judge, he is brought to a room where a dead body lies in a coffin on a table. Victor feels suddenly sick to his stomach as he recognizes the dead man.

Victor Frankenstein: Henry! Henry Clerval! My dear friend! No! It's not possible! That evil brute of a monster! No! Henry can't be dead!

Narrator 1: Victor collapses and is carried from the room in convulsions. For nearly two months afterward, he remains very sick with a high fever. He is delirious and doesn't recognize what's going on around him. Then, one day, he finally comes out of his delirious state and finds his father sitting near his bed.

Victor Frankenstein: Oh, Father! You are safe! And Elizabeth and Ernest? Are they safe also?

Mr. Frankenstein: Yes, yes. They're fine. I left them in Geneva.

Victor Frankenstein: Oh thank heavens! Let's go to them immediately!

Mr. Frankenstein: We cannot, son. Your troubles here are not over. You are in an Irish prison. You have been here for two months. The people here believe that you are Henry's murderer. They have been waiting for you to come out of your delirium so that your trial can begin.

Scene 5

Narrator 2: Fortunately for Victor, he is not convicted of the murder. An eyewitness comes forward who remembers watching Victor board the boat. It is thus proven that he could not have been in Ireland at the time of the murder.

Narrator 3: As Victor and his father head home after the ordeal of the trial, Mr. Frankenstein continues to push for a speedy wedding with Elizabeth. At the same time, Victor continues to be haunted by the monster's words: "I will be with you on your wedding night."

Victor Frankenstein: *(To himself.)* At least I know his plan! The monster intends to wait until a moment when I am completely happy. Then, he will try to kill me. But I will be ready for him! And if I can kill him first, I'll be a free man!

Narrator 1: When Victor and Mr. Frankenstein arrive in Geneva they are welcomed by Elizabeth and Ernest.

Elizabeth: Oh, thank goodness! I've been sick with worry! Victor, you look so pale and thin! But all will be well now. We will be married, and I will look after you. You will find happiness and contentment at last.

Victor Frankenstein: My dear Elizabeth—you are too kind to me. I only wish I were worthy of your love and devotion.

Elizabeth: But of course you are worthy of it, my dear!

Narrator 2: Still mulling the monster's threat, Victor goes ahead and sets a date for his wedding during the days to come.

Victor Frankenstein: *(To himself.)* I'm not sure this is the right thing to do—marrying Elizabeth. If the monster kills me on our wedding night, she will be devastated. But I can't leave her again. I want to be with her. And maybe I can beat the monster.

Narrator 3: Victor and Elizabeth decide that on their wedding night, they'll go to a little cottage on the edge of Lake Como. In preparation for his showdown with the monster, Victor buys a gun but keeps his ownership of it secret. He begins to carry it with him everywhere.

Narrator 1: The wedding is a joyful occasion. Many people gather at the Frankenstein home for the wedding reception. It is after sundown by the time Elizabeth and Victor leave the house and set out for the cottage on the lake.

Narrator 2: As they enter the cottage, drops of rain begin to fall. Soon, the rain is coming down in sheets. Thunder growls in the distance. Victor paces the cottage.

Elizabeth: What's the matter Victor? Your hands are shaking. Tell me what it is that frightens you.

Victor Frankenstein: Shh. Don't worry, my love. After tonight, all will be safe. Go to bed now. I am going to sit up awhile.

Elizabeth: All right, then. But don't stay up too late.

Narrator 3: Once Elizabeth has gone to bed, Victor begins checking in every corner of the house for the monster.

Victor Frankenstein: *(Muttering to himself.)* Where is he hiding? Where is he? Can something have prevented him from coming?

Narrator 1: Suddenly, Victor hears a piercing shriek coming from the bedroom. He rushes in. Across the bed Elizabeth lies dead. Victor can see the marks of the monster's fingerprints on her neck. He runs to the body and lifts it in his arms.

Victor Frankenstein: Elizabeth! Oh no! Please! Speak to me!

Narrator 2: Victor's eyes stray over to an open window as a flash of lightning illuminates the grinning figure of the monster standing just outside.

Narrator 3: Victor immediately jumps up from the bed, grabbing his pistol from his coat. He fires out the window after the monster, but misses. The monster sprints toward the lake. Before he jumps into the water and swims away, he cries out over his shoulder.

Monster: I am satisfied, my creator. You, too, now live in misery, and I am satisfied!

Narrator 1: With a terrible-sounding laugh, the monster disappears.

Scene 6

Narrator 2: Back on the ship in the Arctic waters, the sick and dying Victor Frankenstein finishes telling his story to Captain Walton.

Victor Frankenstein: That is the end of my story. It has been months since Elizabeth's death, and I have followed the monster through Europe, across the Black Sea, through Russia, and finally here to the arctic. He continues to escape me. The day I came aboard your ship, I was very close to catching him. I saw him not more than a mile ahead of me. But then the ice broke and I was left floating while he escaped yet again.

Narrator 3: Victor looks up weakly at Captain Walton.

Victor Frankenstein: And what will happen now? I know that I will never leave this ship alive. Must I die while he still continues to live?

Walton: You are not going to die, my friend. Don't speak that way.

Narrator 1: But Walton knows that Victor is very close to death. He watches the dying man lean back and fall asleep. In his sleep, Victor calls out the names of dead loved ones.

Victor Frankenstein: Elizabeth! William! Henry!

Narrator 2: Victor's breathing slows and then stops. With tears in his eyes, Walton heads out onto the deck of the ship for some air.

Walton: *(To himself.)* At least death will finally bring peace to that poor man.

Narrator 3: After he calms himself in the cold wind, Walton returns to the bedchamber of the dead Victor Frankenstein. There, a terrifying surprise awaits him. By the dead man's bed stands the monster. As soon as it spots Walton, it immediately springs toward a window.

Walton: Wait! Don't run away so quickly! I mean you no harm.

Narrator 1: The monster stops in his tracks. Walton takes a good look at it. He shivers.

Walton: My friend told the truth when he spoke of you.

Monster: *(To Walton.)* He told you our sorry tale, then? *(To the dead body of Victor.)* Oh, Frankenstein! My last victim! I wished to ask you to pardon me for my sins, but it is too late.

Narrator 2: The monster's voice sounds full of tears.

Walton: If you had repented of your crimes earlier, Frankenstein might still be alive.

Narrator 3: The monster nods his head sadly.

Monster: How he hated me! But he didn't hate me more than I hate myself. Do you think the cries of those I killed were music to my ears? They were torment. They haunt me still.

Narrator 1: The monster sighs deeply.

Monster: Once I hoped to find people who would overlook my ugly appearance, but the good in me was destroyed by the cruelty and prejudice of human beings. I longed for love and friendship, but instead I was despised and rejected. Even now my heart fills with anger when I think of the cruelty and injustice of this world.

Narrator 2: A frightening, angry look crosses the monster's face. Then it fades.

Monster: But don't worry. I will do no more harm in this world. My work is now complete. I will leave your ship and head to the North Pole. There, I will build my own funeral pyre. It is with joy that I will throw this deformed body of mine into the flames, and die. The man who created me is dead. I go now to die, as well. When I am dead, both of us will be forgotten. Good-bye!

Narrator 3: The monster springs from the cabin window and onto an ice raft. Walton watches in amazement as he is carried away by the waves and disappears into the distance.

The End

Dr. Jekyll and Mr. Hyde

Robert Louis Stevenson

Adapted by Jennifer L. Kroll

Summary

Gabriel Utterson, a lawyer, becomes concerned after reading the will of his friend, Dr. Henry Jekyll, a scientist. In his will, Jekyll declares that if he should suddenly mysteriously disappear, a man named Edward Hyde will receive all of his earthly belongings and "step into his shoes." When Utterson hears a horrifying story about Edward Hyde attacking a young girl, he becomes convinced that Jekyll is in trouble or is being blackmailed by Hyde. Eventually, Utterson discovers the truth. Through use of a chemical solution, Jekyll has been changing himself into Hyde— the physical manifestation of his hidden, darker side.

Background Information

The writer Robert Louis Stevenson was born in Scotland in 1850. Despite, and sometimes because of, his chronic poor health, he traveled widely during his lifetime. His wife, Fanny Osborne, was American. Stevenson eventually settled in the Pacific on the island of Samoa, where he died in 1894. Among his most famous works are his collection of poems titled *A Child's Garden of Verses* (1885) and his novels *Treasure Island* (1882), *The Strange Case of Dr. Jekyll and Mr. Hyde* (1886), and *Kidnapped* (1887).

Presentation Suggestions

Seat Utterson and Jekyll on stools or chairs in the center. Place Mrs. Poole, Servant, and the two Narrators to the side of Dr. Jekyll. Place Enfield, Miss Guest, Dr. Lanyon, and Witness to the side of Utterson. Place Hyde behind Dr. Jekyll on a higher stool, so that he is visible throughout the reading. Have him come forward to exchange places with Dr. Jekyll during scene 9. You might assign students to pantomime the two attack scenes while they are being described in scene 1 and scene 6.

Props

Dr. Jekyll should dress in white, and Mr. Hyde in black. Dr. Jekyll might wear a lab coat or protective smock. Utterson, Lanyon, and Miss Guest can wear business attire— blazer jackets, or the like. Mrs. Poole can wear an apron and hold up a candlestick in scene 9. If the attack scenes are to be pantomimed, Hyde can use a cane or walking stick during the pantomime.

Characters

- ❀ Narrators 1 and 2
- ❀ Richard Enfield, *Utterson's cousin*
- ❀ Gabriel Utterson, *a lawyer*
- ❀ Dr. Lanyon, *an old school friend of Utterson*
- ❀ Mr. Hyde, *a young man who uses Dr. Jekyll's laboratory*
- ❀ Mrs. Poole, *housekeeper for Dr. Jekyll*
- ❀ Dr. Henry Jekyll, *an old school friend of Utterson*
- ❀ Policeman
- ❀ Witness, *present at the scene of a murder (female)*
- ❀ Miss Guest, *Mr. Utterson's legal clerk*
- ❀ Servant *(male or female)*

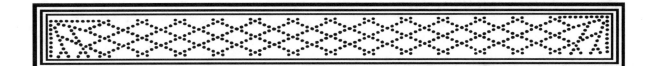

Dr. Jekyll and Mr. Hyde

Scene 1

Narrator 1: Gabriel Utterson and his cousin, Richard Enfield, two middle-aged bachelors, are out for one of their weekly walks through the streets of London. Coming down a street filled with lovely homes and charming little shops, they suddenly come upon an old door covered with peeling paint and graffiti. Enfield points to the door.

Enfield: Did you ever notice that door? In my mind, it is connected with a very odd story.

Utterson: Tell me.

Enfield: I was walking home once, very late at night. Must have been about three in the morning. There was hardly anybody out at that hour, but as I turned the corner and started coming down this street, I noticed two people.

Utterson: At three in the morning?

Enfield: One was a little man stumping along eastward at a good pace, the other was a little girl of about eight or ten who was running about as hard as she could down that cross street over there. The two of them collided.

Utterson: Collided?

Enfield: Yes. And this is the strange part. The little man didn't stop when he hit the girl. He didn't apologize. He knocked her flat over and then he trampled on her body! He seemed almost gleeful as he stomped on her.

Utterson: What kind of a sick brute would do such a thing? Was the girl hurt badly?

Enfield: She was screaming in horror, but she wasn't really hurt.

Utterson: What did you do? Did the man escape?

Enfield: No, I caught him. I ran up and grabbed him. I've got to tell you, there was something about the man. I hated to even to touch him. He gave me the shivers.

Utterson: How strange.

Enfield: In a few moments, the girl's parents or relatives arrived at the scene. They must have been right behind her. All of us went together to visit a doctor and make sure the girl was okay.

Utterson: And was she okay?

Enfield: She was fine—just scared. It was funny, though. The doctor's reaction to my prisoner seemed even stronger than my own. The doctor seemed completely sickened by the vile little man, even before he'd heard our story.

Utterson: Did the villain ever give an explanation for his actions? Did he ever apologize to the girl or her family?

Enfield: No! Through it all, he just sneered. He never seemed sorry in the slightest. He did offer to give money to the child's family, but it was just to keep everybody quiet. In the end, we made him cough up one hundred pounds. We told him that if he couldn't produce that exact amount, we were going straight to the police.

Utterson: Did he have the money? Or did you go to the police?

Enfield: That's where the door over there comes into my story. The little brute whipped out a key, went in through that door, and in a few minutes came back with a check for the money.

Utterson: You took his check? I don't think I would have trusted such a person to be good for the money.

Enfield: We knew the check was good, if in fact it was genuine. You see, the check was signed by Dr. Henry Jekyll,

Utterson: By Jekyll! How strange! Jekyll is an old friend of mine from school, you know. I'm his attorney.

Enfield: I know it. Jekyll is well known in the community as a trustworthy and upstanding—not to mention wealthy—gentleman. Everyone knows all the charities he supports. If the check was genuine, we knew it would be good.

Utterson: Jekyll is one of the dearest, most honest, and good-hearted men I've ever known. It's so strange to think that he would in any way be associated with a man like this despicable little child trampler . . . What did you say the villain's name was again?

Enfield: I didn't tell you his name. I guess, though, it can't hurt for you to know it. The man was named Hyde.

Utterson: Hmmm . . . That name sounds familiar.

Scene 2

Narrator 2: When Utterson returns from his walk with Enfield, he goes to his business room. There, he opens a safe and takes out a document labeled "Dr. Jekyll's Will."

Utterson: (*Reading.*) In case of the death of Dr. Henry Jekyll, or his disappearance or unexplained absence for any period over three months, Mr. Edward Hyde shall step into Henry Jekyll's shoes without further delay, and free from any burden of obligation.

Narrator 1: Utterson scowls.

Utterson: Whatever can this all be about? I am beginning to fear that Jekyll must be in some kind of trouble. Has he disgraced himself somehow? Is he being blackmailed? What's going on?

Narrator 2: Utterson puts the will back in the safe and goes to get his coat and hat.

Utterson: If anyone knows the answer, it will be Dr. Lanyon.

Scene 3

Narrator 1: Utterson pays a visit to his friend, Dr. Lanyon. After some rambling talk, Utterson brings the discussion around to the subject of Henry Jekyll.

Utterson: I suppose, Lanyon, that you and I must be the two oldest friends that Henry Jekyll has?

Lanyon: I wish the friends were younger! *(He laughs.)* But I suppose we are. And what of that? I see Jekyll very seldom these days.

Utterson: Really? I thought you two talked often. You share so many interests, both being medical doctors and scientific researchers.

Lanyon: We used to discuss our medical interests pretty frequently. It's been more than ten years, though, since Jekyll's research became much too fanciful for me. He began to go wrong, wrong in mind. And though I continue to take an interest in him for old time's sake, I see very little of the man. Such unscientific rubbish!

Utterson: Did you ever meet this friend of his, a young man named Hyde?

Lanyon: Hyde? No, never heard of him.

Narrator 2: Utterson returns home and spends the night tossing in turning in his bed, trying to guess at the sort of trouble his old friend Jekyll might be in. Enfield's story about Hyde plays over and over in his mind.

Utterson: Mr. Hyde. Hmm. I guess I will just have to become Mr. Seek! I've got to find out what's going on with Jekyll!

Scene 4

Narrator 1: In the days to come, Utterson takes to lurking around the battered door that his cousin, Enfield, pointed out to him. He comes to realize that the door is actually a back passageway into Jekyll's home, an entrance into Jekyll's laboratory.

Narrator 2: After a few days of waiting around the door, Utterson's patience is rewarded. At ten o'clock one night, he hears an odd, light footstep drawing near and then sees a small man approaching. The man removes a key from his pocket, like a person returning home. Utterson steps forward.

Utterson: You're Mr. Hyde, I think.

Hyde: *(Rudely.)* That's my name. What do you want?

Utterson: I see that you're going in. I'm an old friend of Dr. Jekyll's—Mr. Utterson. I'm sure you've heard my name. I thought you might let me in.

Hyde: Dr. Jekyll's not at home.

Narrator 1: Hyde looks at Utterson suspiciously.

Hyde: How did you know me?

Utterson: I knew you by description. We have common friends.

Hyde: Common friends? Who are they?

Utterson: Jekyll, for instance.

Hyde: He never told you about me! You're lying!

Narrator 2: Hyde enters through the door and slams it after himself.

Utterson: Hmm. What should I do now? Perhaps I'll go around the block and pay Jekyll a visit through his front door.

Narrator 1: Utterson rings the bell at Jekyll's front door. A housekeeper answers the door.

Utterson: Is Jekyll at home, Mrs. Poole?

Poole: I'll see, Mr. Utterson. Will you wait here by the fire, sir?

Narrator 2: Mrs. Poole returns some minutes later.

Poole: Dr. Jekyll must have gone out.

Utterson: I saw Mr. Hyde go in by the old laboratory door, madam. Is that all right, when Dr. Jekyll isn't home?

Poole: It's quite all right. Mr. Hyde has a key.

Utterson: Your master seems to have a lot of trust in that young man.

Poole: Yes, sir. He does indeed. We all have orders to obey him.

Utterson: I haven't ever met Mr. Hyde before, have I? At a dinner or some such affair?

Poole: No, sir. He never *dines* here. In fact, we see very little of him on this side of the house; he mostly comes and goes by the laboratory.

Utterson: Well, goodnight, Mrs. Poole.

Poole: Goodnight, Mr. Utterson.

Narrator 1: Mrs. Poole closes the door.

Utterson: *(To himself.)* Poor Henry Jekyll! He must be in deep water! This Hyde seems like a devilish character. It gives me the chills to think of him creeping around the house while Henry's sleeping! And what if Hyde knows about the will? He might grow impatient to inherit and murder Henry! I've got to do whatever I can to stop that from happening!

Scene 5

Narrator 2: Two weeks later, Dr. Jekyll throws a small dinner party and invites Utterson. After the other guests are gone, Utterson and Jekyll sit beside the fire chatting.

Utterson: I have been wanting to speak to you, Jekyll. You know that will of yours—

Jekyll: You poor fellow! You are unfortunate to have a client like me. I've never seen anyone as upset as you were when you first read my will. Except maybe that stodgy old Lanyon. He used to get so upset over what he called my scientific heresies.

Narrator 2: Utterson frowns and takes a sip of his tea.

Jekyll: I know Lanyon is a good fellow; you don't need to frown like that. And I always mean to see more of him. But he is so narrow-minded about everything. I've never been as disappointed in any person as I've been in Lanyon.

Narrator 1: Utterson changes the topic back to the will.

Utterson: You know I never approved of that will.

Jekyll: Yes, certainly, I know that. You've told me so.

Utterson: Well, I'm telling you so again. Lately I've been learning something of young Hyde.

Narrator 2: Dr. Jekyll's face goes all pale.

Jekyll: I don't care to hear more. I thought we had agreed to drop this matter.

Utterson: What I heard about Hyde was horrible.

Jekyll: I can't change the will, Utterson. You don't understand my position. I'm in a very strange spot. And this is not one of those matters that can be mended through discussion.

Utterson: Please, Jekyll. You can trust me. Let me help you get out of whatever trouble you're in.

Jekyll: You have always been a great friend. I would trust you before any man alive, even before myself. But there is nothing you can do for me. The only thing you can do is promise that if anything happens to me, you will do your best for Hyde. It means a great deal to me. Please—will you promise?

Utterson: I can't pretend that I'll ever like him.

Jekyll: I don't ask that. I only ask that you help him for my sake, when I am no longer here.

Utterson: *(Sighing.)* I promise.

Scene 6

Narrator 1: About a year later, Utterson is wakened one morning by a pounding on his door. Throwing on a robe, he answers the door.

Policeman: Sir, I regret to report that a terrible crime has been committed. A man is dead. There was no identification on the body, but the murder victim was carrying this.

Narrator 2: The policeman hands Utterson a letter addressed to himself.

Policeman: Because you obviously knew the victim, we are hoping that you can help us identify the body.

Utterson: This is horrible! Horrible! Did anybody witness the murder?

Policeman: Yes. There is one witness. A young woman. She is down at police headquarters.

Narrator 1: At the police station, Utterson identifies the body.

Utterson: Yes. I recognize him. I am sorry to say that this is Sir Danvers Carew. He was a client of mine, and a very good man.

Policeman: He was a member of the government! This affair is going to make quite a lot of noise. I hope perhaps you can help us find the man responsible.

Utterson: May I speak to the young woman who witnessed the murder?

Policeman: Of course.

Narrator 2: In another part of the police station, Utterson listens as the young woman describes what she saw.

Witness: I had gone upstairs to bed at about eleven, but it was a beautiful starry night, so I sat down at the window for a few minutes, just looking out. That's when I saw a man coming down the street, an aged gentleman with white hair. After a few minutes, I noticed that coming toward him from the other direction was another very small gentleman.

Utterson: Did the two exchange words?

Witness: When they came upon one another, the old gentleman bowed and started speaking to the small fellow. He looked like he was just asking for directions or something. I recognized the small man as a Mr. Hyde, who had visited the office I work in. I really couldn't stand that Mr. Hyde. Something about him gave me a chill.

Utterson: Hyde! Again! Tell me the rest of what happened!

Witness: As the two men were talking, Mr. Hyde was playing with a heavy walking cane. All of a sudden, for some reason or other, he broke out in a great fit of anger. He started stamping his foot and started waving his cane around like a madman.

Utterson: What did Sir Danvers, do?

Witness: He seemed shocked. He took a step back. And then Mr. Hyde just leaped on him and clubbed him to death. And when the old man had been brutally battered and was lying in the road, Hyde trampled on his body! That's when I ran to call for the police.

Policeman: We did not get to the scene in time to catch the murderer.

Scene 7

Narrator 1: That afternoon, Utterson pays a visit to Dr. Jekyll. Jekyll's housekeeper, Mrs. Poole, leads Utterson through the main part of the house and down a long corridor, to Jekyll's office and laboratory. In his office, Jekyll sits by a fire, looking sick.

Utterson: Sir Danvers Carew is dead. Have you heard the news?

Jekyll: The newspaper boys were crying it in the square. I heard them in my dining room.

Utterson: You haven't been mad enough to hide this Hyde fellow, have you?

Jekyll: Utterson, I swear I will never set eyes on him again! I swear I am done with him! It is all at an end. He is safe, far away, and will never more be heard of.

Utterson: You seem pretty sure of all this. I hope, for your sake, that you're right. If it came to a trial, your name would probably appear in connection with the murder.

Jekyll: I am quite sure Hyde is long gone and won't be seen again. But there is one thing about which I need advice. I have received a letter from Hyde, and I am not sure whether to show it to the police. I'd like to leave it in your hands. I know you will judge wisely.

Utterson: You're afraid the letter might lead to Hyde's discovery?

Jekyll: I don't care what becomes of Hyde. I'm totally through with him. I was thinking of myself.

Utterson: Let me see the letter.

Narrator 2: Utterson takes the letter and starts reading aloud.

Utterson: *(Reading.)* Dr. Jekyll, I owe you so much for all of your generosities, and I am ashamed to pay you back as I have done. Please do not worry for my safety. I have a sure means of escape.

Narrator 1: Utterson notes the strange, upright signature on the letter: "Edward Hyde."

Utterson: Do you have the envelope this came in?

Jekyll: I burned it before I realized the contents. But it didn't have a postmark on it. A messenger handed in the note at the door.

Utterson: Well, it's been a long day. I'm going to go home and rest. But first I want to know one last thing. Was it Hyde who dictated the terms in your will about your possible disappearance?

Narrator 2: Jekyll looks faint. He shuts his mouth tight and nods.

Utterson: I knew it. Hyde meant to murder you. You're lucky you've escaped.

Jekyll: I have learned my lesson! And what a lesson I have learned!

Narrator 1: Utterson excuses himself from the doctor and leaves the study. At the front door of Jekyll's house, he holds up the letter from Hyde and asks Mrs. Poole.

Utterson: When this letter was handed in today, what did the messenger look like?

Poole: I'm sorry, sir, but the only letters delivered today came from the postman. No messenger handed anything in.

Utterson: *(To himself.)* Strange . . . very strange.

Scene 8

Narrator 2: At home, Utterson sits in his office with Miss Guest, his legal clerk and one of his good friends.

Utterson: This is a sad business about Sir Danvers.

Guest: Yes, indeed. There is a lot of public emotion over the whole affair. The man who committed the murder must be crazy, of course.

Utterson: I'm interested in your opinion on that. I know that you're good at guessing things about people's character from looking at their handwriting and signatures. I have a document here in the murderer's handwriting. What do you think of his autograph? Is Hyde insane?

Guest: No—I wouldn't say he's crazy, but it is an odd signature.

Utterson: And by all accounts a very odd writer.

Narrator 1: A servant enters with a note. Mr. Utterson takes it and reads it to himself. The servant leaves.

Guest: Is that from Dr. Jekyll, sir? I thought I knew the writing. Is it something private?

Utterson: No, no. Just an invitation to dinner. Why? Would you like to see it?

Guest: Yes, I would, if you don't mind.

Narrator 2: Miss Guest takes the note from Jekyll and holds the sheet of paper alongside the note from Hyde. She studies the contents of the two notes.

Utterson: Why are you comparing them? What do you see?

Guest: There's a very strong resemblance between these two signatures, don't you think? In fact, they look pretty much identical, except that they are sloped differently.

Utterson: Hmm. Interesting.

Guest: Yes, indeed.

Utterson: I have to ask you not to speak of this to anyone.

Guest: Yes. Of course.

Narrator 1: For the rest of the evening, Utterson is worried and restless. Only when he is alone in his bed for the night does he finally speak the thought that is troubling him.

Utterson: I can't believe that Henry Jekyll would forge a note for a murderer!

Scene 9

Narrator 2: In the weeks ahead, nothing more is heard of from Hyde. Henry Jekyll becomes more social than he has been for several years. He is seen all over town attending parties and dinners. He makes huge contributions to charities and begins doing more volunteer work. Utterson enjoys seeing his old friend so full of life and hope.

Narrator 1: Everything seems to be going well, until one evening. Mr. Utterson is sitting by his fireside after dinner, when he is surprised to receive a visit from Mrs. Poole.

Utterson: Bless me, Mrs. Poole, what brings you here?

Narrator 2: Utterson notices that Mrs. Poole looks very distraught and pale.

Utterson: What ails you? Is the doctor ill?

Poole: Mr. Utterson, there is something wrong.

Utterson: Take a seat, madam. Now take your time and tell me plainly what you want.

Poole: You know the doctor's ways, sir, and how he sometimes shuts himself up. Well, he's shut up again in the laboratory and I don't like it, sir. . . . Sir, I'm afraid.

Utterson: What exactly are you afraid of?

Poole: I've been afraid for about a week, and I can't bear it anymore.

Utterson: Come, Mrs. Poole. I see there is something seriously wrong. Try to tell me what it is.

Poole: I think there's been foul play.

Utterson: Foul play! What foul play?

Poole: I don't dare say, sir. But will you come along with me and see for yourself?

Narrator 1: Mr. Utterson and Mrs. Poole make their way through the chilly March night to Dr. Jekyll's house.

Poole: Well, sir, here we are.

Narrator 2: Mrs. Poole knocks on the door.

Servant: Is that you, Mrs. Poole?

Poole: It's all right. Open the door.

Narrator 1: The hall, as they enter, is brightly lit up. A fire is blazing in the fireplace and all the house servants are huddled around it. They look extremely frightened.

Servant: It's Mr. Utterson! Oh thank goodness!

Utterson: Why are you all huddled in the front room? What's going on?

Poole: They're all afraid. *(To the servant.)* Reach me a candle. We're going down to the laboratory.

Narrator 2: Mr. Utterson and Mrs. Poole make their way through the long hallway toward the sealed laboratory door. The shadows from the candle bounce eerily off the walls.

Poole: *(Whispering.)* Now, sir, come as quietly as you can. I want you to hear, and I don't want you to be heard.

Narrator 1: Near the end of the hallway, Mrs. Poole sets the candle down, and slowly makes her way up the steps to the laboratory door. With an uncertain hand, she knocks at the door.

Poole: Mr. Utterson, sir, is asking to see you.

Narrator 2: The muffled sound of a whiny voice is heard within. The voice sounds nothing like Jekyll's.

Poole: Thank you, sir. I'll tell Mr. Utterson that you don't wish to see him.

Narrator 1: Mrs. Poole retreats to where Mr. Utterson is standing.

Poole: Sir, was that my master's voice?

Utterson: I couldn't hear it clearly, but it did seem different.

Poole: Different? Yes, I think so! Have I been this man's housekeeper for twenty years to be deceived about his voice? No, sir! My master is gone. Somebody did away with him or made away with him eight days ago, when we suddenly heard him cry out as if he was in agony. Who is there instead of him and why it stays there is what I cannot understand.

Utterson: This is a very strange tale, Mrs. Poole.

Poole: All this past week, him—or it—whatever it is that lives in that laboratory, has been crying night and day for some sort of medicine that he cannot get. It was sometimes Dr. Jekyll's way to write his orders on a sheet of paper and throw it on the stair. We've had nothing else this whole week—nothing but papers and a closed door, and the meals left there to be smuggled in when nobody was looking.

Utterson: What was written on the papers that you found on the stairs?

Poole: Requests for a kind of drug. I've been to all the wholesale chemists in town. But every time I brought the stuff back, there would be another paper telling me to return it, because it was not pure, and another order to a different firm. This drug is wanted very badly—whatever it's for.

Utterson: May I look at one of those papers?

Poole: Certainly sir.

Narrator 2: Mrs. Poole retrieves one of the papers for Mr. Utterson to see.

Utterson: *(Reading.)* Dr. Jekyll presents his compliments to Mr. Maw and Company. He assures them that their last sample is impure and quite useless for his present purpose. Four years ago, Dr. J. purchased a somewhat large quantity from your company. He now begs you to search with the greatest care, and should any of the same quality be left, to forward it to him at once. Expense is no consideration. The importance to Dr. J. cannot be exaggerated. Please! I beg you! Find me some of the old!

Poole: A strange note isn't it? Especially those last lines. When I presented the note at Maws' chemists, it made the clerk very angry. He assured me that the sample he'd sent had been perfectly pure.

Utterson: I'm starting to formulate a theory about Dr. Jekyll. What if he has one of those types of diseases that both torture and deform the sufferer? That might explain why he is trying to get a special drug and doesn't want to be seen by anyone. It might also explain why his voice seems changed.

Poole: Somehow, I don't think that's what's going on. Whoever is in there sounds and acts nothing at all like Dr. Jekyll.

Utterson: Well, we must find an answer somehow, even if it means breaking the door down. Dr. Jekyll needs our help and support. Send two of the servants around to the other entrance and have them guard that door, then find me something that I can use to break this door down.

Narrator 1: Mrs. Poole leaves and after some minutes returns to the inner laboratory door bearing an axe. She hands the axe to Utterson.

Utterson: *(Calling out to the door.)* Jekyll, I demand to see you!

Narrator 2: For a moment, all is dead silent.

Utterson: I give you fair warning. . . . We are going to break this door down if you won't let us in.

Hyde: Utterson! Leave me alone! Have mercy!

Poole: That's not Jekyll's voice—it's Hyde's!

Utterson: We're coming in!

Narrator 1: Utterson swings the axe on the wooden door panels again and again, until finally, after much effort, the door falls inward onto the carpet. Mr. Utterson and Mrs. Poole cautiously peer into the room. In the middle of the chamber, on the floor, the contorted body of a man lies twitching. The two draw near to the body on tiptoe.

Utterson: It's Edward Hyde! He's dead. He must have taken his own life just now! Poison—I think.

Poole: Look! He was wearing the doctor's clothes! See how big these clothes were on him! How strange!

Utterson: And where is Dr. Jekyll?

Poole: We have to find his body!

Utterson: Perhaps he is still alive. Let's search the chamber here for clues.

Narrator 2: They begin to search the chamber.

Poole: Here, on the table, is a packet addressed to you, sir.

Narrator 1: Utterson rips open the packet and begins reading.

Utterson: *(Reading.)* My dear Utterson, when this shall fall into your hands, I shall have disappeared. If you wish to understand the circumstances of my disappearance, read my enclosed confession. Your unhappy friend, Henry Jekyll.

Poole: A confession! What does the doctor confess?

Utterson: This looks long, Mrs. Poole. Perhaps we should sit down and go over it carefully.

Poole: Shall I call the police, sir?

Utterson: Let's have a look at this so-called confession first.

Scene 10

Narrator 2: Mr. Utterson and Mrs. Poole sit in Jekyll's library. Utterson studies the "confession." As he reads it, he imagines his dear friend Jekyll speaking to him.

Utterson: On the early pages, Jekyll describes how "divided" he always felt.

Poole: Divided? What does he mean?

Utterson: Here's what he says . . .

Jekyll: Even as a young man, I was aware that I possessed two distinct sides. One side of me was wild and selfish. It sought after and reveled in the pleasures of life. I was always somewhat ashamed of this side of myself. I tried not to let others see it. To the eyes of most, I appeared to be very serious and responsible, concerned for the welfare of others. I was proud of this controlled, intellectual part of myself.

Poole: This is no confession of wrongdoing! Everyone has the different sides that Dr. Jekyll describes.

Utterson: True enough, Mrs. Poole. But most of us are content to let these opposite aspects of ourselves exist simultaneously, side by side. Jekyll, according to his own confession, was not.

Jekyll: The controlled, intellectual, moralistic part was constantly being made miserable by its awareness of the pleasure-seeking, selfish part. And my wilder half was always becoming frustrated when its plans and desires were held in check by my moralistic side. I thought to myself, if only I could divide these two parts from each other entirely, both halves would be happier. And so it was, many years ago, that I first began my research.

Utterson: (*Reading.*) He says here that he began seeking for a way to divide the two opposite sides of himself, so that each could exist independently.

Jekyll: I discovered, through my scientific research, that certain chemical agents could accomplish this goal, and so I set out to assemble these agents. The last ingredient I needed to create the transformative potion was a particular salt. I purchased, all at once, from a firm of wholesale chemists, a large quantity of this salt, and finished assembling the potion. For weeks, I did not test the substance. Finally, I got up the courage.

Poole: Where can this tale be going?

Utterson: I think I am beginning to see.

Jekyll: After I swallowed the compound, I was wracked with pains. I felt a grinding of my bones, terrible nausea, and a horror in my heart. I thought perhaps I was dying.

Poole: The poor doctor!

Jekyll: But, finally, the pains subsided. And when they did I felt younger, stronger, and more energetic. But I also was aware of the fact that I was much more wicked and ruthless than I had been before. As strange as it may sound, I was also much smaller than I'd been before. My pants legs were dragging on the ground. My shirtsleeves were drooping. I raced to the mirror and for the first time saw the face and figure of Edward Hyde.

Narrator 1: Mrs. Poole gasps in alarm.

Utterson: I can scarcely believe this to be the truth!

Poole: But it must be. No other explanation exists. Please, keep reading.

Jekyll: I was able to take a second swallow of the potion and, after more pains and contortions, turn back into my ordinary self. I was very pleased with the results of the experiment, even though I had expected a slightly different outcome.

Poole: What other outcome?

Utterson: He says that he had hoped to be able to cast the two opposite parts of himself into separate bodies. As it turns out, he was only able to separate out the ruthless, wicked part of himself that he named Edward Hyde.

Poole: So Dr. Jekyll turned into Mr. Hyde? He must have performed this experiment dozens of times, for we saw a great deal of Mr. Hyde. Why would the doctor do such a thing?

Utterson: He apparently enjoyed being Hyde. As Hyde, he felt no guilt, no sense of responsibility. He had a younger, lighter body and felt free to do whatever he pleased. And so, he kept changing himself back and forth between Jekyll and Hyde. But, after some time, the transformation process seems to have stopped working properly.

Poole: What happened?

Utterson: Let me read it to you . . .

Jekyll: Some two months before the murder of Sir Danvers Carew, I had been out for one of my adventures, had returned at a late hour, and transformed myself back into my ordinary self. But the next morning, I woke up feeling some very strange sensations. Looking down at my hand, I noticed that it was much smaller, leaner, and hairier than it had been the night before. I realized that I had turned back into Hyde while I slept.

Utterson: After this event, Jekyll says that he began spontaneously turning into Hyde more and more often. This greatly alarmed him. He felt that the Hyde part was growing stronger and stronger and taking over his life. He began to find that sometimes he would have to take two or three times the usual amount of the potion to transform himself back to his ordinary shape.

Poole: And eventually, his supply of the transformation potion began to run low.

Utterson: Exactly. But not until after Hyde had killed Sir Danvers.

Poole: It is so difficult to believe that my dear master could be responsible for that brutal murder!

Utterson: But, indeed, it seems to be the case.

Poole: I see now what has been going on. The doctor has been desperately trying to get some more of the salt he used in his original potion. But something must have been wrong with that first batch of salt, some impurity must have been in it, and so he hasn't been able to get any more exactly like it.

Utterson: Without that salt, Jekyll was trapped forever in the body of Edward Hyde. And Edward Hyde was wanted for the murder of Sir Danvers Carew. He couldn't show his face beyond the laboratory or he would have been arrested, tried, and put to death.

Poole: *(Sadly.)* Should I call the police now, sir? What shall I tell them?

Utterson: Tell them anything you please. They are not going to believe us in any case.

The End

The Lady, or the Tiger?

Frank R. Stockton

Adapted by Suzanne I. Barchers

Summary

In this adaptation of a classic short story, a semi-barbaric king in an unknown kingdom discovers his daughter has fallen in love with a courtier. He declares that the young man will be subjected to the king's favored method of justice in which the accused chooses his own fate. A tiger is placed behind one door. If this door is chosen, the accused is considered guilty and becomes victim to the tiger's vicious nature. Behind the other door, a carefully selected lady waits. If chosen, the entire kingdom celebrates the couple's marriage. The king's daughter learns which door holds the lady and the tiger, and she wrestles with the decision to allow her beloved to be killed or to be rewarded with marriage to an alluring woman. She indicates her choice of doors to the young man, and the audience is left to speculate on her choice for her beloved: the lady, or the tiger.

Background Information

Frank R. Stockton (1834–1902) was born in Philadelphia and became a wood engraver. By 1867, he began to write children's stories, followed by stories for adult magazines. This is his most famous story, appearing in the *Century* magazine in 1882. People have debated the ending ever since the story first appeared.

Presentation Suggestions

Arrange the characters in the following order: Narrator 1, Julius, Leto, Marcus, Helen, King, Princess, Mira, Narrator 2. Place the king in a chair on a raised dais.

Props

The kingdom's historical setting is unspecified, giving the players an opportunity to choose the style of dress. Although the kingdom is described as semi-barbaric, the tone of the story suggests a sense of tradition or ritual. The king and princess should be dressed in clothes befitting royal status.

Characters

❀ Narrators 1 and 2
❀ Julius, *nobleman*
❀ Leto, *nobleman*
❀ Marcus, *Julius's cousin*
❀ Helen, *Julius's cousin*
❀ King
❀ Princess
❀ Mira, *the princess' friend*

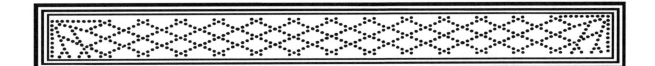

The Lady, or the Tiger?

Scene 1

Narrator 1: The time is of olden days. There lives a semi-barbaric king who is a man of exuberant fancy and of great authority. When everything moves smoothly, he is bland and genial.

Narrator 2: But whenever there is a little hitch, he is blander and more genial still, for nothing pleases him so much as to make the crooked straight and crush down uneven places. How he does this will soon be made clear.

Narrator 1: Listen now to the story of how this ruler's unusual practices affected lives of people who were lucky—or unlucky—enough to live within his rule.

Julius: Welcome, Cousin Marcus and Helen.

Leto: Make yourselves comfortable while I order refreshments. Tell me about your journey. Was it terribly tedious?

Marcus: It was long, but we saw many wondrous things along the way.

Helen: We are grateful to be here, Julius and Leto. We're looking forward to a long rest and a congenial visit before we return home.

Narrator 2: Just then, the king sweeps into the room.

King: Where is my daughter? Someone find her immediately.

Narrator 1: The king's daughter quietly enters from a side room. She is a beautiful woman, the apple of his eye. The king loves her above all humanity.

Princess: Father, I am here. How can I serve you?

King: Daughter, are the rumors true? Have you been consorting with a common courtier who professes to serve me?

Princess: Yes, Father. It's true.

King: How can you even think of such behavior? He's not worth your attention. He is of a low station, and you are royalty.

Princess: Father, he is brave and handsome. He has served you faithfully. And Father, I love him dearly.

King: Do you really love him? Well, daughter, your love is about to be put to a test.

Princess: What do you mean?

King: He's in the prison this very day. His trial will be held as soon as the most savage tiger in the kingdom has been found.

Princess: Please, Father. Spare him. His only crime was to love me.

King: It will be done as I command. You know that my justice is impartial.

Scene 2

Narrator 2: The king leaves, and his daughter turns away, quietly contemplating her beloved's future.

Helen: Julius, what has just happened? What is going to happen to this young man?

Julius: Unfortunately, the king has decided to subject this young man to his version of justice. Whenever a subject is accused of a crime of sufficient importance to interest the king, public notice is given that the fate of the accused person will be decided in the king's arena.

Marcus: Is he put on trial in front of the entire citizenry? Why would people want to watch a trial?

Leto: It's a rather unusual version of a trial. Everyone gathers in the galleries, with the king and his court sitting high above. On his signal, the accused steps out from a lower door into the amphitheater.

Julius: Directly opposite the accused are two doors, exactly alike and side by side. The accused walks to these doors and opens one of them. He can open either door he pleases. He is subject to no guidance but that of impartial chance.

Helen: What is behind the doors?

Leto: You heard the king mention a tiger. That fierce and hungry tiger will be behind one door. If the accused opens that door, the tiger will tear him apart and feast on him. The accused is considered guilty, and this is his punishment.

Helen: This is horrifying!

Julius: Indeed, and the audience mourns this dire fate, while iron bells clang.

Marcus: What's behind the other door? I hope it's not another beast.

Julius: Quite the opposite. His Majesty chooses the most suitable lady for the accused that he can find among his subjects. If the accused selects this door, the woman comes out, and the celebration begins. A priest and dancing maidens playing golden horns enter from another door, and a wedding is promptly held.

Leto: Brass bells ring forth, and the people cheer while children strew flowers on the newly wedded couple's path as they make their way home.

Helen: What if the man is already married?

Leto: It matters not that he might have a wife, family, or someone he loves. The king considers this fair and decisive. The accused person is instantly punished if he finds himself guilty.

Marcus: I see—and if innocent, he is rewarded on the spot, whether he likes it or not.

Julius: That's right. There's no escape from the judgment of the king's arena. No matter how this turns out, the king has disposed of the problem of this young courtier who presumed to fall in love with his daughter.

Leto: It won't take long before the trial. You'll be here to watch with us.

Scene 3

Narrator 1: While the king makes the final preparations for the trial, his daughter discusses her dilemma with her trusted friend Mira.

Princess: Mira, thank you for helping me.

Mira: I'm not sure this knowledge is advised, but it's your decision now. You know which door hides the tiger, and you know who is behind the other door. Do you know what you will do?

Princess: I don't know. My father chose the loveliest damsel of the court. I've seen her throwing glances at my love for months. She knows I love him, yet she sought him out. How could she dare to raise her eyes to him? He is mine! The thought of her having him is unfathomable. But the thought of seeing him torn to pieces by a tiger tortures me.

Mira: Either way, your father has ensured that you have lost him.

Princess: I know, I know. What is worse? To watch him die or to see his look of delight when he opens her door? I can just see her now, flushing with triumph as the priest and dancers come out, the people cheer, and the bells ring.

Mira: He would be alive at least.

Princess: Yes, but if he dies at once, perhaps we will be reunited in death.

Mira: You have some time to think. The trial is some days off.

Princess: Time to think? That's all I've been doing. Every day and night is full of anguished deliberation.

Scene 4

Narrator 2: Finally, the appointed day arrives. From far and near the people gather and throng the great galleries of the arena. Crowds who are unable to gain admittance wait in masses outside the walls.

Narrator 1: Julius, Leto, Marcus, and Helen watch from the gallery near the king.

Julius: The king has given the signal. There's the courtier coming out of the door below.

Helen: Look, he's searching for the princess.

Marcus: They are looking at each other! What do you think he's going to do?

Narrator 2: The young man assumes that his beloved has learned behind which door the tiger crouches and behind which door the lady waits. He knows her nature and understands that she would never rest until she had learned the secret, hidden to all others, even to the king.

Narrator 1: As he gazes at the princess, he can see in her eyes that she knows what is behind each door. He looks at her anxiously, as if asking the question, "Which?" The question is asked in a flash; it must be answered in another.

Narrator 2: Her right arm lies on the cushioned parapet before her. She raises her hand and makes a quick, slight movement toward the right. None but he sees her. All other eyes are fixed on him.

Julius: Look! He is choosing!

Leto: It's the door on the right!

Narrator 1: Now, dear listeners, what happened? Did the tiger come out of that door, or did the lady? Think on it a minute. The princess is semi-barbaric. She struggles between despair and jealousy. She has lost him, but who should have him?

Narrator 2: How often, in her waking hours and in her dreams, has she started in wild horror and covered her face with her hands as she thinks of her beloved opening the door on the side where the cruel fangs of the tiger waits!

Narrator 1: But how much oftener has she seen him at the other door! How in her grievous reveries has she gnashed her teeth and torn her hair, when she sees his start of rapturous delight as he opens the door to the lady!

Narrator 2: Would it not be better for him to die at once, and go to wait for her in the blessed regions of semi-barbaric futurity? Her decision has been indicated in an instant, but it has been made after days and nights of anguished deliberation. She knew she would be asked, she had decided what she would answer, and, without the slightest hesitation, she moved her hand to the right.

Narrator 1: And so I leave it with all of you: Which came out of the opened door—the lady, or the tiger?

The End

The Prince and the Pauper

Mark Twain

Adapted by Suzanne I. Barchers

Summary

In sixteenth-century England, a poor boy and a prince happen upon each other. Envious of the other's life, they decide to change clothes briefly. Circumstances intervene, and the young boys find themselves thrust into each other's roles. The true prince must learn to survive on the streets, while the pauper copes with the impending assumption of the throne. Through a series of serendipitous events, each regains his rightful place.

Background Information

Mark Twain was born Samuel Langhorne Clemens in Florida, Missouri, in 1835. He intended to write a sequel to *The Adventures of Tom Sawyer* and began writing *The Adventures of Huckleberry Finn* in 1876. After sixteen chapters, he set aside the manuscript and undertook other projects. He wrote *The Prince and the Pauper* in 1883.

As a young man in Hannibal, Missouri, Twain was an avid reader. He worked as an apprentice in a printing shop until he left Hannibal to find work as a journalist in Philadelphia. Other jobs he held before becoming a writer included working on riverboats, working as a miner, and working as a newspaper reporter. Twain died in Redding, Connecticut, in 1910.

Presentation Suggestions

Arrange the stage with a combination of chairs and stools. The following characters should sit on stools: Narrator 1, Narrator 2, Edward, Tom, and Hendon. The following characters should sit on chairs in front and to the right of the stools: Soldier, Canty, Mother Canty, Child 1, Child 2, Hermit, Justice, Woman. The following characters should sit on chairs in front and to the left of the stools: Jane Grey, Henry VIII, Lord Hertford, Lord St. John, Elizabeth, Lord Chancellor, Hugh, and Edith. If preferred, the characters with short parts could stand to the side and step offstage after reading.

Props

The stage can be decorated with a somewhat impoverished décor to the right (behind Canty, Mother Canty, and so forth) and a more royal décor to the left. Members of royalty can wear rich clothing, with the other characters in plain clothing.

Characters

- Narrators 1 and 2
- Soldier
- Edward, *prince*
- Tom, *poor lad*
- Canty, *Tom's father*
- Jane Grey, *Lady*
- Henry VIII
- Lord Hertford
- Lord St. John
- Elizabeth, *Lady*
- Lord Chancellor

- Mother Canty, *Tom's mother*
- Hendon, *Tom's friend*
- Child 1
- Child 2
- Hermit
- Justice
- Woman
- Hugh, *Hendon's brother*
- Edith, *Hugh's wife*

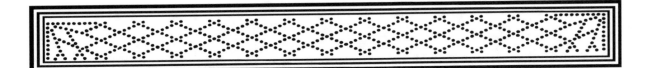

The Prince and the Pauper

Scene 1

Narrator 1: In the city of London in the sixteenth century, a boy is born to a poor family of the name of Canty, who does not want him. On the same day another English child is born to a rich family of the name of Tudor, who does want him.

Narrator 2: All of England wants Edward Tudor, and people are mad for joy. All of England rejoices in the Prince of Wales. But there is no talk about the other baby, Tom Canty, wrapped in his poor rags.

Narrator 1: Some years later, in Offal Court, Tom's father, John, a thief, and his mother, a beggar, are raising Tom. Tom has a hard time, but he manages to learn to read and write, thanks to Father Andrew, a local priest, who tutors him.

Narrator 2: Each night Tom loves to dream of living in faraway, romantic lands, in a vast palace. He creates elaborate pretenses of royalty. Each morning he looks at the sordidness of his surroundings with bitterness. One morning he wanders to the Temple Bar, outside the walls of London on the Strand, to the village of Charing.

Narrator 1: He approaches the palace of Westminster, where he spies a comely boy in silks and satins—a real prince. A soldier sees him watching and throws him aside.

Soldier: Mind your manners, you young beggar!

Narrator 2: The young prince springs to the gate, eyes flashing.

Edward: How dare you treat a poor lad like that! Open the gates and let him in.

Narrator 1: The soldier opens the gates and allows Tom Canty to enter.

Edward: You look tired and hungry. Come with me. What is your name?

Tom: Tom Canty, if you please.

Edward: Where do you live?

Tom: In the city—Offal Court, out of Pudding Lane.

Edward: Do you have parents?

Tom: Yes, sir, and a grandma and twin sisters.

Edward: Is your grandmother kind to you?

Tom: There are times that she holds my hand, being asleep or overcome with drink. But she later makes up for it with beatings.

Edward: Beatings?

Tom: Oh, indeed.

Edward: I shall have her punished! Is your father kind to you?

Tom: Not more than grandmother.

Edward: My father has a heavy hand, but he spares me. How does your mother treat you?

Tom: She is good, sir. She gives me neither sorrow nor pain. My sisters are like her in this.

Edward: You speak well. Are you learned?

Tom: Father Andrew teaches me from his books.

Edward: Do you have a pleasant life there?

Tom: Yes, except when I'm hungry. There are Punch and Judy shows, monkeys all dressed up, and plays. We lads of Offal Court play games with each other.

Edward: That I would like! Tell me more.

Tom: We have races. In summer we wade and swim in the canals and in the river. We duck under, dive, and shout, and—

Edward: It would be worth my father's kingdom to enjoy that once! Go on!

Tom: We dance and sing around the Maypole in Cheapside. We play in the sand, and sometimes we make mud pies.

Edward: Say no more! It sounds glorious. If I could only wear clothes like yours and strip my feet and revel in the mud once. I would forego the crown for that!

Tom: And if I could clothe me once, sweet sir, as you are clothed—

Edward: Then it shall be! Take off your rags and don these splendors. We will have a brief happiness and then change back before anyone knows better.

Narrator 2: A few minutes later the Prince of Wales wears Tom's rags, and the little pauper wears plumage of royalty. The two stand side by side in front of a mirror. They stare at each other, puzzled. There does not seem to be any change.

Edward: You have the same hair, the same eyes, the same voice and manner, the same face that I have. If we were naked, no one could tell which is you and which is the prince. And look, you are bruised where the guard struck you. Wait one moment. I'm going to speak to that guard.

Narrator 1: The prince sets aside a royal object that was on the table and flies through the grounds in Tom's rags. He reaches the gate, shouting.

Edward: Open the gates!

Narrator 2: The soldier obeys, and as the prince bursts through the gate, the soldier knocks him to the road.

Soldier: Take that for getting me in trouble with His Highness!

Edward: I'm the Prince of Wales! You shall hang for striking me!

Soldier: *(Mockingly.)* I salute your gracious highness.

Narrator 1: The crowd jeers and hoots, closing around the prince.

Soldier: *(Angrily.)* Be off, you crazy rubbish.

Narrator 2: The crowd hustles the poor little prince down the road.

Scene 2

Narrator 1: The crowd pursues the prince, tormenting him as he utters royal commands. When they finally abandon him, he cannot recognize where he is. He wanders the streets, looking for something he knows, hoping to find Offal Court, as Tom mentioned.

Narrator 2: A group of boys gather around and torment him, teasing him when he claims to be the prince. Escaping from this latest torture, he is suddenly seized by a rough hand.

Canty: Out so late? And I bet you have not brought a farthing home! If I don't break all the bones in your body, then I'm not John Canty!

Edward: Oh, you're his father! Will you fetch him away and restore me?

Canty: I don't know what you mean. I am your father, you shall soon realize!

Edward: Don't tease me. Take me to my father, the king. I am worn and wounded. I can't bear any more. Save me! I am indeed the Prince of Wales.

Narrator 1: John Canty stares at him, bewildered.

Canty: You've gone stark mad. But mad or not, you'll soon learn your lesson.

Narrator 2: John Canty begins to strike Edward, and when a kind observer tries to intervene, Canty strikes the man away with his cudgel. Then Canty drags Edward away from the crowd.

Narrator 1: Meanwhile, Tom enjoys admiring himself in the great mirror. He practices walking with a princely carriage and plays with the jeweled dagger that hangs at his thigh. He begins to wonder at the prince's absence and feels lonely.

Tom: *(To himself.)* I do wish the prince would return. What if someone catches me in his clothes? They might hang me at once. I need to find him.

Narrator 2: Tom opens the door and six servants rise and bow before him. Tom steps back quickly, shutting the door.

Tom: *(To himself.)* Oh how they mock me! They will tell someone. What shall I do?

Narrator 1: The door swings open and a page announces the arrival of Lady Jane Grey, who speaks to Tom.

Jane: What is wrong, my lord?

Tom: I'm no lord, but only poor Tom Canty of Offal Court in the city. Let me see the prince. He'll restore me to my rags and let me go. Save me!

Jane: Oh, my lord, what is wrong?

Narrator 2: Lady Jane Grey flees in fright. She spreads the word that the prince is mad. Everyone whispers in dismay until an official commands that the foolishness end. Tom finally comes out of the room, walking slowly until he finds himself at the bedside of Henry VIII, where he kneels. A physician and other attendants stand near the ailing ruler.

Henry VIII: Now my prince, explain this jest to your father, the king.

Tom: You are the king? Then I'm ruined.

Henry VIII: The rumors must be true. Come to me, my son.

Narrator 1: Tom trembles as he approaches the king.

Henry VIII: Don't you know me? Don't break my heart, son.

Tom: Yes, you are my dread lord the king.

Henry VIII: True, but do not tremble so. No one will hurt you. Do you know yourself again?

Tom: Please believe me. I speak the truth when I say I am one of your most common subjects, a pauper born. It's only by accident that I am here. I am too young to die, sir.

Henry VIII: Die? You shall not die!

Narrator 2: Tom jumps up joyfully.

Tom: *(To the others.)* I'm not to die! *(To the king.)* May I go now?

Henry VIII: Stay a while. Why would you go?

Tom: I thought I was free to return home to my mother and sisters. Please let me go.

Henry VIII: *(To himself.)* He seems to be well, except for the belief that he is a pauper.

Narrator 1: The king and the physician question Tom and decide that he is mad, but that the condition is not permanent. They decide to confirm him as prince the following day.

Henry VIII: My son, kiss me, your loving father. Go amuse yourself so I can rest.

Narrator 2: Tom turns to leave, thinking about how his dreams of royalty had been so pleasant. This reality is dreary!

Scene 3

Narrator 1: Tom is taken to a suite where he begs the many waiting men to be seated. His "uncle," the Earl of Hertford and the Lord St. John assist him. Various men come forward with their requests, and the earl encourages Tom to just signal his wishes. When Tom is reminded of an upcoming banquet, Tom blames his forgetfulness on his poor memory.

Narrator 2: Lady Elizabeth and Lady Jane Grey enter the room.

Lord Hertford: *(To the ladies.)* Please, ladies, try not to show surprise when his memory lapses. It sticks at every trifle.

Lord St. John: *(To Tom.)* Remember all you can, and pretend to remember the rest. Don't let others see how you've changed. It will only upset your followers.

Narrator 1: Tom signals his understanding. He is determined to do the best he can.

Jane: *(To Tom.)* Have you visited the queen today, my lord?

Narrator 2: Tom hesitates, and Lord St. John smoothly responds for him.

Elizabeth: Don't worry, sir. This distemper will soon disappear.

Tom: You are a comfort, sweet lady.

Narrator 1: Time moves on, and Tom grows more at ease. He is happy to know that the ladies will be at the banquet. After they leave, Tom asks if he can rest. A page escorts him to an apartment where attendants remove his clothes and dress him in a rich robe. His head is too full to sleep. Meanwhile, his guardians discuss his state of mind.

Lord St. John: What do you think?

Lord Hertford: The king is near death, and my nephew is mad. But he will take the throne and remain there. God protect England, since she will need it.

Lord St. John: Have you no misgivings? His manner and speech are princely, but they differ from what he was previously. The difference is slight and hard to identify. It seems to have taken away the customs he should know. He can speak Latin, but his Greek and French are gone. It haunts me, how he claims not to be the prince.

Lord Hertford: Peace, my lord. Have you forgotten the king's command? He is to be confirmed. He is my sister's son. I've known his face and voice since he was an infant. Madness can do odd things. Don't worry, my lord. This is the prince—and soon he will be king.

Narrator 2: Lord St. John departs, and Lord Hertford paces the floor, thinking of all he has seen.

Lord St. John: *(To himself.)* He *must* be the prince. There can't be two in the land who look like twins. And even if there were, it would be a miracle if they were to change places. And if he were an imposter, would he deny being the prince? Of course not. This is the true prince, gone mad!

Scene 4

Narrator 1: Tom struggles through dinner, retiring after to his new room. In a closet he discovers a book about etiquette of the English court. He settles down to read.

Narrator 2: Henry VIII awakes from a nap, feeling troubled. An attendant informs him that the Lord Chancellor is waiting to see him.

Henry VIII: Admit him! Admit him!

Lord Chancellor: I have ordered everyone to gather. They are waiting for you to confirm the Duke of Norfolk's doom.

Henry VIII: Lift me up! I will go before the parliament and use my seal on the warrant that will rid me of him. It is time to be rid of my enemy.

Narrator 1: The king pales and falls back on his pillows.

Henry VIII: I have longed for this moment, but now I will have to send you instead. Take the seal and compose the warrant.

Lord Chancellor: As you command, sir. Will you give me the seal so that I can take care of this business?

Henry VIII: Don't you have the seal?

Lord Chancellor: You took it from me two days ago. You said you'd use it next on the Duke of Norfolk's warrant.

Henry VIII: So I did. What did I do with it? I am very feeble . . .

Lord Hertford: Sir, I remember that you gave the Great Seal to the prince to keep until—

Henry VIII: True! Fetch it. Go—before it's too late.

Lord Hertford: Sir, I'm sorry to tell you this, but I have already inquired, and the prince can't recall having gotten the seal.

Henry VIII: Then fetch the small seal that I use when I go abroad. It's in the treasury. Don't return until the Duke of Norfolk has been executed!

Scene 5

Narrator 2: While Tom faces the challenges of royalty and attendants who refuse to believe he is anyone but the prince, gone slightly mad, the true prince has been coping with John Canty. The prince finds himself in the Canty's home, where he spies two girls and a middle-aged woman cowering against the wall. An old hag sits in the corner. John Canty stands over Prince Edward.

Canty: Now, enough of your foolishness. Say thy name! Who are you?

Edward: You are ill bred to command me to speak. I tell you again, I am Edward Prince of Wales, and none other.

Mother Canty: Oh, my poor boy. All that foolish reading has taken your wits away. I warned you not to read so much. You've broken my heart!

Edward: Your son is well and has not lost his wits. Take me to the palace, and the king, my father, will restore him to you.

Mother Canty: The king—your father! Son, shake off this terrible dream. Look at me. Am I not your mother who gave birth to you and loved you?

Edward: Truly, I have never seen you before.

Narrator 1: The youngsters plead with John Canty to let Tom rest, but Canty has other thoughts.

Canty: Tomorrow we must pay our rent—two pennies for a half-year's rent. Otherwise we leave this hole. Show me what you've gathered!

Edward: I tell you, I am the king's son!

Narrator 2: John Canty strikes the prince, who falls back against Mother Canty. As she tries to protect him, the hag joins Canty in striking out at Edward. The prince springs away, speaking to Mother Canty.

Edward: Let this swine do their will on me alone!

Narrator 1: Canty and the grandmother waste no time in beating the boy, including the mother and girls in their work.

Canty: Now to bed. This entertainment has tired me.

Narrator 2: Mother Canty tries to sleep, but something about the boy's manner nags at her mind. She begins to wonder if he is indeed Tom.

Mother Canty: *(To herself.)* Ever since Tom was little, he has thrown his hand, with the palm turned outward, over his eyes whenever startled out of his dreams or his thoughts. Others always turn their palms inward. That would be a test!

Narrator 1: She takes a candle and flashes the light in his face and strikes the floor by his ear. Edward's eyes spring open and he looks up, startled. But he makes no movement with his hands.

Mother Canty: *(Softly to Edward.)* Shh, shh. Go back to sleep. *(To herself.)* His hands could not unlearn so old a habit. This is a sad day. Where is my son?

Narrator 2: During the night, sharp raps on the door awaken the miserable group. The man who tried to intervene during Edward's beating is dying from the blow, and a priest has come to warn them that the police are coming for Canty.

Canty: Everyone get up! Take to the streets! If we get separated we'll meet at London Bridge. Keep quiet and don't speak our name. I'll give us a new name later. Then we'll flee to Southwark.

Narrator 1: The family flees into the street, where Edward takes the first chance he sees to slip away in the crowds.

Scene 6

Narrator 2: While the true prince flees, Tom spends the evening transported in grand style along the Thames and through London to the Guildhall where all of royalty and attendants gather for a grand banquet.

Narrator 1: Prince Edward makes his way to Guildhall as well, standing outside, proclaiming that he is the true Prince of Wales. Miles Hendon, a kindly bystander, takes pity on the youngster, rising to his defense when the crowd becomes rowdy. Just as Prince Edward is about to be struck, a troop of horsemen, the king's messengers, ride urgently through the crowd. Hendon flees with the prince.

Narrator 2: Inside Guildhall, the messengers announce that the king is dead. After a moment of silence the assemblage looks to Tom, shouting, "Long live the king!" Tom, who has learned that the Duke of Norfolk is to be executed, speaks to the Earl of Hertford.

Tom: Tell me truly. If I were to utter a commandment, would it be obeyed?

Lord Hertford: You are the king. Your word is law.

Tom: Then the king's law shall be one of mercy, not of blood. Release the Duke of Norfolk from the Tower. He shall not die!

Lord Hertford: The reign of blood is ended. Long live Edward, King of England!

Narrator 1: As Hendon and Edward flee the crowds, Edward hears the shouts that the king is dead, but he hardly has time to reflect on the fact that he is now king. They arrive at Hendon's lodgings on London Bridge, only to be stopped by John Canty who reaches for Edward, raising his hand to strike him.

Canty: So there you are!

Hendon: Not so fast! Who is the lad to you?

Canty: He is my son!

Edward: That's a lie!

Hendon: I believe you, but even if he is your father, he need not beat you. Do you prefer to stay with me?

Edward: I do! I loathe him and will die before I go with him!

Hendon: Then it's settled.

Canty: We'll see about that. I'll take him now!

Hendon: If you touch him, I'll split you like a goose! I kept this lad from being hurt by a mob. Do you think I'll give him over to you?

Narrator 2: Canty moves off, muttering threats. Hendon takes Edward upstairs, ordering a meal on the way. The prince falls into the one bed, just as if he owns it.

Edward: Wake me when the food is here.

Hendon: *(To himself.)* Poor lad. He thinks he's the Prince of Wales. Of course now he'll call himself the king! Ah well, it won't hurt to help him a bit.

Narrator 1: The food arrives and Hendon humors Edward when commanded to wash and serve him. While Edward eats, he asks Hendon to tell about himself.

Hendon: My father was one of the smaller lords, Sir Richard Hendon. My mother died while I was a boy. I have two brothers. Arthur is kind and my elder, but Hugh, my younger brother, is mean and treacherous. My father was guardian to Edith, heiress to a great fortune. We were in love, but she was betrothed to my older brother from the cradle.

Edward: Did they marry?

Hendon: No, my brother loved another, and hoped that one day it would all work out. But Hugh loved Edith as well, or at least he loved her fortune. My father trusted Hugh and believed him when he told many lies about me. He put a silken ladder in my room and convinced our father that I was about to elope with Edith, in defiance of my father's will.

Edward: What happened next? Why are you here?

Hendon: I was banished. My father thought that being a soldier might make a man of me. I became a soldier and in the last war was taken captive and held in a foreign prison for seven years. I most recently fled—and here I am! I am poor in purse and in the knowledge of what has happened during the past seven years.

Edward: You have been treated shamefully. But I will right this wrong! The king has spoken!

Hendon: *(To himself.)* What an imagination he has! His poor ruined little head won't lack for shelter. I'll take care of him.

Edward: You have saved me from injury and shame, perhaps my life and so my crown. Name your reward.

Narrator 2: Hendon is startled at the notion and almost turns down the offer. Then he thinks for a moment and speaks, dropping to one knee.

Hendon: My service was my duty and deserves no reward. However, because you believe me worthy of reward I ask only one thing: that I and my successors may have and hold the privilege of remaining covered in the presence of the kings of England and that I may sit in the presence of the majesty of England.

Edward: Rise, Sir Miles Hendon, Knight. Rise and seat yourself. Your petition is granted.

Hendon: *(To himself.)* That was a wise thought. My legs are very weary. If I hadn't thought of that I'd have to stand for weeks or until his wits have returned . . . And so I am a knight of the Kingdom of Dreams and Shadows! I must not laugh, for this is real to him. And it reflects the sweet and generous spirit within him.

Scene 7

Narrator 1: Meanwhile, at the palace Tom tries to cope with his assumption of the kingship. When he discovers that some prisoners are punished by being boiled alive in oil, he abolishes the practice. He shows compassion when dealing with the accused, winning loyalty among the wrongly convicted.

Narrator 2: The morning after being declared a knight, Hendon leaves Edward alone long enough to obtain clothing for him, and John Canty has a youth lure Edward away on the pretext that Hendon has sent for him and is waiting in a barn. Upon arrival at a barn, Edward asks for Hendon.

Edward: Where is he? Who are you?

Canty: This disguise is not that good. You can't pretend you don't know your father.

Edward: You aren't my father. I am the king! If you've hidden my servant, find him for me.

Canty: You are mad. But listen, my name is changed. It is John Hobbs. Your name is Jack. Remember this. Sit and be quiet. Eat.

Narrator 1: Edward, exhausted, falls asleep. A group of vagabonds gather, and when Edward awakes, they make sport of his claims of royalty.

Narrator 2: Hendon returns to the inn and discovers that Edward has been abducted. He sets off through the woods in search of the boy.

Narrator 1: When Hendon searches, the vagabonds press Edward into service as a thief, and when he makes poor work of it, they abandon him in the barn. Once again, he falls into a deep sleep, curling up next to a calf. The next morning he awakens to children's voices.

Child 1: He has a pleasant face.

Child 2: But his clothes are poor.

Child 1: And look how starved he seems.

Child 2: Who are you?

Edward: I am the king.

Child 1: The *king?* What king?

Edward: The king of England.

Narrator 2: The children argue a bit, trying to decide whether to believe Edward.

Child 1: If you are truly the king, then I believe you.

Edward: I am truly the king.

Narrator 1: The children discuss how Edward came to be in their barn and take him to their mother for breakfast. She tries to get to the truth of the matter, but finds she cannot shake his story. Edward appreciates his plentiful food and accedes to her startling request to clean the dishes.

Narrator 2: Shortly thereafter he sees John Canty and a companion, Hugo, approaching and he slips away, speeding toward the nearby woods. He comes to a hermit's hut, knocks, and is bid to enter.

Hermit: Who art thou?

Edward: I am the king.

Hermit: Welcome, King! Welcome! Many have sought sanctuary here, but they were not worthy, and were turned away. But a king who casts his crown away and clothes himself in rags to devote his life to holiness—he is worthy! He is welcome!

Narrator 1: The king tries to explain, but the hermit continues.

Hermit: You shall be at peace here. You shall pray. You shall study the Book and meditate. And I shall tell you a secret. Shh! I am an archangel.

Edward: *(To himself.)* The outlaws would be better than this! Now I'm prisoner of a madman!

Narrator 2: The hermit rambles on about being archangel for an hour, finally stopping to cook supper and care for the exhausted boy. He tucks him into a bed as lovingly as a mother might. Then he recalls an earlier thought and speaks to the boy.

Hermit: You are the king?

Edward: Yes.

Hermit: What king?

Edward: Of England.

Hermit: Then Henry is gone?

Edward: Yes, I'm his son.

Narrator 1: As Edward falls asleep, the hermit mumbles about how Henry made him homeless. His anger at his condition slowly builds. He begins to sharpen a knife, watching, and mumbling. Then the hermit quietly binds Edward's arms, legs and mouth, so that when Edward awakens he finds he cannot move. He struggles helplessly while the hermit watches.

Hermit: Son of Henry the Eighth, pray the prayer for the dying!

Narrator 2: Just as the hermit raises the knife to gain retribution for his pitiful state, there is a knock at the door.

Hendon: Open! Hello!

Narrator 1: The hermit moves out of the boy's room and answers the door.

Hendon: Where is the boy?

Hermit: What boy?

Hendon: Don't try to trick me. I tracked him here. Others saw him arrive, and his footprints still show in the dust.

Hermit: That ragged vagrant? He'll be back soon. He's on an errand.

Hendon: I don't believe you.

Narrator 2: Edward struggles, making some small amount of noise.

Hendon: What was that?

Hermit: The wind! Yes, that's what it is.

Hendon: Which way did he go on this errand?

Hermit: That way—I'll go with you.

Hendon: Yes, ride the mule while I walk.

Narrator 1: As their voices fade, Edward despairs of being rescued, but soon he hears the door open. In horror he sees it isn't Hendon, but finds himself being carted off by John Canty and his companion, Hugo.

Scene 8

Narrator 2: Edward finds himself among ruffians and vagabonds again, part of a thieving band. When Hugo snatches a pig from a woman, Edward refuses to divert the pursuers and finds himself caught. Hugo and Canty dart off, leaving Edward in her grasp.

Edward: Unhand me! I didn't steal your goods!

Narrator 1: The crowd grows ugly, crowding in. Suddenly, a sword flashes in the air, arresting all movement.

Hendon: This is a matter for the law. Let loose of the boy, goodwife.

Edward: Carve them to rags!

Hendon: Softly, my prince. Trust me and all shall go well.

Narrator 2: A constable approaches.

Hendon: Constable, withhold your hand. He shall go peacefully.

Narrator 1: In a short time, Edward is in front of the justice of the peace, where the woman makes her claim.

Justice: What is your property worth?

Woman: It was my pig, worth three shillings and eight pence, your worship.

Justice: This is a poor ignorant lad. He was perhaps driven by hunger. He doesn't have an evil face, and these are hard times. Don't you know that anyone stealing above the value of thirteen pence shall hang for it?

Woman: Oh! What have I done! I would not have you hang the poor thing! What can I do?

Justice: Perhaps you can revise the value, since it is not yet written on the record.

Woman: Then call it eight pence so I won't have this day on my conscience.

Narrator 2: The justice sentences Edward to a short imprisonment, followed by a public flogging. Edward gasps, but heeds Hendon's signal to remain silent. After a brief imprisonment, Hendon manages to outwit the constable, and Edward finds himself once again escaping with Hendon.

Narrator 1: While they travel, Hendon explains how he and the hermit waited all day for Edward. Edward explains how he was stolen away by Canty and Hugo. They pass through a village, arriving at Hendon Hall, Hendon's family home.

Hendon: Welcome to Hendon Hall, my king! My father, brothers, and the lady Edith will be mad with joy to see me.

Narrator 2: They enter the hall. Hendon seats Edward and rushes to his brother.

Hendon: Embrace me, Hugh! Call our father! Home will not be home until I touch his hand and see his face.

Hugh: Poor stranger, your wits seem touched. You seem to have suffered greatly. Who do you think I am?

Hendon: Why you are Hugh Hendon!

Hugh: And who are you?

Hendon: How can you pretend to not know your brother?

Hugh: My brother? Why, he was lost to me years ago. Let me look at you in the light.

Narrator 1: Hugh begins to study him closely while Hendon prepares to celebrate their joy.

Hugh: Ah, what a disappointment. I fear the letter spoke the truth.

Hendon: What letter?

Hugh: The one that came some six or seven years ago, stating my brother had died in battle.

Hendon: That can't be true! Call my father. He will see the truth of this.

Hugh: One may not call the dead.

Hendon: Dead? This is heavy news. Let me see my brother Arthur.

Hugh: He also is dead.

Hendon: Gone! Both gone! Do not tell me the lady Edith—

Hugh: No, she lives.

Hendon: Bring the servants. They will recognize me.

Hugh: All are gone but five.

Narrator 2: Hugh excuses himself and returns in a short time. Lady Edith and several servants enter with him.

Hendon: Oh, my Edith, my darling.

Narrator 1: The woman's cheek flushes.

Edith: I do not know you.

Narrator 2: She departs, sobbing. The servants shake their heads, claiming not to recognize him.

Hugh: The servants and my wife know you not.

Hendon: Your wife! I see it now. You wrote the letter yourself, stealing my bride and all my goods.

Narrator 1: Hendon begins to attack Hugh, who commands the servants to seize Hendon. Having no weapons, they hold back.

Hugh: *(To the servants.)* Leave, you cowards. Get weapons and guard the doors while I send for the authorities. *(To Hendon.)* I advise you not to try to escape.

Hendon: Escape? Don't worry. I am master of Hendon Hall and will remain, doubt it not.

Narrator 2: While Hugh leaves, Edward looks up at Hendon.

Edward: This is strange. I cannot account for it.

Hendon: It's not strange. My brother was a rascal from birth.

Edward: No, I mean that no one is looking for me. The land should be filled with couriers and proclamations describing me and searching for me.

Narrator 1: Hendon continues to humor his ward.

Hendon: Most true, my king, I had forgotten.

Edward: But I have made a plan. I will write a paper in three languages—Latin, Greek, and English—you will take it to London in the morning. Give it to my uncle, the Lord Hertford. He will know I wrote it and send for me.

Hendon: It might be best to wait until I prove myself. Then I will be better able to help you.

Edward: What is your estate compared to my throne? Obey and I will make things right.

Hendon: *(To himself.)* I think Edith knew me. I believe Hugh has commanded her to lie. I will find her and discover the truth. She loved me in those old days. She won't betray me.

Narrator 2: Edward finishes his work, handing over a paper, which Hendon pockets. Hendon steps toward the door just as Edith enters.

Edith: Sir, I have come to warn you. I think there is some truth to this dream of yours, but it is dangerous. It is more dangerous because you are much like what our lad would have been had he lived.

Hendon: But I *am* he!

Edith: I know you think it, but I warn you. My husband is master in this region. The people prosper or starve as he wills. I know him well; he will say to all that you are but a mad imposter. If you *were* Miles Hendon and he knew it and the region knew it—well, you would be in the same peril.

Hendon: I do believe that. He must have great power to command a lifelong friend to betray and disown another.

Narrator 1: Edith's cheeks color.

Edith: I have warned you. This man will destroy you.

Hendon: Grant me one thing. Look at me and answer. Am I Miles Hendon?

Edith: No. I know you not.

Hendon: Swear it!

Edith: I swear. Now, don't waste precious time! Save yourself.

Narrator 2: At that moment, the authorities burst into the room and lead Hendon and Edward to prison.

Scene 9

Narrator 1: Hendon and Edward are chained to a large cell, crowded with other prisoners. Several days pass while Hendon puzzles over all that transpired. One day the jailer brings in an old man who quietly lets Hendon know that he is an old family servant who recognizes him.

Narrator 2: The servant, Andrew, shares the story of Hendon's family—how Hendon's brother and later his father had died, asking for Hugh to marry Edith on his deathbed. The marriage was unhappy, and Sir Hugh turned into a pitiless master.

Narrator 1: Later, Andrew describes how the new king is gaining favor through his kindness. Edward begins to suspect that the urchin he met has taken his place. He becomes desperate to reach London.

Narrator 2: One morning, the prisoners are forced to watch women prisoners burned to death for their crimes. Edward swears to himself that he will never forget this horrible scene.

Narrator 1: Finally, their trial arrives. Hendon is sentenced to sit in the pillory for two hours, and Edward is let off with a lecture. Upon Hendon's release, they decide to head for London. Perhaps the new king will hear the truth of Hendon's story and offer his help. But as they try to cross London Bridge, the weary travelers are separated, and Hendon is struck down.

Narrator 2: While Edward struggles through the crowds to the palace, Tom Canty is drawn into the pageantry for his official crowning. He proceeds among the people, enjoying their adulation. Then a voice cries out.

Mother Canty: Oh my child, my darling!

Narrator 1: As a guard pushes the woman away, Tom recognizes his mother. Shame falls on him, consuming his pride. Royalty is no longer sweet.

Tom: *(To himself.)* Would that I were free of my captivity!

Narrator 2: His demeanor becomes somber, and Lord Hertford notices.

Lord Hertford: Your highness, shake off this sadness. Did that crazy pauper disturb you?

Tom: She was my mother!

Lord Hertford: God help us! He has gone mad again.

Narrator 1: The coronation plans proceed, while Tom struggles with his conscience. At last the grand moment is at hand and the Archbishop of Canterbury lifts the crown of England off the cushion and holds it over the mock king's head.

Narrator 2: A deep hush settles over the Abbey, and at this very moment, a bareheaded boy, clothed in coarse rags, raises his hand.

Edward: I forbid you to set the crown of England upon that head. *I* am the king!

Narrator 1: Several indignant hands are laid upon the boy, but Tom Canty steps forward.

Tom: Let him go! He *is* the king!

Narrator 2: The assemblage stares in astonishment.

Lord Hertford: Pay him no mind. He is mad again. Seize the boy!

Tom: Do not touch him. He *is* the king!

Narrator 1: Tom Canty falls to his knees before the true king.

Tom: Oh my lord the king, let poor Tom Canty be first to swear loyalty. Put on your crown and become your own self again.

Narrator 2: Lord Hertford sees the remarkable similarity between the two boys and hesitates.

Lord Hertford: By your favor, sir, I would like to ask some questions.

Edward: I will answer them.

Narrator 1: Lord Hertford asks various questions that only one intimate with royalty would know. The true king answers all the lord's questions, but Lord Hertford remains unconvinced.

Lord Hertford: You've answered well, but this is not proof. Wait—I know how we can settle this. *(To Edward.)* Where is the Great Seal? Only the Prince of Wales can answer that riddle.

Edward: *(To Lord St. John.)* Go to my private cabinet in the palace. Look in the left corner, close to the floor. You'll find a nail. Press on it and a little closet will open that no one knows of. You'll see the Great Seal.

Narrator 2: Lord St. John departs, but returns empty handed.

Lord St. John: Sire, the Seal is not there!

Lord Hertford: Throw the beggar in the street.

Tom: No! Touch him and your life is in danger.

Lord Hertford: *(To Lord St. John.)* Did you search well? Surely you know what it looks like, a golden disk—

Tom: Wait, that's enough. Was it round? And thick? With letters engraved on it? Now I know what this Great Seal is. I know where it is, but it was not I who put it there first.

Lord Hertford: Who then?

Tom: The rightful king. He shall tell you himself where it is. *(To Edward.)* Think, my king. It was the last thing you did before you rushed from the palace, wearing my rags, to scold the soldier that threw me down.

Edward: I remember it all, except for the Seal.

Tom: Wait! Think! Remember how I told you of my grandma and sisters, the rough games of the lads in Offal Court. Remember how you gave me food and drink and how we changed garments as a jest? When you realized the soldier had hurt me, you rushed from the room to reprimand him. Just before you left, you snatched up the Seal and looked about for a hiding place—

Edward: Yes! Go, St. John. You'll find the Seal in an armpiece of the armor that hangs on the wall. God be thanked!

Narrator 1: The entire assemblage waits uneasily but with great excitement. A hush falls upon the house and St. John appears, holding the Great Seal aloft in his hand.

Lord St. John: Long live the true king!

Tom: Now, my king, take these garments and give me my rags again.

Lord Hertford: Let the pretender be stripped and flung into the Tower!

Edward: No, without him I would not have my crown again. None shall lay a hand on him to harm him!

Scene 10

Narrator 2: Miles Hendon struggles through the crowds, his pockets thoroughly picked by now, still searching for the boy. He tramps endlessly, finally making his way to the palace. He begs to have a message sent to one of the lords, when an officer arrests and searches him. The officer discovers the message in three languages from Edward and takes Hendon for another pretender to the throne.

Hendon: Now I've had more bad luck. I shall be hanged and what shall happen to my lad?

Narrator 1: The officer leaves him in custody, taking the note with him. To his astonishment, when the officer returns, Hendon is treated respectfully and asked to follow the guard. Soon he is standing in front of the true king.

Hendon: Is this a dream? Are you really on the throne? How can I understand this?

Narrator 2: Then Hendon remembers a promise Edward made. He gathers a chair, places it in front of the king, and sits in it.

Lord Hertford: Up, you mannerless clown. Would you sit in the presence of the king?

Edward: Touch him not. It is his right! Listen. This is my trusty and well-beloved servant, Miles Hendon, who saved his prince from bodily harm and possible death. He is a knight by my voice, a peer of England, Earl of Kent. He shall have gold and lands for this, plus the privilege, which he just exercised, is his by royal grant. I have ordained that all in his line shall have and hold the right to sit in the presence of the Majesty of England henceforth, age after age, so long as the crown shall endure.

Hendon: *(To himself.) This* is my pauper? This is who I adopted and tried to make respectable? Would that I had a bag to hide my head in!

Narrator 1: As the king looks at the group, he spots Sir Hugh, Hendon's brother.

Edward: Sir Hugh! You are to be stripped of your stolen estates. You'll be imprisoned until I have need of you.

Narrator 2: Sir Hugh is led away. Tom Canty, now dressed in decent clothes, kneels before the king.

Edward: I have heard the story of these past few weeks and am pleased with you. You have ruled with gentleness and mercy. Your sisters and mother shall be cared for, and your father shall hang if you wish it. All you who hear me, know that everyone who lives in his company shall be fed and clothed well. He is in the throne's protection and shall be given the honorable title of the King's Ward.

Narrator 1: The proud, happy Tom Canty rises, kisses the king's hand, and runs to tell his mother and sisters the great news.

Narrator 2: Miles Hendon learns that his brother had forced Edith to deny that she recognized her long lost love, threatening to have him killed if she did not cooperate. Miles will not testify against him, and Hugh deserts his wife for the Continent, where he soon dies. Miles and Edith marry, to great rejoicing.

Narrator 1: Tom Canty's father is never heard of again. King Edward sets about rewarding those who had helped him during his time as a pauper. He spends hours telling the stories of his adventures for the rest of his life.

Narrator 2: Tom Canty lives to be a very old man, honored and respected. King Edward VI lives until he is just 25 years old, but he lives with dignity and compassion, never forgetting the lessons he learned as a pauper.

The End

ALPHABETICAL INDEX OF PLAYS

ABOUT THE AUTHORS

Suzanne I. Barchers is the author of twenty teacher resource and textbooks and more than twenty books for children. She earned a doctorate of education in curriculum and instruction at the University of Colorado, Boulder. After working as a teacher and administrator in public and private schools for fifteen years, she began a second career in publishing and as an affiliate faculty member at the University of Colorado, Denver. Since 1999, Barchers has been Managing Editor at Weekly Reader in Stamford, Connecticut, commuting between Stamford and her home in Arvada, Colorado.

Jennifer L. Kroll received her BA from the University of Notre Dame's Program of Liberal Studies. She holds an MAT in English Education from Boston College and a Ph.D. in English from Auburn University. After teaching English for a number of years, she is now the Senior Editor of and a contributing writer at Weekly Reader's *Read* magazine. Jennifer lives in Hamden, Connecticut, with her husband, Carl James, and dog, Buck. She enjoys hiking and photography.

DATE DUE

Nov. 20	2009